DAVID WRAGG

# SIGNAL

## POLITICS & BRITAIN'S RAILWAYS

# FAILURE

SUTTON PUBLISHING

First published in 2004 by
Sutton Publishing Limited · Phoenix Mill
Thrupp · Stroud · Gloucestershire · GL5 2BU

British Library Cataloguing in Publication Data
A catalogue record for this book is available from the British Library.

ISBN 0-7509-3293-7

Typeset in 10/13 pt New Baskerville.
Typesetting and origination by
Sutton Publishing Limited.
Printed and bound in England by
J.H. Haynes & Co. Ltd, Sparkford.

# Contents

# Illustrations

(*Between pages 90 and 91*)

# Introduction

It was what the military might have described as a 'pre-emptive strike'. The railways struck the first blow. Unfortunately, it could also have been described as a 'friendly fire' incident, since the victim was a keen supporter of the railways. Either way, the opening of the Liverpool & Manchester Railway on 15 September 1830 was marred by the death of the Liverpool Member of Parliament, William Huskisson. His death was a loss to the new mode of transport as, in his role as President of the Board of Trade, which at the time was what would now be described as the sponsoring department for railways, no one had been better placed to oversee the spread of the railways. The Liverpool & Manchester was being opened by the Prime Minister, the Duke of Wellington. As the Duke's train stopped for the locomotive to take water, Huskisson was standing beside the Duke's carriage with his back to the other line, when the famous locomotive *Rocket* arrived with another train. *Rocket* knocked the unfortunate MP as it passed, and he died that night from his injuries.

It is tempting to suggest that politicians have never forgiven the railways for the dispatch of one of their number in this way. Yet this wasn't the first death on the railways and, at a time when Parliament rushes to produce new legislation at the slightest excuse, it is worth noting that it took another ten years before the first legislation covering railway safety was published.

In 1830 few people had any experience of railways, although wagons had been propelled on wooden tramways and on flat iron plates for two centuries or more. The railways had been transformed by the arrival of the steam age into a serious mode of transport. Today it is different. Many people have experience of railways, but the trouble is that modern politicians frequently have little experience of anything outside politics, coming to the job far too early in life, whereas their predecessors had made their way in business or the professions, or perhaps the armed forces, and had often learnt the rough trade of politics in local government before trying to run a country.

This is a history of the railways, starting during the nineteenth century when a few highly successful 'smart' companies, such as the Great Western, London Brighton & South Coast, and the Midland Railway, stood out from many more struggling to pay their way. Financial ruin faced many investors, although the financial institutions themselves had earlier shown the way when the banking bubble had burst; hence so many railways in their turn went into what had become known as 'bankruptcy'. Nothing changes, and investors can still be swept up in new schemes to make money, as the so-called 'dot.com' craze at the turn of the twenty-first century reminds us.

Yet, in contrast to most other railway histories, this is a history of the railways and politics covering a period of almost two hundred years, during which the railways were built and came to cover the UK in a scarcely credible short period of time; during which politicians at first opposed railway mergers, and then forced one upon the railways; during which the railways were taken in and out of state control for the duration of two global conflicts; and then nationalised and eventually privatised again, only to have the infrastructure taken back into state control. It is also a saga in which the railways were taxed and then later subsidised, while it is now the road users who are taxed to the extent that they account for roughly a tenth of central government's revenue, all in the interests of them and their goods being forced off the roads and back on to the railways, when no doubt railway travel will be taxed again by some means or other.

The railways themselves have been in and out of fashion throughout their history but, strangely, for most of the time out of favour. They were built largely without significant public subsidy in the UK as in the United States, with the construction of just one of the lines in the north of Scotland being subsidised, while another was promised relief from rates. The first signs of a change came in the 1930s when the government, anxious to create a major works programme to alleviate unemployment and influenced by the economist John Maynard Keynes, offered loans for railway modernisation at an attractive rate. During the late 1930s it was air transport that was actually subsidised, including domestic air services by a government that was concerned that Britain's European rivals were far ahead in the development of internal air services.

How times, and attitudes, change!

David Wragg
Edinburgh, August 2003

CHAPTER 1

# Birth of the Railway

'My fellow-passenger had the highest of all terrestrial qualities which for me a fellow-passenger can possess,' recalled Jane Carlyle, wife of the historian Thomas Carlyle. 'He was silent.'

Jane Carlyle was travelling by coach and, while able to afford the relative comfort of an inside seat, that meant she had to face spending many hours, perhaps a day or two, in accommodation that was small and cramped with her un-chosen fellow passengers.

It is hard today to realise just how important an advance the railway was when it first appeared as a form of public transport, breaking out from its early existence in quarries. The previous century, business had been transformed by the arrival of the canals, dramatically cutting the costs of moving bulky goods such as coal, but canals were slow and expensive to build, facing considerable problems when forced through steep hills or over deep valleys and always demanding the provision of large quantities of water. That the canal system slashed the costs of bulk commodities such as coal so dramatically only shows just how difficult and costly transport was before the eighteenth century. The railway was easier to build and to operate, and from the outset it was far faster than any form of transport then known to man.

The railways arrived on the scene at a time when few people made lengthy journeys, with most going no further than the nearest town. The Christmas-card glamour of the long-distance stagecoach or its rival the mail coach, first introduced in 1784, was in reality so harsh and bleak, as well as being expensive, that it was not to be undertaken lightly. In winter coaches squelched through mud, could be overwhelmed by snow, or could find bridges swept away by rivers in flood, while in summer the roads were baked hard and the coaches banged from one deep rut to another. Coaches could, and sometimes did, overturn or were blown off exposed stretches of road. Competition on the busiest routes could see some wild driving, with more than one stagecoach smashed to matchwood in an accident. The arrival of the turnpike trusts in the early eighteenth century, with their much better road-building and mending techniques, brought a considerable improvement, except that stretches of non-turnpike highway were still to be found between the turnpikes, themselves not wholly popular among those who had always used the roads free of any charge or taxation and who were damned if they were going to pay anything now, even for better roads!

Turnpike or not, passengers froze in winter despite heavy clothing, blankets and foot warmers, and sweltered in summer, longing for the next stop and liquid refreshment. Those outside fared worst, and even on a good road could not seek solace in sleep because to nod off was to fall off! Another consideration on any journey was one's fellow passengers, especially if travelling inside, for which privilege one paid double.

Meals were served at inns, and at many of them passengers were treated to rotten food badly prepared by unscrupulous proprietors well aware that they had a captive market, anxious to absorb some sustenance in an all-too-brief halt – as little as twenty minutes – before being hurried back to their coach. Few people were regular travellers, so it was fair to assume that few of the customers would pass that way again. The hungry customers, perhaps on a journey taking as many as 60 hours, paid their money and were often cheated. Scalding hot soup would be served, so that customers with just twenty minutes or so to eat, drink and doubtless perform other essential bodily functions as well, would not have much time for subsequent courses, for which much of the food, as a result, was often stale. If one was contemplating a journey from, say, Edinburgh or Newcastle to London, it was worth considering going by sea, and coasting voyages were indeed an option. So too was travel by canal barge, on the relatively few routes served, which was slow but comfortable and relatively safe.

In the 1830s, at the dawn of the railway age, a passenger from London to Newcastle on the 'Lord Wellington' coach would be charged £3 10s for the 274-mile journey, a fare of 3d per mile, for an outside seat. Ignoring inflation, this fare was exactly the same per mile as the standard rate for a second-class railway ticket in the early 1960s for a journey of up to 200 miles, after which the rate per mile fell. To put these fares into perspective, a footman in a grand house, by no means the most junior member of the servant class, would have been doing well to earn £20 per annum. Looked at another way, £3 10s in 1830 would be the equivalent of almost £200 today.

Assuming that you decided to stay with the coach for the entire 30-hour journey in order to save money on accommodation along the way, what happened? Leaving London after lunch, your first chance of a break is at Arrington Bridge for dinner, costing 2s 6d, while later you are charged 3s at Huntingdon for sandwiches and cognac, the latter being an attempt to fight off the night cold. There will have been other stops to change horses, but this is done in just two minutes. At Doncaster breakfast awaits, provided that you have the necessary 2s 3d, but also waiting on you before you can get to your breakfast is the guard who is changing, and who expects a tip, usually around 2s 6d, while further on, at Ferrybridge, the driver changes and also expects a tip, another 2s. Lunch at York costs you another 3s 6d, while you give the driver 1s 6d when he changes again at Northallerton. Tea is taken at Rushyford Bridge, and costs just 2s. You reach Newcastle during the evening, no doubt exhausted, cramped, sore and cold. As you alight you are expected to tip both the guard and the driver, 2s 6d and 2s respectively. All in all, your £3 10s trip has cost you £4 17s 3d, or more than £300 in today's money. Drivers and guards were not backwards in seeking a tip: 'I'll be leaving you now, sir . . . your driver who has driven you the past 50 miles.'

All of this was for outside accommodation, exposed to the elements, dirt and dust. If you had opted to travel inside your fare would have been £5 15s, and in addition to your meals, your driver and guard would have expected far higher tips, say 3s for the former and 3s 9d or even 4s for the latter.

All of these costs assume that your journey was a simple affair. If you lived in a village, or even in a small town, away from the main coaching routes, you would have had to make your way to the coach, and perhaps also make your own way to your destination at the end of the journey if that too was off the coaching map. This might mean walking, or perhaps hiring a carriage, at considerable additional expense.

Travelling north from London to Newcastle or Edinburgh, the traveller would have been spared one minor chore – changing the time on his or her watch. For those travelling east or west, it would have been wise to check the time whenever they stopped, as there was no conception of and no need for a single national time.

There is no doubt that the fares charged by the stagecoach operators were high, but the costs of providing this service, for up to six people inside and eleven outside on a stagecoach, with fewer outside on a mail coach as the seats at the back were reserved for the guard, were considerable, and the rewards were by no means guaranteed. On a run from London to Edinburgh, a single coach would need the services of 400 fine horses. Fewer horses were needed pro rata on the shorter routes, say from London to Portsmouth or Brighton. These were the so-called 'short stages', for which smaller teams of horses were used so that the coach, which with a full team was capable of running at up to 10–12mph (16–19kph) on a good stretch of road, did not deposit its passengers at their destination in the middle of the night.

Needless to say, Parliament soon saw an opportunity to raise money. Owners of carriages had been taxed as early as 1747, and their horses were taxed as well from 1785. As early as 1775, an annual duty was levied on each stagecoach of £5, followed in 1783 by a duty of a halfpenny for every mile run, doubled to 1*d* after a few years and then increased later, when a coach licensed to carry fifteen passengers could pay 3*d* per mile. There was also a tax on every coach and carriage produced that had to be paid by the carriage builders. Only mail coaches were exempt from taxation, on the grounds that they were employed on state business. From London to Edinburgh the horses provided by contractors, usually at the inns along the way, would cost another £5, and the turnpikes would charge another £6 15*s*. Interestingly, travel by canal barge or shipment of goods by canal barge was free of taxation, although it had been proposed by William Pitt the Younger who had wanted to tax the carriage of cargo in 1797, but backed down in the face of extremely strong opposition.

Given costs on such a scale for carrying so few people at speeds of around 12mph, it is not surprising that the new railway made an impact and that entrepreneurs could see that there was money to be made. At the beginning of the steam age, there was a number of attempts at harnessing steam to the stagecoach, but none was successful. Steam-powered carriages were heavy and damaged the roads, while the heavily rutted roads in turn produced such a rough ride that mechanical reliability was seriously compromised. In any case, the costs continued to be high given the still small number of passengers that could be carried.

A VAST AND INTRICATE NETWORK

While comparisons with coaching might account for the provision of a network of longer-distance railway routes, a predecessor for 'InterCity', it doesn't explain the vast and intricate network of branch lines and minor routes. Why, for example, in the Isle of Wight was a branch built for less than 3 miles between Brading and Bembridge, so that passengers from Ryde would change at Brading for Bembridge, with a railway journey that was a 'dogleg' of a route measuring 7½ miles between the two towns? The Bembridge branch had originally been built for a short-lived train ferry from the mainland, but it survived because it was still quicker, more comfortable and less expensive than horse-drawn transport. This was why, even on very short runs such as that between St Helier and St Aubin in Jersey, a distance of just 3¾ miles, a railway was viable. The railway largely displaced the horse bus on such a suburban run, and it is worth noting that even Jersey had two railway companies. In Guernsey a railway was even proposed for the 2 miles between St Peter Port and St Sampson's, but sanity prevailed and they built a tramway instead.

One of the best examples of how times have changed since the advent of the railways is in London. Congestion in London is nothing new, and even in the middle of the nineteenth century the streets of the capital were so congested that, in 1867, no fewer than 3.5 million of the 8 million passengers using the terminus at Cannon Street were travelling solely between the City and the West End terminus of the South Eastern Railway at Charing Cross. The new railway was also competitive, charging fares of 6*d* first class, 4*d* second class and 2*d* third class, compared with 3*d* for the horse bus, while, no doubt, first-class travel compared well with a hansom cab on cost, timing and comfort. Until a stop was introduced at Waterloo, this worthwhile business was boosted by ladies of a certain calling who entertained their clients on the 7-minute trip between the City and the West End, presumably using the more comfortable compartments. This, of course, was before the construction of the Circle Line, and one might add that the diversion of all trains running between London Bridge and Charing Cross through Cannon Street must have been an unwelcome delay for travellers from Kent heading for the West End.

Of course, not everything on the railways marked a massive change from coaching practice at the start. Many will have noticed that the early first-class carriages consisted of three stagecoach bodies joined together and mounted in tandem on a railway truck. It took a little time before designers explored the possibilities for the new mode of transport, and even then the preference for the first hundred years or so for compartment stock on Britain's railways can be traced back to stagecoach practice, while in the United States from the early years the open saloon was favoured. Another hangover from long-distance coach travel was that for many years longer-distance trains had to stop at stations to allow passengers to take food and drink, but this continuation of stagecoach practice was made even less desirable by the far larger numbers involved. The quality of the food on offer certainly hadn't improved.

> Until 1879, there were no dining-cars: hence the churning mobs who, like hopped-up dervishes, descended on station refreshment-stalls, hoping to snatch and gobble down a meal before their train steamed off again. Their enthusiasm tended to wane once they had sampled the food; scalding, discoloured water described as tea or coffee, greasy soup, dry buns and biscuits, and endless arrays of musty pork-pies that were almost museum pieces. Unfinished cups of coffee were poured back into the urn ready for the next batch of customers.
> (Ivor Smullen, *Taken for a Ride*, London, Herbert Jenkins, 1968)

Especially on journeys into London, your trip would also have been interrupted by a stop, tantalisingly close to your destination, for tickets to be checked. It took some time before someone thought of checking tickets at the barriers of the London termini, while non-corridor rolling stock remained on some lines, even on express trains as late as the 1920s, limiting the opportunities for on-board checks.

A rearguard action was fought against improving the lot of the unfortunate traveller by the trade publication *Railway News*, which went to great lengths to prove that adding lavatories would put too much extra weight on to a train. There would also be the cost of providing towels, which *Railway News* was certain would be stolen by third-class passengers, and of providing plumbers to fill the roof cisterns. In the circumstances it is not surprising that even into the twentieth century travellers on many lines, including those of the South East & Chatham, had to have strong bladders. The enlightened self-interest that would have improved facilities to enhance the appeal of railway travel was sadly lacking.

## FRAGMENTED

Britain's railways were fragmented from the start. This was not a failure of organisation or even a political decision; more the lack of both. The government of the day did not sit in London and decree that there should be lines linking the capital with this or that town or city, and perhaps later that there should be lines linking provincial cities. As one of only two countries – the other was the United States of America – to leave the development of the railways almost entirely to private enterprise, a means had to be found of raising money from investors. The funds required were so huge, and memories of failure so recent, that this could only be done by offering digestible chunks of railway to the market.

A glance at the railway map in 1830 would have shown a series of lines widely separated and built with no intention of creating a network. This was not a failure of the private enterprise system; rather, it was a sign of the times and of the parochial nature of planning, with the promoters of railway schemes thinking locally. Stockton needed to be linked with Darlington, Liverpool with Manchester, Canterbury with little Whitstable. At first no one thought that there might be a need for a railway across the Pennines, or running from London to Scotland. The Great Western (GWR) had its origins not in some grand scheme in London, but because Bristol business interests thought that London might benefit from being connected with Bristol. One frequently overlooked advantage of this approach was that the UK saw cross-country routes developed as quickly and with as much enthusiasm as the trunk routes linking the provinces with London, in contrast to some European countries in which links between provincial centres were provided late and grudgingly.

While the first specific Parliamentary measures were the private bills designed to authorise the construction of railway lines, or other works such as bridges and major termini, the first public bills did not follow for some time. This was not the practice on the Continent, with Belgium, for example, taking powers to control and direct the construction of railways as early as 1834. This could, of course, have been a reflection of the difference between the UK, 'where everything is permitted unless it is forbidden', and those European countries 'where everything is forbidden unless it is permitted'.

Not only new branch lines or extensions of main lines were built as small isolated projects, but so too were some of the London termini. An extension from London Bridge to Charing Cross was built in this way by the Charing Cross Railway Company, as was that to Victoria and the terminus itself by the Victoria Station & Pimlico Railway Company. Often these schemes were barely disguised as new ventures by a railway; sometimes the connection was less obvious. At a time when the European Union demands that railways in member states should provide 'open access', it is worth reflecting that many of the new ventures floated during the nineteenth century assured would-be investors that their lines would be used by two or more railway companies. This led to some interesting developments, with the Great Western, for example, having a complicated access to Victoria via Southall, so that part of Victoria station was originally laid out to accommodate dual-gauge track for the still-broad-gauge GWR. Many of the convoluted routes taken around London to arrive at a strange terminus were far more useful than one might suspect today, since these preceded the development of the underground network, and especially of the Circle Line, so that one reason for such services falling out of favour was the arrival of mass transport within the centre of London itself. Not all of the new services were convoluted by any means. The extremely hard-up London Chatham & Dover Railway (LCDR) had succeeded in persuading both the Great Northern Railway and the London & South Western Railway (LSWR) to subscribe more than £300,000 apiece towards the cost of its lines to Blackfriars, then known as St Paul's, and the now closed Ludgate Hill, with the promise of through-running powers, which they soon exercised, along with the Midland Railway, which started running trains to Victoria in 1875. The LCDR itself sent trains from Herne Hill to King's Cross and then as far north as Barnet: this was a very useful Victorian north–south 'Thameslink' service, yet without a transport planner in sight!

It was also proof that fragmentation in itself was no obstacle to cooperation and through-running. The arrangements made for different railways to have access to the better placed London termini had their uses, but far more enduring arrangements saw through services from London to Scotland – from Euston starting in 1848 and from King's Cross in 1852. This required cooperation on a grand scale, while there were the occasional, but usually short-lived, outbreaks of competition between the operators of the east coast and west coast routes. Competition and cooperation became more intense when a third route from London to Scotland was opened in the mid-1870s by the Midland Railway, albeit on the longer route to both Edinburgh and Glasgow from St Pancras via Settle and Carlisle. The Midland didn't offer speed, but it did offer comfort and was a very superior railway. Unlike the Great Western and the London Brighton & South Coast, two companies normally associated with having an up-market image, the Midland looked after its third-class passengers, and was the first company to provide third-class accommodation on all of its trains. Prior to the start of its Anglo-Scottish service, the Midland made one of the single greatest advances ever in customer service by the simple expedient of abolishing its second-class fares and at the same time scrapping its third-class carriages, although, to put this into perspective, there were still relatively few of the latter. While it might have seemed more logical to have simply reduced the second-class fare to the third-class rate and scrapped the third-class carriages, thanks to Parliament third class was sacred and such a move was not allowed until many years after nationalisation.

The operation of a service from Euston to Glasgow and Edinburgh required the London & North Western Railway (LNWR) to cooperate with the Caledonian Railway, while King's Cross to these cities required cooperation between the Great Northern, North Eastern and North British railways, while for the passenger heading even further north to Aberdeen, the journey would have been over the lines of the Caledonian Railway. The Midland's partners on the Anglo-Scottish routes included the Glasgow & South Western and North British railways. Given this thrust northwards and the rapid expansion of the railways it is not surprising that by 1848 the first signs of a network were evident on the railway map. The opening of the Forth Bridge in 1890 made the east coast line 16 miles shorter than the west coast for Aberdeen traffic and ended the advantage that the LNWR and Caledonian had hitherto enjoyed. Along the way the traveller would pass through stations shared with other companies. The system worked, and endured until grouping in 1923.

It was not just these grand enterprises that enjoyed collaboration. At Newport on the Isle of Wight, trains from the Freshwater Yarmouth and Newport Railway rubbed shoulders with those from the Isle of Wight Central Railway, which in turn met the Isle of Wight Railway at both Sandown and Ryde, while the line from Ryde St John's Road to Ryde Pierhead was owned jointly by the London & South Western Railway and the London, Brighton & South Coast Railway. This was generally supposed to have been an arrangement to keep the Central and the Isle of Wight from each other's throats, but the Central would have been running over the Isle of Wight's metals between Smallbrook Junction and St John's Road.

Given the time taken to bring major infrastructure projects to fruition today, it is a salutary experience to look back on the expansion of the railway network. In 1844 there were already 2,236 route miles, but just six years later this had grown to 6,084 miles, then by almost half as much again to 9,069 miles in 1860, and this rate of increase was maintained to reach 13,562 miles by 1870. By 1900 the total was 18,506 miles and still it continued to grow, not peaking until 1930 when there were 20,243 route miles, almost twice today's total mileage. The increase between 1900 and 1930 is all the more impressive because a number of lines were closed during the First World War, many of them never to reopen, to conserve fuel, manpower and equipment. New lines continued to appear during the 1930s, such as that to Chessington South on the Southern Railway, built to serve new housing developments.

## THE THREAT FROM ROAD TRANSPORT

The railways swept almost all of the stage and mail coaches off the highways by 1870, leaving just horse-drawn buses in the major towns and cities. Full of confidence, the railways were not too concerned when trams first started to appear as these were at first also horse-drawn, but once the trams became electrified, the advantage swung back to them as they became faster and, of course, were more likely to pick up the passenger close to his doorstep and arrive closer to his destination than the train. After the First World War, with so many redundant War Office vehicles available, and with so many ex-soldiers having learnt either to drive or maintain the now increasingly reliable motor vehicles, a new hazard arrived for the railways: the bus and the lorry. These vehicles offered infinite flexibility regarding routes and economy. For their operators it was not necessary to ask Parliament for approval to establish a new route, raise the money and then wait for it to be built, as with the railways. Instead, a new bus service could appear overnight. Within a few years, many branch and suburban lines were converted into no-hopers. The railways lobbied hard for legislation to protect themselves, but this did not happen until 1930.

Many then, as today, saw road transport as a bad thing, an interloper. Reactions were not always negative, however, as the competition from the electric tramways encouraged many railway companies, including the London Brighton & South Coast (LBSCR) and the London & South Western, to start electrification of their suburban lines, starting with the LBSCR's south London line connecting Victoria with London Bridge, on which electric services started in 1909.

The massive programme of suburban electrification completed by the successor to these two companies, the Southern Railway, between the two world wars succeeded in increasing passenger traffic. Nevertheless, on many routes it simply disguised the fact that the pendulum would in the longer term swing back in favour of road transport simply because railways were unsuitable for such short journeys. The creation of so many lines for short-distance travellers had been due simply to the low speeds and discomfort of many road journeys at the outset of the railway age. Today, most suburban lines are busy only during the peak periods – a reflection of the inability of the road system to carry so much traffic at these times – and, lying idle in between the all-too-short peaks, they now lose money. In less affluent times with poorer roads, the railways could be tolerably busy most of the time, while the peak periods were often longer, perhaps three or four hours a day instead of barely two, and on six days a week instead of five. These were also the days before television, so people of all ages went out more in the evenings and at weekends, with the result that off-peak traffic could be very healthy on many suburban lines.

CHAPTER TWO

# Politics and the Railways

There is no question that politics became involved with the railways right from the start. It was inevitable. Railways, like canals, needed to acquire vast amounts of land and needed compulsory purchase powers, which only Parliament could give. Compulsory purchase suggests that the railways then acquired the right to thrust new routes wherever they wished, but this was never the case. In reality Parliament, usually the House of Commons, received representations through Members of Parliament who would speak for or against the bill authorising a particular stretch of railway, and vote accordingly. There were also opportunities for interested parties to make representations, so that no measure could be regarded as authorised until it had received the royal assent.

Such procedures did not affect the private lines running entirely within a quarry or a coal mine, and in an attempt to simplify the extremely costly procedures so that the railway network would extend to many remote areas, much later, in 1868, the first legislation was passed allowing light railways to be built by virtue of a parliamentary order rather than by Act of Parliament. By this time the railway network was well established. Light railways were defined as having a 25mph maximum speed and 8 ton maximum axle loading. The pace at which the railway network grew meant that very few light railways were in fact built, but those that were were often operated to extreme standards of cheapness, typically lacking signals or level-crossing gates, and with only the most basic station facilities.

## REGULATION

An indirect but significant government interest in the railways had come as early as 1830, when the superintendent of mail coaches of the Post Office attended a board meeting of the Liverpool Manchester Railway to discuss the basis on which mails could be conveyed between the two cities twice a day in each direction. This was forward looking, and showed that the Post Office was not wed indefinitely to its own mail coach system, but was constantly looking for the fastest and most economical means of conveying the mails. In the case of the Liverpool Manchester, agreement was reached that the mails would be carried for the princely sum of 2s 6d per 30-mile trip. This seemingly insignificant start was to become an important source of railway revenues, and it was in many cases to have another impact on the railways, with certain express trains designated to carry mails and earning unofficial titles such as the 'Irish Mail', often denoting that these were among the faster trains, even if timings owed more to the convenience of the Royal Mail than that of the passengers. Nothing much more happened until 1837 and the opening of the Grand Junction Railway, and once again an ad hoc arrangement was negotiated for mail between Birmingham and Liverpool, so that by using an overnight mail coach from London to Birmingham and then transferring to a morning train Liverpool could be reached from London in 16½ hours.

The Post Office was by now firmly convinced that the mail coaches were on the way out and that railways were here to stay, so that the Railways (Conveyance of Mails) Act 1838 gave the postmaster-general the power to require all railways, whether existing or proposed for the future, to carry the mail. The Act required the carriage of mail on both ordinary and special trains, and the latter were to operate at such times as the Post Office might direct. The measure also allowed for the mails to be carried in special rolling stock if the Post Office wished, for already on-board sorting of mail in special carriages was foreseen. In a parallel to the early development of the passenger carriage, in 1838 the Great Western Railway started to carry mail coaches on its ordinary flat trucks as soon as the first sections of its main line opened, and the London & Southampton did the same between Nine Elms and Winchfield, to the south-west of Woking. Just as the stagecoaches transformed themselves during the period of transition from trunk carriers in their own right to feeders for the railways, the mail coaches also changed their role, filling in the gaps in the railway network, for there was absolutely no point in even attempting to compete with the all-conquering power of steam and wheel on rail.

The Post Office seems to have used the Act as a reserve measure, since by 1842, of the forty companies carrying mail, twenty-seven were doing so under notices issued under the Act while the remainder had obviously concluded a voluntary agreement with the Post Office. The Act allowed negotiation on the remuneration to be paid to the railway companies. It can only be supposed that those companies that had to be directed to carry the mails were those with unduly high expectations. Nevertheless, this legislation can be construed as aiding the Post Office, rather than regulating the railways.

Before Parliament even considered regulating the railways, it did what every administration throughout history has done: it considered taxing them! Taxation of railway travel began as early as 1832, when railways were so few and far between, and their routes so short, that it hardly seemed to matter. Railway companies were made to pay what was then the not-insubstantial duty of a halfpenny per mile for every four passengers carried, and the relative significance of the railways compared to stagecoach travel at this time can be judged by the fact that in 1835–7 the Treasury collected £13,000 annually from the railways as against £750,000 (worth about £42 million today) from the stagecoach operators. As duties go, this 'passenger tax' as it became known was a clumsy instrument since it made no distinction between the class of passenger, and so bore more heavily on the poorer passengers than the more affluent travelling in second or first class. It was not until 1844 that the first attempt was made to ease this situation.

By 1833 a growing body of opinion was concerned about the rapid expansion of the railway network, supported by a growing volume of unrelated private bills with no overall shape or form. To give just one example of the problems that were arising even at this early stage was the all-important question of the track gauge. The most famous problem was that of the Great Western and its 7ft broad gauge being incompatible with the 4ft 8½in standard gauge being generally accepted elsewhere a 5ft gauge was adopted on the Eastern Counties Railway until 1844, while the Liverpool Overhead Railway adopted 4ft. In Ireland, all then part of the UK, the debate centred on whether the gauge should be 5ft or 5ft 6in, and, asked to rule on the question, a British Army engineer opted for the compromise of 5ft 3in, which it remains to this day. The absence of any firm commitment to standardisation meant that through running was greatly restricted, although some mixed-gauge track was provided, and at railway centres where the different gauges met, known in railway terms as a 'break of gauge', massive confusion reigned as passengers had to change trains and goods had to be transhipped, with good examples of this being at Exeter and at Gloucester, the latter being especially notorious for chaos, confusion and loss or damage to goods.

As concern rose, the House of Commons established not one but two committees to look into regulation of the railways, with the result being the recommendation from the second committee in 1838 that a new board be established to oversee the railways, and it was suggested that this should be annexed to the Board of Trade (BoT). The result was the first Railway Regulation Act 1840, which established the Railway Department of the BoT, and this was followed by a second measure in 1842. Some commentators have pointed out that the BoT was ill-equipped for its new role, with no knowledge or understanding of the railways, but at the time, just how many people could claim to have this outside the frantic world of the rapidly expanding railways? In fact, the BoT was already the repository of a certain amount of information on the railways, having been collecting statistics on the railways since 1832, and the statistician concerned, G.R. Porter, was put in charge of the new department and given a solicitor to help in the scrutiny of all railway legislation, including the private legislation empowering the construction of new lines and major works. All in all, the new department had just five people in it, but then the entire BoT at the time employed just thirty people. The initial powers of the Railway Department were the essential ones of ensuring that the railway companies provided returns on their traffic, that new lines be inspected before opening and that accidents be investigated. The inspectors were all officers in the Royal Engineers and so well suited to an assessment of the engineering, and especially civil engineering, aspects of the railways, but naturally enough completely ignorant on the operational and financial aspects. Even the knowledgeable Porter was, in 1845, concerned that the fledgling railways would not be able to compete with the arrival of steamboats on the River Thames. He needn't have worried.

The 1840 Act was effectively a safety measure. This was the first of nine so-called 'Railway Regulation Acts' that passed on to the Statute Book between 1840 and 1893. This was not an avalanche of legislation for it compares favourably with the House of Commons today, from which legislation issues in a steady stream, the worst of it not debated but introduced by stealth in the form of Parliamentary orders.

In addition to awarding powers to the BoT, the 1840 Act also provided for the punishment of 'railway servants' for safety transgressions. Such legislation was necessary because the BoT almost seems to have acquired its responsibilities for the railways by default rather than by design, and there was to be no such thing as a Ministry of Transport until after the

First World War. The BoT had originally developed to oversee the country's foreign trade and through this assumed responsibility for shipping. In its original form it was not concerned with the inland transport of the UK, and indeed was none too concerned about domestic trading arrangements.

The 1842 Act dealt with such matters as the conveyance of troops by train and the policing of the railways, the latter being especially important in the early days when much of the role of the railway signaller, as signalmen have become known in these politically correct times, was handled by railway policemen not such a ridiculous concept since comparisons can be made with traffic police. The need to convey troops by train was brought about largely by concerns on internal security, rather than by any external threat.

Nevertheless, it now became apparent that there was much to be done to correct and control the growth of the railways. The European system of central direction was considered, and as President of the BoT Gladstone was especially keen to overhaul the system. No doubt much of this was necessary, but it was inevitable even then that an ambitious politician would be keen to extend the powers of his department.

The famous railway entrepreneur George Hudson's representations to the committee chaired by Gladstone early in 1844 are mentioned in the next chapter. Gladstone had by this time been an MP since 1832, but more significantly he was probably one of the better informed members as far as railways were concerned, since his father, Sir John, had been an enthusiastic promoter of the early railways in Scotland, and by 1843 had accumulated £170,000 (£9.4 million today) of railway investments. The only real question had to be just how impartial did this make his son? On the one hand, it could account for the watering down of the early provisions of the Railway Bill that resulted from the committee's deliberations, but on the other, shortly after the measure was enacted, Gladstone resigned, largely because he was aware of the conflict of interest between his own family's involvement in railways and his powers as their Parliamentary overlord. He maintained this distance between himself and railway regulation for the remainder of his life, attending only two sessions of Cardwell's Committee on Railways which sat in 1852–3, even though he was nominally a member, and avoiding service altogether on the 1865 Royal Commission on Railways. On the other hand, in later life Gladstone did not maintain a physical distance between himself and the railway, being the only prominent British politician to use the railways during electioneering, often addressing crowds at railway stations and even from carriage windows, a style more usually associated with the USA than the UK, and probably possible because at the time it was still a practical proposition for an individual to hire a train.

The Railway Regulation Act 1844 has become more commonly known as 'Gladstone's Act'. It was significant as much for what it failed to do as for what it did, as no attempt was made to enforce gauge standardisation, which would have been a practical measure. The most significant provisions were for cheap railway travel, a predecessor of the later 'Cheap Trains Act', while telegraph companies were enabled to compel railway companies to allow their wires to be carried alongside their lines and, for the first time, the possibility of nationalisation of the railways was enshrined in British law. Gladstone himself felt that the Act had been an opportunity missed, and that the powers contained within the Act were far too weak, largely owing to the power of the railway companies who had many members of both Houses of Parliament among their shareholders and directors.

The importance of the Act should not be underestimated as it authorised the purchase of railway companies by a British government in the future, although it applied only to those companies established after 1 January 1845, and the powers could not be exercised before 1866. The price to the government of a railway company was to be the profits for a 25-year period, averaged out over the preceding three years. As we shall see, by the mid-1860s many railway companies were passing through a bleak period and no doubt the cost of acquisition at the time would have been low, but the railway system was still incomplete. One cannot help speculating had nationalisation occurred at this early stage, would the total mileage have ever reached its ultimate grand total of more than 20,000 miles? Given post-nationalisation experience of the attitude of the Treasury to investment in the railways, one may be excused for doubting it.

CHEAP TRAVEL FOR ALL

The cheap travel provisions of the 1844 Act created what came to be known as 'Parliamentary Trains', establishing certain standards of speed and comfort for these while carrying passengers at very low fares. The combination of certain standards as well as low fares owed its origins to an accident on Christmas Eve 1841, when a Great Western train was derailed at Sonning, just to the east of Reading, killing eight third-class passengers who had been travelling in a goods train's low-sided open wagons. In the ensuing inquiry the inspector pointed out the dangers of travelling in such unsuitable accommodation. This provoked a general investigation by the Railway Department into the provision made for third-class passengers throughout the country, and it was found that the GWR example was more the rule than the exception. Many trains had no provision at all for third-class passengers. As a result, the 1844 Act stipulated that all future railways defined as passenger railways, meaning that they earned a third or more of their turnover from passenger fares, would have to provide at least one daily train, including Sundays, that would call at every station and have an overall speed, allowing for stops, of not less than 12mph, and that the passengers would have to be carried in enclosed carriages provided with seats. It was also stipulated that the fares would not exceed 1*d* per mile, and for this each passenger would be entitled to carry up to 56lb (25.4kg) of luggage, rather more than economy-class passengers are allowed nowadays, and much more still than the 33lb (15kg) of many charter flights. To help the railways provide this basic service, these low fares were exempted from passenger tax, by this time at a rate of 5 per cent, which of course meant that it no longer weighed most heavily on the poorer passengers. On some railways this became the new third class, while others provided both 'Parliamentary Trains' and third-class trains, although strictly speaking, third-class fares were still subject to passenger tax.

This measure was only enforceable on future railways, but most of the railway companies complied with the measure anyway. This was not simply a gesture of goodwill. The way in which new lines and extensions to existing lines were sanctioned by private acts of Parliament meant that any other arrangement would have been cumbersome and impractical. Indeed, there is considerable evidence, especially in Scotland, that many railways bitterly objected to the new measure on the grounds that many passengers who could afford much more were travelling in the 'Parliamentary Trains' and thus depriving them, and, of course, the Treasury, of revenue. In another sense the new measure was itself scarcely a model of common sense, doubtless because the Treasury was anxious to see as few passengers as possible escape paying tax. An ordinary third-class passenger, possibly commuting, although the term was unknown at the time, to a place of employment, was taxed, regardless of his or her circumstances. Then too, while the 12mph speed was good for a stopping train in 1844, later this became slow and unattractive, but a subsequent court decision in 1874 ruled that a train that did not stop at every station along its route could not be classed as a 'Parliamentary Train' and had to pay the tax.

CHAPTER THREE

# The Age of the Railway King

Imagine, if you will, that a former British prime minister has a sister who has invested heavily in a company, one which is active in exploiting a new technology, but she has been seriously embarrassed by a massive fall in the value of her shares. Still a prominent figure, the former prime minister discusses the problem with a leading industrialist, known and respected for his experience in the new technology. The industrialist solves the problem by investing in the company in question and making his investment known. So high is his reputation that other investors hastily follow the great man and invest, so that the share price rises, at which point the prime minister's sister sells her shares and, doubtless with a huge sigh of relief, banks the cash. No doubt the industrialist does the same, for after all, he may have been doing a good deed for an important and influential friend but he himself is not a charity. This would be construed as rigging the share price. Scandalous, is it not? How would the press and Parliament react today?

In fact, the former prime minister in question was none other than the Duke of Wellington, the victor at Waterloo and throughout his lifetime a national hero, while the industrialist was the so-called 'Railway King', the Yorkshireman George Hudson. Neither gentleman comes out well in this little episode, but who would you suggest was the more blameworthy, Wellington or Hudson? I would suggest the former, as a prime minister should be above such behaviour. Yet history has generally been kind to Wellington, rightly a national hero, but far less kind to Hudson, so often portrayed as a villain. Of course, one might suggest that Wellington didn't know how things ought to be done, having been a bluff soldier for so much of his life. That might be true. Certainly, after his first cabinet meeting on becoming prime minister, he remarked what an odd experience it had been, since he had given them their orders and then they had wished to stay and discuss them! On the other hand, Hudson also did much that would be frowned upon today, so perhaps we are making the mistake of judging the actions of those in the past by modern standards, always a serious error and one that if it does not actually rewrite history certainly interferes with a true understanding of it.

The railway age did not simply improve communications and provide for the first time a single standard time across the British Isles, as the railways required a national time, or 'railway time', which became the direct predecessor of Greenwich Mean Time. It did not even simply allow people to move out from overcrowded slums and into less crowded and more congenial dormitory towns or the rapidly expanding suburbs, known as the 'Metroland' effect. The impact of the railways was far more pervasive than this for they materially affected the way in which business functioned in its most basic sense, the raising of capital. While this was happening the railways also dramatically increased the extent to which Parliament felt it could, indeed should and would, intervene in business activity. Because the railways were often seen as having a monopoly, at least locally despite the multitude of companies, some compared the iron road with the public highway, especially when at first many railways were meant to be open to anyone who wanted to run a train, and so the railways also brought into being the concept of nationalisation, of state ownership, even though the first example of this was in another form of communication altogether, the telegraph system. The railways marked the change from the state providing a service, such as the Royal Mail, to the takeover of a functioning business, or businesses.

In a modern business the shareholders often have little to do with the business itself, and often know remarkably little about it, many seldom bothering to turn up for the annual general meeting, and there are doubtless those who don't bother to read the annual report, and certainly many who find the accounts impenetrable. They can afford to be so relaxed because their liability, if things do go wrong, is limited to their investment in the business. Unlike a partnership, no one is going to pursue them until all of the creditors have been paid, and remember too, that in a partnership, if your partners cannot meet their share of the liabilities and declare themselves bankrupt, then creditors may continue to press for payment from any remaining partners who still may have assets. The loss of an investment is no small thing, but it is reassuring if the liability stops at that. This concept of limited liability, of the joint stock company, was brought about by another piece of legislation, the Joint Stock Companies Act 1862, encouraging investment to fund the continued expansion of the railways. The stock markets and the exchanges (for most large cities, such as Bristol, had their own stock exchanges at this time) that served them developed apace with the railways, which were not simply hungry for capital, but were devouring it at an unprecedented rate. No one had ever seen such massive enterprises, with their demand for large tracts of land, needing not just track and signals, locomotives and carriages or goods wagons, but stations, engine sheds, even their own locomotive and carriage building facilities, as well as massive bridges and viaducts. We saw earlier how such important works as railway termini were often built as separate projects in order to ease the raising of capital, and this even applied to such structures as the Forth Bridge, completed in 1890. The huge sums needed meant that the railways had to be promoted and funded in manageable chunks.

It is difficult to assess the attitude of the times after almost two centuries have passed. As early as the sixteenth century groups of people would band together to pay for a ship to make a trading voyage, and if it came back after a successful trip, would share any profits. Rather than leaving new ventures of single entrepreneurs or partnerships, the concept of the company emerged as early as 1555 with the creation of the Muscovy Company, which was given a Royal Charter in London that year. The creation of the statutory companies for exploration and exploitation of overseas territories, such as the Hudson's Bay Company and the even more famous British East India Company, formed in 1600, removed some of the element of gambling from such enterprises, but could never remove all of it. In their turn, many of the railway projects were a gamble. For every worthy attempt to get coal from A to B, or to link the manufacturers of one town with the shipping at another, there were some that might best be described as being created in an atmosphere of heady over-optimism. My favourite for the most impractical and least-likely-to-be-viable railway project of all time was the Don Farm to St Peter's Church Railway in Jersey, which was meant to connect the small parish of St Peter's with the Jersey Railway at Don Bridge. It was never built.

All that can be said about many of these lines was that the technology was new and exciting, and other forms of communication so uncomfortable, unreliable and expensive, that the railway was seen as a saviour for all. Railways could bring bankruptcy, but they could also bring prosperity. York was jealous of the impact of the industrial revolution on Leeds and Bradford, but retained its earlier prosperity, built on being at the heart of an agricultural area, by becoming a railway city; otherwise it would have remained something of a backwater as in the case of, to take another great cathedral city as an example, Lincoln. It is simply little short of miraculous that York retained all of its beauty and dignity despite becoming a great railway city with workshops and a major station, itself contributing to the city's architectural glory. No other railway city can have been so important yet so unspoiled. Elegant Bristol was never a railway city in the accepted sense, despite having two locomotive builders, partly because Swindon was the Great Western's railway town and also because of the diversity of the local economy.

## THE RAILWAY KING ARRIVES

The story of no one man quite encapsulates the roller-coaster ride that was the lot of the early railway entrepreneur than that of George Hudson, who at the peak of his powers was the chairman of four railway companies covering a wide geographical spread. By 1850 he controlled a quarter of the nation's railway route mileage, then over 6,000 miles, itself probably equalling the total route mileage in the rest of the world at the time. Those interested in business management might like to reflect on the situation of someone like Hudson, since he managed his empire, which included docks and property interests as well as railways, without a telephone, fax, e-mail, typewriters, calculating machines or computers, and without a massive head office. Perhaps the absence of these 'essential' tools of modern management held the key to his success. The late Charles Winter, when chief executive of the Royal Bank of Scotland, once gave a speech in which he compared modern management techniques with those of the British East India Company. In the latter case it could take a year for a communication to reach India from London, and a year for a reply to get back to London. This meant that those on the ground, as it were, had to take decisions themselves. Today decisions are referred upwards, and Winter himself complained that his car phone (he was usually chauffeur-driven) was forever ringing as a senior manager or a fellow director afforded him the courtesy of letting him know what they had done, or what they were proposing.

The modern manager works within two frameworks. One is the regulatory framework that has grown up over the years, whether it be regulation by legislation or by, for example, the stock exchange rules. The other is the network of specialists with which he is surrounded. The only specialist for George Hudson was the great railway engineer George

Stephenson, for he was a civil engineer as well as a mechanical engineer, and doubtless much else as well. This was usual at the time. Brunel went a stage further, and built ships as well. Today the different engineering roles are all specialisations of their own. Maunsell during the 1920s and 1930s, as chief mechanical engineer for the Southern Railway, wanted to build large 4–6–2 Pacific steam locomotives to move ever-heavier trains at higher speeds, but couldn't do so because of objections from the civil engineer. Combining the different engineering roles wouldn't be possible today, but it did mean that problems were seen in the round rather than in isolation.

George Hudson was no business school graduate. He was from a farming family and was born in 1800 in the small Yorkshire village of Howsham, which he left under a cloud at the tender age of fifteen years after fathering an illegitimate child by a local girl. He made his way to York, where he worked in a draper's shop, married the owner's daughter and later, in 1827, received the then considerable inheritance of £30,000 (about £1.38 million today) from a distant relative.

He was later to say that the inheritance was the worst thing that could have happened to him. It enabled him to become active in local politics (becoming Mayor of York three times) and also to invest in local railway schemes. In 1836 he was elected chairman of the York & North Midland Railway, the first successful scheme to link his adopted city with London, albeit by a circuitous route via Derby and Rugby of 217 miles, but nevertheless offering four through trains a day, with the journey from York to London taking 10 hours as against around 20 hours by stagecoach. The company leased and then later absorbed adjoining lines, as well as building a number of extensions itself, including, in 1845, to Scarborough and Pickering, with 49 track miles laid down within a year. The York & North Midland Railway from the outset seemed to be prosperous and, suitably encouraged, Hudson pressed for a major trunk route up the east coast to Scotland. This was a more difficult ambition to realise. Part of the problem was that the line being built by the North of England Railway from York to Newcastle was in serious difficulties, and by 1841 it had exhausted its capital, but still had only managed to reach as far north as Darlington. The directors had no option but to open the 45 miles between York and Darlington to generate some income, something that should have been planned from the outset. The route between York and Darlington had been easy to build, but further north the terrain became more difficult, while the line was crossed by a number of smaller companies, including the pioneering Stockton & Darlington, who were alarmed by the arrival of the larger and more ambitious newcomer.

Hudson was dismayed by this situation, as not only was his vision of a line to Newcastle and beyond compromised, but the BoT had finally started to take an interest in creating strategic routes and, wanting to link London with Scotland, had opted for a route from Carlisle to Edinburgh using a competing route that had already reached as far north as Lancaster. It was left to Hudson to bring the various assorted railway interests involved in a line between York and Darlington to a meeting, from which he obtained their cooperation.

All Hudson now had to do was finance the scheme, but the £500,000 (£27.65 million today) needed was, Hudson felt, unlikely to be raised on the open market, so he suggested that each of the companies present should offer shares in the proposed line to their own shareholders, almost what would today be described as a rights issue, with a guaranteed dividend of 6 per cent. A new company was formed, the Newcastle & Darlington Junction Railway, with Hudson, of course, as chairman. It was not until 1842 that the necessary legislation was passed through Parliament, and the difficulty of the process and its importance was undoubtedly a factor in Hudson deciding to become an MP.

Meanwhile, the York & North Midland had been doing well, paying a 10 per cent dividend at a time of recession, but the North Midland, over which much of its traffic proceeded, was suffering. Hudson headed a committee enquiring into the affairs of this company, and within a week proposed a dramatic reduction in expenses, cutting these from £44,000 weekly to £27,000 through a combination of redundancies and reducing wages, as well as looking for economies elsewhere. This decisive action saved the company, but its neighbours, the Midland Counties and the Birmingham & Derby Junction, were also suffering difficulties, having been built during a boom and by this time being involved in ruinous competition with each other. With remarkable clarity of purpose, Hudson proposed a merger of all three companies – one that would achieve still further savings – the new Midland Railway and formed in September 1843, was having the then considerable capital of £5 million (£277 million today).

This was the height of the railway mania that was gripping the country. Speculators and small investors alike with their hard-earned savings headed into the new railway stocks, and Parliament was in danger of being swamped by the tidal wave of private bills, each of which was intended to authorise a railway, often only for short stretches of line. Some were links in a grander and more ambitious scheme, some satisfied a local need, some seemed to be a whim. It was this 'activity' almost as much as the Sonning accident on the Great Western that had sparked the 1844 legislation. Gladstone planned to regulate the railways 'for the public benefit'. Hudson appeared before the Commons select committee and forecast that the railway bubble was about to burst and that many of the new and proposed lines would turn out to be unviable. He staunchly maintained that 'the public would rather [the railways] be in the hands of companies than . . . government'.

Nevertheless, Gladstone's bill, when published, foresaw a form of state control. Hudson was asked by the directors of the other railway companies to head resistance to the measure, and so it was that when the Parliamentary process was complete, the Railway Regulation Act 1844 saw most of the troublesome and unwelcome clauses of the original bill omitted.

On 18 June 1844 the 39 miles of the Newcastle & Darlington Junction Railway opened. The railway journey from York to London had taken 10 hours in 1837, but by 1844 the much longer journey from Gateshead to London took just 8 hours, a clear indication of progress. The next step was for Hudson's friend and colleague George Stephenson to build a bridge across the Tyne, while two separate companies were promoted in true railway expansion fashion, with one for the line between Newcastle and Berwick on Tweed, and the other to link Berwick with Edinburgh. Later, Hudson was to consolidate his position at Newcastle by taking control of the line from Newcastle to Carlisle, and from Carlisle to Maryport.

Hudson became Conservative MP for Sunderland in 1845, largely because his railway ambitions could be helped by a seat in the House of Commons. While he did much to improve the town's docks, he was also driven by a desire to sabotage the plans for a direct line between York and London, which later became the Great Northern Railway, and in 1846 this drew him into taking over the Eastern Counties Railway, which was struggling financially and also failing to provide a safe service. This was not a disinterested move by Hudson, for he saw the Eastern Counties line from London to Cambridge as the first link in a feasible alternative to the Great Northern route to York. The route via Cambridge would, he estimated, cost £4 million, but that was just half the estimated cost of the Great Northern route. Hudson won over the Eastern Counties shareholders by trebling dividends and although operations improved under Hudson's stewardship it soon became clear that he was paying dividends out of capital. This was unacceptable but a fairly commonplace practice at the time. In 1849 an inquiry found that no less than £200,000 (£13 million today) had been paid out in this way. This raised questions among those concerned with Hudson's other companies, and it was soon found that the same practice was being applied, so that by the end of 1849 he was forced to resign all of his chairmanships. By this time the Great Northern route was open and, pragmatic to the end, Hudson decided to use the new route and abandoned his own plans to extend the Eastern Counties line, with the result that he was also under pressure from angry Midland Railway shareholders who objected to the diversion of traffic away from their route and on to the more direct route.

Earlier, in 1847, Hudson had supported a move by Lord George Bentinck to cut unemployment and help the poor in Ireland through building a railway network using £16 million (£886.4 million today) of taxpayers' money, which would have met two-thirds of the estimated cost, but the measure, designed to make the most of Ireland's meagre resources, was defeated. This had been a blow to Hudson, who had been seen as the most suitable person to drive the Irish railway forward. The paradox was that the failure of the bill was not simply a case of a government being concerned, as always, about the cost, but instead a growing realisation that the end of the railway boom, predicted by Hudson himself in 1844, was not far away.

Had the railway boom continued, Hudson could have avoided the problems that beset him over paying dividends out of capital. His ruse would have been disguised as money continued to flood in from enthusiastic investors, while the seemingly insatiable appetite for railway travel on the most suitable lines would have seen revenues develop to the stage where his misuse of capital would no longer be necessary. It was not to be. Claim after claim was lodged against Hudson, who continued to the end to attract warm local support in both Sunderland and Whitby, as the inhabitants of both towns saw him as a local benefactor. Initially, Hudson was able to fight off the threat of bankruptcy by selling his extensive estates, which he had acquired to leave to his sons, and afterwards because as a sitting MP he could not be arrested for bankruptcy. When he lost his Parliamentary seat he was forced to flee to France, and spent many years in and out of exile. He was rescued in the end by legislation ending imprisonment of debtors, and by an annuity from capital raised by his friends.

Opinions over Hudson differ, and no more spirited and credible defence has been raised on his behalf than in *The Railway King* by Robert Beaumont. It is true that he committed fraud by paying dividends out of capital, and in some cases sold shares between his companies at an inflated price. Using capital to pay dividends was not uncommon at the time, and faced with the need to keep fickle investors on board long enough to complete projects, many succumbed to this temptation, which could escape notice if all went well. The concept of an independent auditor was unknown at the time, although no doubt Hudson's manoeuvrings expedited its adoption.

On the other hand, Hudson was a man of whom it could be said that he got things done, and provided well-paid jobs for many thousands of workers, as well as creating many miles of much-needed railway line, and who appreciated the importance of a network. Indeed, his feeding traffic on to the rival Great Northern route was in recognition of the basic fact that traffic would follow the quickest and most direct route, so better by far to cooperate than to compete to the discomfort and inconvenience of passengers. Hudson also had many rivals, some of whose methods and motives were suspect, but in contrast to Hudson, many of them such as George Leeman, the York solicitor, were also hypocritical. There can be no doubt that many anxious and greedy investors benefited from his behaviour, including a number in high places, and when faced with his difficulties he could have eased the pressure on himself by naming names, or perhaps paid his way out of his own debts by calling in debts, or even blackmailing, those who had done well by him. He did none of these things. In the end he even came to arrangements with his remaining creditors, and was considering a return to Parliament when he died suddenly in 1871.

The spirit of the age was that many entrepreneurs saw investors' money almost as their own, and if they were doing something for the benefit of the company felt free to use it at will. While stock-market and accountancy regulations were at an early stage, Hudson was not the first, and certainly not the last, to feel that the end justified the means. On the other hand, while amassing what was at one stage a great fortune for himself and for his heirs, all of which was lost, he did not rob people. The involvement of the Duke of Wellington's family, if not the Iron Duke himself, shows clearly the extent to which railway mania had spread throughout the country. Everyone felt that they should share in this boom, no one saw the dangers, and the pressure was on. The country in

28

return gained a massive railway network without public expense, so much so that during the Second World War, even though on occasions the London termini were closed by bombing, routes created in the days of competition were always available between London or the Midlands and the Channel coast. Today, despite the UK having only 44 per cent of the land area of France, it still has 7 per cent more railway miles, even after the closure of half the system, and 24 per cent more railway than Japan, despite that country being 54 per cent larger.

CHAPTER FOUR

# Taxation, Cheap Travel and Monopoly

To start in the darkness of a winter's morning to catch the only third-class train that ran; to sit, after a slender breakfast, in a vehicle the windows of which were compounded of the largest amount of wood and the smallest amount of glass, carefully adjusted to exactly those positions in which the fewest passengers could see out; to stop at every roadside station, however insignificant; and to accomplish a journey of 200 miles in about ten hours – such were the ordinary conditions which Parliament in its bounty provided for the people.

(F.S. Williams, *Our Iron Roads*, 1883)

Having been compelled to provide a train for the poorest classes, the railways were determined not to make it too comfortable, doubtless reasoning, as mentioned earlier, that it shouldn't undermine the second-class market. Indeed, at first, second-class passengers had also had to endure open wagons on some railways, but at least they had seats and high-sided wagons. Now that the most basic class was to have covered accommodation and seats, many railways adhered to the letter of the law rather than its spirit, putting perhaps no more than a couple of windows high up, just a single door on each side, and often providing no light at all. It might be thought that third-class passengers had simply been moved off the low-sided trucks and into cattle trucks!

Of course, before the railways few ordinary people would have made long journeys, and if they did they would have gone on foot or taken the carrier's wagon. The railways not only changed the appearance of the country, but in doing so changed the habits that had become ingrained over a thousand years or more. People no longer needed to live close to their place of work, and the prospect of being able to afford better accommodation in less crowded surroundings led to the spread of the suburbs and the creation of the dormitory town. At the time of 'Gladstone's Act' in 1844 it was estimated that the average person in Great Britain made 1.3 railway journeys per year, but by 1869, just twenty-five years later, this figure had risen to 7.8, a six-fold increase. Yet the fallacy in this figure was the counting of each railway ticket sold as being for a single journey, and the small but steadily growing number of season-ticket holders meant that the real average number of journeys could have been around ten, and possibly more.

## TAXATION AND CHEAP FARES

'A tax on the means of locomotion is as bad a tax as any that can be devised' stated Robert Lowe when Chancellor of the Exchequer in 1869. Bold words, and from a chancellor as well! The subject of taxation has always been controversial. It is not simply a case of whether or not to tax, but there is also the argument that keeping taxation as low as possible discourages evasion and increases the overall revenue to the state. Lowe was proposing the abolition of the tax on railway travel, the first chancellor to propose this, but his plans came to nothing since in return for removing the tax, he intended to impose certain terms on them which the railway companies rejected. In any case, the tax had yielded £315,000 in 1855 (£21 million today) and by 1883 this had risen to £810,000 (£56.7 million today), a significant sum for the late Victorian treasury. Lowe had to content himself with abolishing the taxation of stagecoaches, which he did the following year, by which time there were so few left that the tax probably yielded less than the cost of collection and enforcement. The turnpike trusts were also on the way out.

The large number of railway companies, many of them serving markets that differed considerably in both their extent and their characteristics, could barely agree a common approach, and it would certainly have helped their new trade body, the Railway Companies Association, in its dealings with the government had a consensus emerged. There was all the world of difference between, for example, the London Brighton & South Coast, primarily a passenger railway with a growing commuter trade and little freight, and the Taff Vale, built to transport Welsh coal to the docks. The railway companies included those who wanted the tax to be abolished altogether, and those who were more interested in what they saw as the more practical step of exempting the growing number of workmen's trains from the tax. The tax became a rallying point for the emerging socialist reformers, notably G.J. Holyoake and C.D. Collett, who were behind the formation of a Travelling Tax Abolition Committee in 1874. Eventually a compromise was reached between the Committee, the Railway Companies Association and the government, with the Cheap Trains Act 1883 setting out new conditions under which certain types of travel could be exempted from the tax. Instead of the plodding progress of the 'Parliamentary Trains', the growing number of commuters in urban areas was recognised and the Act specified certain urban areas in which an adequate service of trains for workmen had to be provided, and which were exempt from the tax, which continued to be levied on all other fares of more than $1d$ per mile.

'Workmen's trains' were not new, and indeed from 1864 the House of Lords decided that all bills authorising new railways into London should include provision for workmen's trains. There were sound reasons for this. London was burdened with terrible slums by the early nineteenth century and the railways, in their attempts to push as close as possible to the West End and the City, had had to demolish many houses. A good example was the London & South Western Railway that had initially fixed on a terminus at Nine Elms because of the difficulty and cost of getting closer, and when it decided that it needed to reach Waterloo in 1854 it required the demolition of 700 houses for a much narrower spread of tracks than we see today. The Great Eastern extension to Liverpool Street built during 1861–4 was passed by Parliament on condition that it ran workmen's trains from Edmonton and Walthamstow at a return fare of $2d$ per day for the journey of 6–8 miles, and was one of the few to pierce what almost amounted to a surface railway exclusion zone, possibly because the final leg of the extension was in tunnel.

While the 'Cheap Trains Act' further encouraged the development of workmen's trains, as early as 1846 the solicitor to the Corporation of London, Charles Pearson, had advocated cheap trains to carry workers, described as the 'mechanic population', to and from their work. Pearson's vision was one of moving the slum dwellers into better accommodation, what might be described as the 'Metroland vision', and indeed he was a keen supporter of the Metropolitan Railway. Nevertheless, the ill-starred Eastern Counties takes the credit for the first workmen's trains in 1847, which linked Canning Town with North Woolwich, convenient for the Woolwich ferry, and were patronised by dockyard workers. Next appears to have been the Stockton & Darlington with a service between Middlesbrough and Eston in 1852. There were others as well in advance of the Cheap Trains Act, with the Metropolitan Railway introducing workmen's trains in 1864, and followed by the London Chatham & Dover Railway in 1865. In the latter case it was not so much the public interest that moved the directors but their own, as this commitment was offered to obtain Parliamentary sanction for their planned expansion to Blackfriars; this was one of the last pieces of railway private legislation with no clause written into it for cheap trains. Nevertheless, the fares charged on many of these trains were such that they only made a profit if full, and initially this rarely happened. By 1899, when the London County Council was formed, there were 104 workmen's trains running in to and out of the capital and carrying 23,000 passengers daily.

A different type of workmen's train emerged in Birmingham, where the train ran from the city centre carrying workers to Bournville for the large Cadbury's chocolate factory, and also in Glasgow, where the trains carried workers for the Singer sewing machine factory further down the Clyde. The great industrial cities of the north also had their workmen's trains. Later, instead of special trains for workmen, it was found to be more practical to offer special cheap workmen's tickets for those starting their journey before a certain hour, and this helped to ensure both the extension of the peak period by starting it earlier and the utilisation of rolling stock, rather than using special stock just for the workmen's trains. In the Southern Railway's timetable book for summer and autumn 1947, workmen's tickets were offered on the Waterloo & City tube line for just 3*d* return, as opposed to the normal fare of 7*d* return, provided that the outward journey was started before 08.00 on weekdays. The Southern clearly wanted to discourage bankers and brokers from having a bargain! The return journey could be made at any time during the day.

While there is no doubt that the movement of many working people from the city and town centres to the suburbs was an enlightened measure, it was not without its critics as it hastened the depopulation of the centres, something that has continued to this day. From the point of view of the railway companies the move was a mixed blessing. What started as an imposition and then, by the early twentieth century, had become a worthwhile business proposition, later became a burden for the railways as peak period traffic demanded more and longer trains and additional track had to be laid and platforms extended, all for the traffic of a couple of hours a day. Off-peak, many trains lay idle in the sidings, losing money. In working towards such a situation, the railways had made a rod for their own backs.

Of course, one might question just who might be described as a 'workman', since strictly speaking the term could be said to refer to anyone who works, no matter how little manual toil is involved, or how well paid. The other end of the spectrum was catered for by often considerable luxury. This did not simply mean first-class accommodation, although most trains offered this, including inner suburban trains until first class on these was abolished as a wartime austerity measure in October 1941. Nor did it necessarily even mean Pullman accommodation with extra comfort and a service of food and drink at the seat on payment of a special supplement, which was in addition to any refreshment taken, and which had become fairly widespread before the outbreak of the First World War. Indeed, until the Second World War, it was possible to travel in a Pullman even on the Metropolitan Line! Between the wars, first-class and Pullman accommodation was so important that the Southern Railway not only built the all-Pullman 'Brighton Belle' as part of its electrification of the Brighton line and included Pullman cars in many of its main-line electric multiple units, but also commissioned special electric multiple units for its trains to the City of London with a higher proportion of first class accommodation. Grander still were the 'club' trains, but not everyone could travel in such comfort.

The club trains had their origin in passenger demand. There was no need for an expensive trains act! During the 1890s first-class season-ticket holders commuting from Blackpool to Manchester approached the Lancashire & Yorkshire Railway (L&YR) asking that a special carriage should be provided for their exclusive use in return both for a guarantee that a minimum number of annual season tickets be purchased and for payment of a supplementary fare. This was to be a genuine club, and certainly not to be compared with the so-called airline 'club class'. As in any decent club, members had to be elected by a committee – whom one imagines must have been the founding members at first – and the members, once elected, had to abide by the club rules. In 1895 the L&YR introduced the first club car operating from Blackpool in the morning and home again in the evening. The members of the club had their own reserved seats and were served cups of tea from a small galley while, to ensure comfort, one rule was that the windows of the club car had to be kept closed while the train was in motion. This venture was so successful that by 1902 a second club car had been added to the main

Blackpool–Manchester commuter express and, echoing the experience in the south of England with Pullman stock, eventually a third-class club car was also provided. The club carriages were carefully marshalled in the train so that on arrival at Manchester they would stop close to the exit barriers.

The London & North Western Railway was the next to adopt the concept, introducing club cars on the main morning and evening trains on services between Llandudno and other coastal towns in North Wales, and between Liverpool and Manchester, all before the outbreak of the First World War, by which time a further club car was in service between Windermere and Manchester. The North Eastern Railway was next, with a club car on the service from Bridlington into Hull.

Grouping did not disturb the concept, although one might question the economics of a specially built or adapted carriage that made just one return journey daily, but no doubt on occasion such rolling stock found other uses, as when railway company directors ventured out to view their empire. Certainly, in 1935 the London Midland & Scottish commissioned a specially built club car, but this, and all the other club cars, fell victim to the drastic reductions in service and catering introduced as an austerity measure during the Second World War. Unlike the Pullman services, club cars were not reinstated after the war, although apparently a few were used for trains on 'rail cruises' in the 1950s. Despite this, the Blackpool to Manchester commuter trains continued to be loosely described as 'club trains' for several decades after the war had ended, so that the title survived into a more egalitarian age.

## DISABLED RIGHTS

In recent years the railways and bus operators in particular have been subjected to legislation on the rights of disabled passengers, but there is nothing new about the railways making special provision for passengers with mobility problems. This is despite the marked absence of ramps at many older railway stations, or those instances in which ramps have been provided, but only for those boarding or alighting from trains going in just one direction! To be fair, many older buildings do not lend themselves to easy conversion, while space and safety considerations often limit just what can be done. It is also worth noting that the peculiar British tradition of using raised platforms, in contrast to the practice in many countries of having very low platforms with a climb up into the train, does make access to railway carriages far easier in the British Isles than abroad.

The first instance of provision for disabled passengers on Britain's railways came as early as 1850, when the London & North Western Railway introduced a special 'invalid carriage', which included a saloon with seats that could be moved together to form a bed, and with access to a water closet, an extremely rare amenity on the railways at that time. It is worth noting, however, that this was really for passengers who were too ill or too weak to sit upright in an ordinary railway carriage, and certainly did not cater for what today would be described as 'disabled but able-bodied', for whom the guard's van seemed to be the location at this time and for most of the next century and a half. The South Eastern Railway was next to offer an invalid carriage in 1860; this must have been something of an achievement for a company that, along with its rival, the London Chatham & Dover, seemed to expect passengers generally to have strong bladders and was among the tardiest at introducing corridor stock when a good number of journeys in the south-east of England could have taken two hours or more. Perhaps more practical and of wider benefit still was a special carriage introduced by the Great Northern Railway in 1872, which had an open platform at one end to facilitate the loading and unloading of passengers either being carried on a stretcher or in a wheelchair.

Quite clearly the big drawback of these carriages was that there were so few of them, so that considerable advance notice would have to be given before undertaking a journey. It was not unusual at the time for the wealthy to book a saloon of their own, and one could hire even a train at fairly short notice, so this must not have been seen as an insurmountable problem. There is little left to indicate what the cost of such provision must have been, but most railway historians believe that a substantial supplementary charge must have been made on top of what would have been the first-class fare, or that a special rate must have applied. In short, there was nothing for the less wealthy disabled person anxious to travel, although doubtless later those unable to sit up could have made use of overnight sleepers.

The ambulance trains built in two world wars were for the use of repatriated wounded service personnel, and at the outset of the Second World War some were built anticipating the evacuation of patients from civilian hospitals, but on the return of peace the rolling stock was converted back to other uses. No attempt seems to have been made to provide any special rolling stock in later years, and certainly the earlier invalid carriages already mentioned would have been withdrawn by the early twentieth century.

The old railway companies simply requested advance notice of a disabled passenger travelling, but with them and with British Railways it was a question of using the guard's van and having a porter ready to help a wheelchair to be safely trundled across the tracks using the boards laid down for the movement of luggage trolleys. British Rail formalised these arrangements with a booklet, *British Rail and the Disabled Passenger*, giving details of the facilities available and special fares for holders of a disabled person's railcard. Other concessions included free travel for guide dogs.

In more recent years, Parliament has taken an interest in the problems of the disabled, with legislation providing for the Disabled Persons' Transport Advisory Committee (DiPTAC), which has laid down certain minimum requirements to improve access to railway carriages and buses, and to make destination and other displays easier to read, as well as ensuring that such items as grab poles are brightly coloured to ease recognition. Toilet facilities on new trains are also required to be large enough for a disabled passenger to use, with extra handrails and, for ease of access, sliding doors. These facilities have often proved more popular and comfortable for able-bodied passengers anyway, especially with the inclusion of a fold-down table for baby changing.

Nevertheless, echoing Victorian opposition to improving the lot of the traveller, the disabled rights requirements have resulted in considerable controversy in railway magazines. Those advocating greater provision for disabled people might be shocked at how vehement some of the letters and leading articles can be, but many of the criticisms have some validity. The first big criticism concerns the requirement that destination displays on the sides of vehicles be at waist level so that those in wheelchairs can read them easily, but this also means that on a crowded platform few other passengers can do so. There have been few complaints about the provision of special toilets for disabled persons on main-line trains, but on many local services an inordinate amount of seating is lost to toilets on a typical two-car train, leading some to speculate that train operating companies may eventually abandon toilets. Once again, rigid provision for a small minority of passengers is having an adverse effect on the majority.

## LOCAL TAXATION

Today, many railway services are subsidised not just by the government but by local authorities. It wasn't always so. In common with any other business the railways were liable for local authority rates, even though they always argued that their lines provided an immense benefit to the communities that they served, and indeed, for a community to be by-passed by the railways, or even simply served by a branch line, meant that it became a backwater. It is also worth bearing in mind that, since rateable values were based on the notional value of a property, the arrival of a railway in a community immediately increased the value and therefore the total rateable value of the properties there. On the other hand, the rating system actively discouraged the railways from building new stations as the suburbs grew.

It does seem that the railways were rated very heavily for the amount of land that they occupied, and that many local authorities saw the railway as a cash cow to be milked. One of the best examples of this was at Huyton, near Liverpool, where in 1849 the London & North Western Railway provided 35 per cent of the rates paid into the parish council, despite occupying less than 1 per cent of the land.

The system of rating for the railways had to evolve, and it took case law to decide on a fair basis. The rental value of stations and other premises was used as a basis for the rates, but for the actual length of line. The local authorities based their charges on the companies' receipts, making it more of a local tax or duty than rates. In the end the railways paid more than twenty times as much per employee as any other kind of business, and this was only affected to a degree by the Local Government Act 1858 that limited rating assessments for railway property to a quarter of the net value. Even so, this did not stop local authority valuers arguing that a major through line was worth more than a secondary route because it carried a greater volume of traffic and earned the railway greater revenue, though usually this approach was unsuccessful on appeal. The problem simply would not go away. A good example of just how important this was arose in 1935, when the directors of the Southern Railway were able to report that a rating appeal had caused the Net Value Rating Authority to reduce the value of the company from £2,180,000 to £1,077,131, saving the Southern £300,000 (£18.45 million today) per annum. To put this into perspective, just a few years earlier, at a time of zero inflation, it had cost the Southern Railway £2.7 million to electrify the lines to Brighton and West Worthing, including the cost of a new fleet of trains, so the amount was significant.

This is to jump ahead somewhat. The jumbled mess that constituted the means of financing local government itself needed clarification. In some areas, the railways also had to pay dues to turnpike trusts where their land had been acquired. Some cities had an ancient right to levy a toll on all goods entering and leaving, and a through goods train was not exempt. In some cases, goodwill and common sense prevailed, as in Carlisle, which happily commuted this imposition to an agreed annual fee – in 1880 it was £615 – but in Newcastle there was heated discussion and resentment on both sides. Even small towns and some villages could impose such a toll, and many did until the practice was scrapped in 1889.

The creation of school boards in 1870 to establish a formal nationwide network of schools was accompanied by the right to levy rates additional to those levied by local authorities. This brought out the fighting spirit in many railways and other major businesses, who sought a way around this further expense by offering a subscription, in some cases to prevent a local school board being established, but in others as a one-off payment to help build a new school, and infinitely preferable to an indefinite rating liability.

All in all, with national and local taxation of the railways, and restrictions on the fares that could be charged, it seems incredible that so many railways managed to be profitable. In fact, the railway boom bubble did burst on occasion, especially in about 1850, as we can see from George Hudson's story, and again in the 1860s.

## MONOPOLY

When first mooted, the railways were not expected to exercise a monopoly, for after all, there was road transport with which to contend, and on certain routes there would be the option of canal barges or coastal shipping. Parliament was opposed to monopoly, as was public opinion. At no stage did the scrutiny of the private bills set out to allow any one railway company a monopoly; indeed, it could be argued that, by allowing the London Chatham & Dover and the South Eastern Railway to compete so vigorously with one another, Parliament prevented a monopoly but encouraged both railways to beggar themselves. In this case the result was that the quality of service, the track and stations, and the equipment all suffered, and it was not until 1899 that the two companies combined under a management committee to form the South Eastern & Chatham Railway. Indeed, the prevailing mood was against mergers and amalgamations, and it says much about George Hudson's skill that the Midland Railway was able to come into existence.

As already mentioned, many railway operators, especially at first, actually hoped that other railway companies would use their lines, paying a toll for this purpose or coming to some other arrangement, such as a contribution to the capital costs. There were a few cases in which the promoter of a line expected to be able to operate rather as a turnpike trust, with all and sundry paying for the privilege of using the line, but this soon proved to be impractical, especially as signalling systems and junctions became more complex. Another problem lay in the provision of locomotive power, which was beyond the means of many would-be users of the railways, and they certainly could not afford the provision of the many engine sheds required for a far-flung railway network. Many in Parliament, at first knowing little about railway operation, assumed that the railways would indeed operate as a variant on the turnpike trust. The one instance in which this concept came close to being fulfilled was in the question of private owner wagons, usually belonging to coal mine owners. To the end the railways found these to be a nuisance and many companies actually tried to buy out the private owners whenever they could, although, interestingly, the practice has re-emerged for cement and oil traffic in particular in recent years.

One non-railway periodical pronounced on the question of monopoly quite succinctly in 1841, pointing out that the railways had only acquired a monopoly through 'superiority', meaning that they were faster, cheaper and more comfortable than road transport, but they certainly enjoyed no legal privilege. This situation lasted until the early years of the twentieth century for suburban services, and until after the First World War for rural and longer distance services.

Until the grouping, areas in which a monopoly existed were relatively few, and were often created to build a single strong enterprise in areas in which the competition had either been so vigorous as to be ruinous, or where the potential traffic could not justify two operators. The creation of the Midland Railway in the mid-nineteenth century and the South Eastern & Chatham at the end of it were two examples of the former.

This is not to suggest that mergers or amalgamations of railway companies were as rare as these two examples. The most obvious example was in those instances when a major extension of a route came about by creating a new railway for that section of track, including some of the London termini arrangements already mentioned, easing the raising of funds, but only making sense operationally when worked as a single entity.

Even where companies collaborated to share lines, this was to ensure operational efficiency rather than to create a local monopoly. A good example of this was the collaboration of the London & South Western and the London Brighton & South Coast at Portsmouth, on the Portsmouth–Ryde ferry service and on the line from Ryde Pier Head through Ryde Esplanade to Ryde St Johns. The London & South Western and the Midland collaborated on the Somerset & Dorset line partly to compete with the Great Western on traffic between the South Coast and the West Country and the Midlands, and partly because the line ran through such sparsely populated territory that its only hope of viability lay as a link for important longer-distance routes for trains such as the Bournemouth–Manchester 'Pines Express'.

In fact, at first Parliament seemed to favour competition, so much so that the members were happy to authorise the Clarence Railway to compete with the original Stockton & Darlington, and a competitor was also mooted for the Liverpool & Manchester. There was certainly competition as the trunk networks established themselves between London and Scotland, across the Pennines, between London and Birmingham and between London and Exeter, and for a while the latter also included Plymouth until the Great Western built a cut-off that shortened its route and left the London & South Western (LSWR) meandering around Dartmoor.

One of the best examples of monopoly was that of the London Brighton & South Coast (LBSCR) main line to Brighton, but this was simply because this, the first line between the two cities, was so direct that nothing else could rival it. The LBSCR had to face competition for traffic between London and both Portsmouth and Hastings, the two destinations at its western and eastern extremities.

The truth is that at the outset the very term 'monopoly' was anathema to public and politicians alike. Despite the investment made in the port by the railway, in Southampton the civic leaders were anxious to attract a second railway to compete with the London & South Western, which was certainly not always the most enterprising company, while at Plymouth there was great rejoicing when the LSWR broke the Great Western monopoly in 1876, although the latter always managed to hold the upper hand by insisting that all LSWR trains had to stop at Exeter St David's on journeys through that city. Yet by the middle of the nineteenth century opinion had begun to swing the other way. By this time, however, Parliament had already approved not only the mergers that led to the creation of the North Union Railway and allowed the Grand Junction Railway to acquire the Warrington & Newton, and then the merger of three companies to form the Midland Railway, but also the merger of four companies to make the North Eastern Railway. Later it was to approve the mergers that led to the creation of the Great Eastern, which had an effective monopoly in much of East Anglia, other than for traffic between London and Southend, and between London and Cambridge.

The great nineteenth-century economist Walter Bagehot found the British situation confusing and wasteful, comparing it with the major regional monopolies that had already emerged in France, albeit as a result of greater state direction and involvement. He maintained that the major companies were 'competing monopolies'. This meant that in the heart of their territories, usually along the route of their main lines, they were monopolies, but that they fought for business in the areas that abutted on to those of the next big company, building many unnecessary branches, as at Midhurst in West Sussex, at the end of three branch lines, or buying out smaller companies. This was an over-simplification since, as already mentioned, there were many major centres that enjoyed competing main-line services. It was the towns and cities along the way that faced a monopoly, and of the dozen or so largest British cities only Newcastle-upon-Tyne was served by a single railway from London. At the same time it was certainly true that there were some strange branches, such as the long and winding South Eastern route to Reading, or, perhaps more plausibly, two lines to Windsor and the London & South Western route to Reading. Midhurst, already mentioned, was served by the London & South Western from Petersfield, and from both Pulborough and Chichester by the London Brighton & South Coast. Even after grouping in 1923 the London & North Eastern Railway faced competition from the London Midland & Scottish, of all companies, between London and Southend!

In fact Parliament could not, and would not, make up its mind over whether it was pro-competition or pro-monopoly, especially when the latter offered some useful rationalisation. Despite the mergers already mentioned, when the London Brighton & South Coast Railway and the South Eastern Railway proposed a merger in 1868 it was rejected by the House of Lords, and criticised in the House and in the press as a measure that would allow the merged company to raise its fares, despite competition in Kent from the London Chatham & Dover. The same thing happened when the London & North Western (LNWR) and the Lancashire & Yorkshire (L&YR) came forward with proposals for a merger during 1872 and again during 1873. By this time Parliament had established a joint committee of both Houses to examine the whole question of amalgamation. The committee heard of proposals to merge the railways into six companies, an early approach to the post-First World War grouping, possibly to be followed by the creation of a single, large railway company. The idea of a single operator was also seen by some as a step towards nationalisation. The committee hadn't liked the idea of a monopoly supplier of railway services and saw the merger of the LNWR and the L&YR as a step towards this, so rejected the proposed merger for a second time. Yet by the end of the decade the waste of competition was being criticised as leading to fares and freight rates that were unnecessarily high, rather than, as many might argue, keen competition keeping charges to the minimum.

In fact, the 312 route miles between London Paddington and Penzance came into the ownership and operation of a single company, the Great Western, by a series of amalgamations, one at a time, and with five companies involved altogether, between 1866 and 1889. Overall, Parliament felt that no new monopolies were being created by any of these mergers.

This tendency for Parliament to face both ways continued. In 1899 it approved the merger of the London Chatham & Dover (LCDR) and the South Eastern (SER) companies under a management committee to create the South Eastern & Chatham Railway (SECR). Almost ten years later it refused to approve a similar merger in the east of England, involving the Great Northern, Great Eastern and Great Central companies, and another in South Wales, that would have brought the Taff Vale and the Cardiff Railway together! A little later, in 1910, Parliament allowed three out of the then eight London underground railways to merge, and then allowed another one to join them in 1912 and another two in 1920, creating what became known as the Underground Group.

It was not until the grouping after the First World War that Parliament took the initiative on mergers. Before then it was always up to the individual companies to agree what should be done among themselves, and then to seek Parliamentary approval. The merger to create the SECR was a good case in point. The two companies had impoverished one another and, finally recognising this, a working union had been proposed as early as 1890, by which time the LCDR, which at one time had been bankrupt, was, if anything, in a stronger financial position than the SER. As a result the SER, which had objected to the LCDR demanding 37 per cent of the overall receipts in 1890, eventually had to accept the LCDR having 41 per cent in 1899. In 1898, before the combining of the two companies, the LCDR had receipts of £142 per mile per week, against £87 on the SER. On the other hand, the SER had far better rolling stock, and especially locomotives. Had the SER taken a more comprehensive approach to the provision of railway services throughout Kent, the outcome could have been different, and it could even have enjoyed a local monopoly.

   The areas that did experience a railway monopoly before the First World War were:

1.  The Highland Railway north of Inverness.
2.  The Great North of Scotland Railway to the north and north-west of Aberdeen.
3.  The North British Railway between the rivers Forth and Tay.
4.  The North Eastern Railway north from Beverley and Selby to the Scottish border at Berwick-on-Tweed, and west as far as Harrogate.
5.  The North Staffordshire in the Potteries and towards Macclesfield and Burton-on-Trent.
6.  The Great Eastern in Suffolk and in Norfolk south of Norwich.
7.  The London & South Western west of Portsmouth and in the eastern part of Dorset, with collaboration with the Midland Railway on the Somerset & Dorset.
8.  The London Brighton & South Coast Railway east of Portsmouth as far east as Bexhill-on-Sea.
9.  The South Eastern & Chatham Railway in Kent.
10. The Cambrian Railway in mid-Wales from Shropshire to Aberystwyth and Pwllheli, although there were some non-Cambrian minor lines.

In most of these the railways were local and serving areas that were sparsely populated, but often with through trains provided by other companies. The exceptions were services to Newcastle and the three monopolies in the south of England, which more or less fitted with Bagehot's claim of competing monopolies. As we will see later, even after the grouping the companies were often extremely slow to rationalise as dramatically as might have been expected, while after nationalisation sometimes rationalisation was taken to extremes, often as a result of the attitude of the Ministry of Transport and the Treasury. On the other hand railway interest in bus services, once Parliament authorised this in 1929, saw genuine public transport monopolies emerge in many areas, including the Isle of Wight where the acquisition of Dobson Brothers' Vectis concern, promptly re-named Southern Vectis by the Southern Railway in a classic example of a 'branded' corporate identity, left passengers on the main routes with the choice of a Southern train or a Southern bus, except on one or two minor routes left to a dwindling band of independent bus companies.

CHAPTER FIVE

# *Safety*

Safety prompted the first public legislation on railways. One of the earliest concerns of Parliament with regard to the railways was that of accident investigation, and not simply because one of their number had fallen victim to the new mode of transport! The earliest known railway accident occurred long before politicians took an interest, and seems to have been the fate of two boys, one in April 1650 (yes, 1650) and one that July, both of whom were buried at Whickham in County Durham after being run down by a wagon running on a wooden tramway linking coal mines with the River Tyne. Durham seems to have been ill-fated in its railway connections, as in 1815 a locomotive boiler exploded at Philadelphia killing sixteen people. This was the first recorded locomotive boiler explosion, but it was not the last, and the Stockton & Darlington suffered two in 1828 alone. Durham did not have a monopoly on accidents. The Liverpool & Manchester had no fewer than twelve accidents on the Sutton incline between 1831 and 1843, an average of roughly one a year.

The law of the land was well able to take care of cases of accidental death and negligence, since by this time the coroners' courts were well established, and, if they had the money, the injured, or the dependents of those who had been killed, could sue the railway company. The trouble was that the courts lacked the expertise to assess technical matters. This was still a time when many were fearful of being carried along at speeds of 30mph! The Railway Regulation Act 1840 required the railway companies to report all accidents, no matter how minor, involving personal injury to passengers but not necessarily staff to the BoT, which had the duty to appoint inspectors who had the power to enter and inspect railway premises, track and rolling stock but, strangely, did not have the power at this stage actually to investigate an accident! The first railway accident report dates from the year of the act, 1840. Even the subsequent Railway Regulation Act 1842 did not authorise the inspectors, who, with one exception, were all serving or recently retired officers from the Royal Engineers, to investigate all accidents: only serious accidents had to be investigated, meaning those inflicting serious injury to a member of the public. Nevertheless, at the time accidents generally resulted in serious injury, simply because of the circumstances. Frail wooden bodies on brittle iron underframes meant that even a minor collision could be serious, and this was compounded by the use of oil or gas-fired lighting within the carriages, a practice that persisted on some lines into the twentieth century. Modern rolling stock with its integral monocoque construction and couplings or buffers designed to prevent carriages being pushed on top of one another can mean that even a high-speed derailment can occur without causing serious injuries, especially if all-steel construction is used in the carriages and no trackside obstacle, such as a bridge or other structure, is hit.

The 1842 Act brought one significant advance: no passenger-carrying railway line could be opened without the approval of an inspector. This meant that if the inspector was not satisfied opening, and hence revenue-earning, could be delayed. There were also provisions covering the premature opening of a line before an inspector had given his approval, with railway companies liable to a fine of £20 for each day of operation. This was a year's pay for many a working man and the lengths of line were often relatively short. The inspector's powers were not inconsiderable and were used, with one of the most notable early cases being when the London & South Western Railway extended its line from Nine Elms to Waterloo in 1848. The inspector was concerned about the safety of one of the bridges and refused to allow the line to open as planned on 1 July, so opening was deferred for ten days.

Inevitably, when so much depended on the judgement of a single inspector, some veered on the side of caution. In 1850 the Manchester Sheffield & Lincolnshire Railway, a predecessor of the Great Central, complained about an inspector's recommendation that it should not be allowed to open Torksey Bridge, and was allowed to proceed once other engineers declared that the inspector had been over-cautious.

In 1880 it took an accident on a very short stretch of line opened by the Midland Railway in 1872 for it to be realised that this important link in the network, had never been submitted for inspection, making the company liable for accumulated fines totalling £60,000 (more than £3 million today). Under pressure from the Board of Trade the Midland acknowledged its error, ensured that the line was of a suitable standard and then sought a formal inspection, after which the BoT waived the fines.

The army officers on whom the burden of investigation fell were certainly far better qualified to investigate a railway accident than any intelligent layman, but they too had much to learn about the new science, or perhaps it really should be sciences, brought into widespread use by the railways. Metallurgy was almost unknown, and non-destructive means of testing, especially on such things as track and boilers, was simply not available. The inspectors were helped in the case of boiler explosions by the BoT seconding experts from its Marine Department. Then there was so much to discover about signalling and the management of a busy stretch of railway line, and a number of practices that had to be understood fully before an improvement could be considered. The inspectors were not above criticism, but they have been universally regarded as having been diligent and honest, and they built up a massive body of experience and expertise through their work. The reports were never secret and always presented to Parliament, and after 1860 they could be bought by the public. Yet the inspectors had no power to compel the railways to adopt their recommendations, which had to remain no more than advice. It was also the case that sometimes a new precautionary device would resolve one danger, but introduce a new one that would not immediately be apparent until exposed by a further accident. This was trial and error, simply because so much had to be learnt. The system endured the passage of time, including grouping and nationalisation, so that officers of the Royal Engineers continued in this role until 1982.

Nevertheless, as mentioned elsewhere in the background to the Parliamentary Trains, the reports did influence and motivate Parliament. The serious accident on the Great Western Railway at Sonning in 1841 had led directly to the so-called Gladstone's Act of 1844 after much discussion and concern over the conditions in which the poorer members of society were being conveyed.

Technological advances away from the railways sometimes came to the rescue. For example, on the early railways the distance between a train and the one following it was regulated by time alone. This meant that if there was a mishap or the first train failed to maintain the distance between it and the following one, assuming that the driver of the latter could not always count on being able to see sufficiently far ahead to be able to stop in time, an accident could only be prevented by the guard of the first train setting back along the track to stop the following train. If the guard did not do this quickly enough a serious accident could occur, and did so on several occasions. The electric telegraph improved communications so that staff at railway stations knew where trains had passed or were being delayed, and led ultimately to the block system, in which trains were kept apart by distance rather than by time. The system was initially expensive and rejected by some companies on the spurious grounds that it would make enginemen and signalmen less alert! Nevertheless, as early as the 1860s not only the block system but interlocking of points and signals as a further step forward in safety were both possible, and the 1870s saw the spread of both systems throughout the railway network with varying degrees of enthusiasm from railway managements. Anxious that best practice was implemented as quickly and as widely as possible, in 1869 the BoT asked railway companies to provide an annual return showing the extent to which each of them had adopted the block system. Many of the leading railway companies were indignant, and one, the North Eastern, decided that it would ignore the BoT's request completely. The company's reward came in late 1870 with four serious accidents occurring on its track, of which three could have been prevented if the block system had been in use with interlocking. The directors sacked their general manager.

Yet, as in more recent times with controversy over the Train Protection and Warning System, accidents continued to occur, and again as today many could not have been prevented by the safety measures available. The Tay Bridge disaster in 1879 resulted in a court of inquiry in which the railway inspector sat with another representative of the BoT and a distinguished engineer.

The need to ensure that the worst railway managements did not drag down the industry and instead performed closer to the best resulted in a further flurry of legislation. The Railway Regulation Act 1871 for the first time required the railway companies to notify the BoT of any accident involving death or injury to anyone, meaning that for the first time railway workers, or 'railway servants' as they were known, were covered by the legislation. This measure was overdue as goods trains and shunting movements could be involved in accidents without any member of the public getting hurt: the period 1874–8 saw an annual average of 35 passengers killed in accidents, but the five-year total was 682 railwaymen killed. Many of the accidents were due not just to the absence of safety precautions, but to many railwaymen working excessively long hours, and a number of inspectors highlighted this in their reports. The 1871 Act also gave the BoT the authority to establish a court of inquiry to investigate a major accident if the Board saw fit. The Railway Regulation Act 1873 finally gave the BoT the power to compel railway companies to provide an annual return of the track mileage covered by the block system. These measures were so successful that the number of railwaymen killed in the nine years between 1879 and 1888 fell to 479.

The inspectorate and accident investigation were also able to highlight problems over unrestricted competition, especially after the investigation in 1871 of the derailment of a London to Scotland night express at Wigan because of excessive speed. The London & North Western Railway maintained that the high speed had been forced upon it by the need to compete with the East Coast group of companies. Even so, when a Royal Commission was appointed to investigate railway safety in 1874, taking three years, it amassed a considerable volume of evidence, but produced little in the way of results. Typical of the way in which the Royal Commisson worked was the question of the provision of continuous braking to passenger trains, which was now becoming more extensive as speeds rose, but was subjected to different and incompatible technologies. In 1876 the Commission members watched trials of the different systems at Newark, but failed to decide on a standard system, largely because it was hard to see any decisive advantage from one system or another. Nevertheless, in 1878 further legislation at last compelled railway companies to provide twice-yearly returns showing the number of passenger carriages fitted for continuous braking, while the absence of adequate braking ensured higher compensation for the victims or their families.

Many measures that needed legislation to enforce their adoption were appallingly simple, such as the Railway Employment (Prevention of Accidents) Act 1900, enforcing measures for the safety of permanent way workers and for adequate lighting on stations and in sidings. It took an order under this Act to enforce the provision of handbrakes on both sides of new goods wagons as late as 1907, suggesting that previously, brakemen working in sidings either had to be stationed on both sides of wagons, or had somehow to cross over while a train was being shunted, or, most likely, hope that they could brake sufficient wagons on one side of the goods train to stop it running away!

It took the Armagh accident of 12 June 1889 for the government to take powers, the Regulation of Railways Act 1889, to ensure that the railway inspectors at last could insist that all passenger trains employed continuous braking and all passenger lines operated on the block system with full interlocking of signals and points. Irish railways were often operated as cheaply as possible. The accident had occurred on a little-used and steeply graded cross-country route on the Great Northern Railway of Ireland. It involved a Sunday school excursion headed by a small 2–4–0 locomotive, but at the last minute the length of the train was increased to fifteen six-wheeled carriages despite objections from the driver who was unhappy at the heavy load. The train left Armagh 15 minutes late and started the 1:75 climb away from the town. A short distance from the summit the engine stalled, and it was decided to split the train, with the locomotive taking the first five carriages to the next station. This meant that once the brake pipes were disconnected there was no braking power for the rest of the train, which relied on the handbrake screwed down in the rear guard's van and stones placed under the carriage wheels. As the locomotive started to take the first five carriages forward it slipped back slightly, bumping the remaining ten carriages so that the guard's brake failed to hold them and they started to roll back, crushing the stones as they rolled over them. Lacking block working, the discredited time interval system was still in force, and at 10.35 a second train was sent forward from Armagh. As it tackled the steep gradient the fireman saw the carriages of the earlier train running towards them. The driver applied the brakes, but before he could stop his train the runaway carriages hit his locomotive at around 40mph, smashing the wooden guard's van, full of standing passengers, and two carriages, and throwing the locomotive down an embankment. Eighty passengers, twenty-two of them children, were killed and more than 260 seriously injured, making this the worst accident on Britain's railways until Quintinshill in 1915. Amazingly, the accident could have been worse, for as his locomotive rolled over, the driver jumped on to its tender, and by applying its handbrake was able to save his carriages from rolling backwards out of control.

Safety soon became associated with efficient working, and the steady flow of new safety systems provided profitable business for the manufacturers. The block system, for example, worked well when signalmen were conscientious, but a further safety measure was track circuiting, first introduced in the UK in 1901 and an essential ingredient in any automatic signalling system. The enginemen also had to be alert to ensure safety but, of course, often could not see signals in fog, so the next safety device was an audible warning of a distant signal set at caution, available in 1906. Yet, when the Great Western started introducing automatic train control (ATC), which stopped a train passing a signal set at danger, on its main lines from 1929 onwards, it was the only company to do so.

Well before this, at Quintinshill near Carlisle in 1915, Britain experienced its worst ever railway disaster involving no fewer than five trains owing to the criminal negligence of two signalmen on the Caledonian Railway, although, of course, the railways were under unified state control at the time. One of the trains was packed with troops heading for the war in France, and as a result of the serious fire that followed, which destroyed the military records, the exact death toll has never been established, but it is generally accepted that around 227 people lost their lives and another 245 were injured. Had routine operating practices been observed and staff been at their posts on time the accident would never have happened, but neither would it have happened had automatic signalling and track circuiting been in use.

The remote Quintinshill signalbox covered not just the main line but two passing loops to allow expresses to overtake the slower goods trains and local stopping train. At the time both loops were occupied by goods trains, so that a northbound local train had to be reversed on to the southbound main line to allow two expresses to pass it on their way to Edinburgh and Glasgow, and the local was promptly forgotten by the signalman. On to this unhappy scene a crowded troop train raced downhill from Beattock with no fewer than twenty-one carriages, mainly elderly six-wheelers of largely wooden construction and with gas lighting, striking the local train with such force that the troop train was compressed to a quarter of its original length. Worse was to follow, as the first of the two northbound expresses ran into the wreckage before it could stop, and glowing coals from the firebox created an inferno as they ignited the ruptured gas pipes for the lighting of the troop train. Such was the severity of the fire that it did not die down for 24 hours. The accident itself did little to endear the railways to the public mind. The troop train was composed of obsolete rolling stock set aside for the purpose, with little protection for the occupants in even a minor accident.

The continued absence of ATC led to Britain's second worst railway accident, at Harrow in 1952. A late-running express from Perth in Scotland on a misty morning, but with low sun, missed a colour light signal set at danger and ran at high speed into the back of a waiting Up suburban train, with the express locomotive ploughing through the three carriages at the back. A Down express to Liverpool and Manchester, running double-headed, ploughed into the wreckage, with the two locomotives rearing up and demolishing a footbridge before careering on their sides across a crowded platform and onto an electrified line, where a fourth train just managed to stop in time. The total death toll was 112 people. Later, in 1957 at Lewisham St Johns, a main-line express passed two signals set at danger, again in fog, and ran into an electric suburban train with such force that the two carriages at the back were telescoped. This was bad enough, but meanwhile the steam locomotive's tender had swung off the track and hit a support for a railway overbridge, bringing it down onto the carriages behind it. The result was that 90 people were killed and another 109 seriously injured. Both accidents could have been avoided had ATC been in service. The accident at Lewisham hastened installation of the new postwar system known as automatic warning system (AWS), which alerted the driver when passing a signal set at caution or at danger.

The importance of ATC cannot be over-estimated. Today many parts of Great Britain remain notorious for fog, but in the past the situation was far worse because of the lack of any restraint on the burning of coal, at one time the main fuel for industry and every household. Very thick fogs were a frequent winter occurrence in many industrial areas, with days without a breath of wind and such dense pollution that the death rate among the elderly and those with chest infections soared. On the streets people wore smog masks and young urchins earned pennies by walking in front of vehicles with a torch to guide drivers across junctions and on to the right road. The Clean Air Acts reduced this problem almost beyond belief, so that a genuine 'pea-souper' became a thing of the past, while on the railways the spread of colour light signalling marked an improvement over semaphore signals.

The spate of accidents that followed privatisation of the railways has tended to cloud judgment and obscure the memories of the accidents on the nationalised railway. The recent disaster at Hatfield, when a Great North Eastern Railway (GNER) express was derailed owing to a broken rail, has allowed politicians and journalists to overlook the far worse accident at Hither Green, also caused by a broken rail, in 1967, in which 49 passengers were killed and almost 80 injured. The accident was caused by deficiencies in inspection, as at Hatfield, and appalling standards of maintenance, again as at Hatfield. At Hatfield the track had been in a visibly poor state for some months, while at Hither Green short lengths of 'infill' track had been used to link longer lengths, with some track on wooden sleepers and others on concrete, leading to uneven stresses that had increased the chance of a broken rail.

The accident at Clapham in 1988 also showed what could happen with a shortage of qualified staff, with many signalling engineers working for weeks at a stretch with hardly a day off, and poor supervision of work. It was this accident that led to a review of railway safety by a public inquiry chaired by Mr Justice Hidden, recommending a completely automatic train control, ATC, and protection system.

In many ways Clapham was a watershed in British railway safety and accident investigation. It was the last major accident in which priority was given to two things; firstly, clearing the tracks and getting the service running again as quickly as possible, and secondly, investigating the causes of the accident before deciding on any further action, such as prosecution.

The first significant accident to be subjected to a new investigative approach occurred at Southall, where a high-speed train (HST) collided with a freight train that had been cleared to cross its path while the HST's driver was distracted and its AWS was inactive. On the 'old' railway the freight train would have been held back and priority accorded the express. The Southall accident was followed by an accident again on the old Western Region route into Paddington close to the terminus itself when a Down local train overran a red signal into the path of an Up HST. The severity of the almost head-on collision was worsened by the presence of the overhead wires for the 'Heathrow Express' that turned fuel vapour released by the severity of the impact into an inferno as the power car reared up and struck the wires.

In the Southall accident prosecution preceded full investigation and, not surprisingly, failed. The skewed logic of this approach was that an inspector's findings could jeopardise a court hearing, ignoring the fact that it required an inspector's findings to provide the necessary grounds for a prosecution! The role of the accident investigators was usurped by the Health & Safety Executive (HSE) and by the British Transport Police, who treated each accident as a scene of crime and took a leisurely approach to their task. Instead of getting services back to normal, accident sites were cordoned off and cocooned. At Harrow in 1952 the suburban lines were reopened late on the following day. At Hatfield it took weeks. When a single electric multiple unit was involved in a fatal derailment at Potters Bar the media were told that the line would re-open in ten days! Those who advocated greater use of the railways and less use of the roads for environmental and safety reasons happily ignored the fact that tens of thousands of railway passengers had to switch to the roads. Travellers want safety, but they also want reliability. Even leisure travellers want to get to their destination at a reasonable time.

Reasons for the changes in the way accidents were handled can be attributed to several factors. One of these was that in 1990 responsibility for railway safety was passed to the HSE, which took over Her Majesty's Railway Inspectorate. The HSE's interventions not just on the railways but also in other industries have been criticised for their excessive zeal and lack of realism. Another reason has been the growing role of the British Transport Police which, instead of treating an accident site as something to be protected while investigators carry out their task, see it as a scene of crime. At Clapham the reasons for the accident were known within hours. Many also blame the growth in the compensation culture, but it would be wrong to over-emphasise this too much as the victims of serious accidents have always had access to the courts.

Prompt discovery of the cause of an accident brings one major benefit, the most important of all, in that it enables action to be taken to prevent a recurrence as quickly as possible. It is also the case that often accidents occur for reasons other than criminal intent, and sometimes for reasons other than neglect.

The HSE suffers from not treating railway safety as an issue in its own right, and almost certainly doesn't understand railways. HSE strictures on trains arriving at a terminus provide a good example of this. To avoid trains hitting the buffers at stations, trains have had to slow as they approach the platform, often so severely that the driver then had to apply power to reach the stop point, itself usually just short of the buffers. This meant that instead of the train being driven into the terminus with the brakes on, and the experienced driver judging the distance to make a smooth stop, trains now power towards the buffers!

Inevitably Parliament was soon back on the scene. The Railway and Transport Safety Act 2003 finally introduced a Rail Accident Investigation Branch (RAIB), amid doubts among insiders about an overlap with the HSE, but at least with a brief to improve railway safety and prevent accidents. The new RAIB is not to apportion blame or liability, but instead to report on the cause of an accident. The HSE, meanwhile, was empowered by the Act to levy the industry for its services.

Responsibility for the British Transport Police (BTP) was also covered by the Act, making the BTP a completely independent police force, albeit one funded by the railways, with the train operators and infrastructure provider meeting its costs through a series of service agreements that will determine their shares.

# CHAPTER SIX

# The Growing Control of the State

In 1844 Gladstone's Act clearly established Parliament's intent to maintain a close interest in the railways. The next significant measure came only two years later, and this was the very necessary, indeed long overdue, Gauge Act. In 1845 Parliament had established a Royal Commission on track gauges, and this heard and saw for itself the terrible disruption and chaos caused by the break of gauge, most especially that between the Great Western and the other railways. The Gauge Act in theory forbade, with certain exceptions, the construction of new lines to any gauge other than 4ft 8½in, which from this time onwards became known as the standard gauge. Following the Act, anything wider became known as broad gauge and anything narrower as narrow gauge. This was one measure that only applied to Great Britain, as in Ireland the standard gauge remained at 5ft 3in, and a considerable mileage of narrow gauge, 3ft 6in, was also laid, especially in Donegal. In practice, the Great Western and its satellites continued to expand their track mileage for some time on the 7ft gauge.

As far as the Railway Regulation Acts were concerned the next measure did not appear until 1868, and concerned such mundane matters as keeping accounts and the companies' obligations as carriers, and also ensured that all trains included some non-smoking accommodation. Further legislation followed in 1871, with two acts in 1873, then again in 1889 when matters such as overtime for railwaymen and passenger evasion of fares were tackled, while the 1893 Act returned to what was obviously becoming an increasingly vexed question of hours of work.

At the height of the railway mania in 1846 Parliament created the Railway Commissioners, removing the supervision of railways from the

BoT to what was in effect a standing commission appointed by Parliament, chaired by an MP, and including a member of the House of Lords, a retired judge and two officers from the Royal Engineers. The balance of capabilities provided by this grouping seems at first sight to be almost ideal, although one could argue that the addition of one or two railwaymen could have made a difference, but no doubt these were all very busy either making money or persuading would-be backers to part with some. Either way, the Railway Commissioners made little impact on the burgeoning industry, while Parliament could not let go of its rights and, for that matter, the very real need to examine the massive volume of private legislation coming forward to authorise new lines. In 1851 the Railway Commissioners were disbanded, and the BoT regained responsibility for the railway. While the first of the two acts of 1873 also dealt with a proposed Railway Commission, it was not until 1891 that the body was formally created, and on this occasion it was within the BoT itself and replaced the Railway Department. A further measure occurred in 1896, when the Board was commanded to establish a commission to examine the construction and working of light railways, since Parliament felt that these had much to offer in extending the railway network, although very little use had been made of the earlier legislation.

## TRAINS OR HOUSES?

Parliament had set up another Royal Commission in 1846 to look at the London termini, since there was a scramble between railway companies to find locations as close to the centre of London as possible and Parliament thought that some order should be brought to bear on the situation. It was not successful, despite the enterprising ideas of some of the railway companies that would, for example, have seen a north–south link between Charing Cross and Euston, which would not only have eased the capacity problems at the former, but would have made it far easier to run trains through from the Channel ports to the Midlands and beyond. The disruption being caused by the railways as they gouged routes through the heavily built-up inner suburbs of London and as lines, especially south of the River Thames, crossed one another, was another factor that concerned Parliament. The terms of reference for the Royal Commission were: 'whether the extension of railways into the centre of the metropolis is calculated to afford such additional convenience or benefit to the public as will compensate for the sacrifice of property, the interruption of important thoroughfares, and the interference with the plans of improvement already suggested'.

The team of commissioners charged with this exercise were once again the victims of their age. Their brief was well considered by any rational assessment, but no one understood the true nature of the problem, and the impact that the railways would have on the travelling and indeed the working habits of the population could not be foreseen. Here we have the paradox that it was too early to predict the best way forward, and yet once the matter really could be examined sensibly with the benefit of experience, opportunities had been lost, and the further development of the London area meant that any attempt to alleviate the problem would be prohibitively expensive and the disruption immense.

One could argue that this was no bad thing. For example, one matter considered was the creation of a single large terminus for all of the railway companies. This begs the questions of where and just how large? After all, there were still fewer than 5,000 route miles in the country as a whole, less than a quarter of the eventual total, and there was no such thing as an underground railway network at the time. Fortunately, the Commissioners were adamant that there was no advantage in a single terminus since the number of through passengers across the centre of London was negligible – true at the time. They also foresaw problems of congestion at and around such a terminus, while its management, divided between what would eventually be twelve* companies, would be extremely difficult. The convenience for long-distance passengers of a central London terminus seemed of little importance to the Commissioners when set against the disruption that it would cause, and we should bear in mind that the various stagecoach departure and arrival points had usually been just outside the centre.

If the convenience of long-distance passengers took second place to that of those whose lives and property would be disrupted by any

* Taken from Paddington and running clockwise, these were: Great Western, Paddington; Great Central, Marylebone; London & North Western, Euston; Midland, St Pancras; Great Northern, King's Cross; North London, Broad Street; Great Eastern, Liverpool Street; London, Tilbury & Southend, Fenchurch Street; London Brighton & South Coast, London Bridge and Victoria; South Eastern, Cannon Street and Charing Cross; London Chatham & Dover, Blackfriars, Holborn Viaduct, Ludgate Hill and Victoria; London & South Western, Waterloo. There was also the Waterloo & City Railway, but this was taken over by the LSWR.

extension into the central area, that of short-distance passengers weighed still less. In their final report the Commissioners recommended that no railway should enter the central area on the north side of the River Thames. By 'central area' they meant from Park Lane in the west to the City Road and Moorgate in the east, and from Euston Road in the north to what would now be the Embankment, but additionally this extended south of the Thames to Borough High Street. Any plans to allow the railways to intrude into this box in the future should only be allowed under an overall plan that had been carefully considered and 'sanctioned by the wisdom of Parliament'. Then, as now, property south of the river was less valuable than that to the north of it, and the Commissioners also felt that the disruption to highways and to property would be far less. The Commissioners were happy with the already authorised construction of Waterloo and felt, wrongly as many passengers would suggest, that London Bridge was convenient for the City, but they accepted the need for the lines from Kent to be extended from London Bridge to Waterloo and Charing Cross.

A glance at a street plan for London will show that for lines from two (north and west) of the main compass points the Commissioners' recommendations held good, even though it left many of the main termini, and especially Paddington, not well sited for either the City or the West End, with only Charing Cross and then Marylebone, the last to be built, anywhere near convenient for the latter. Only Cannon Street and Liverpool Street were well sited for the City, the latter having been built as 'an exception to the rule'. The winners were the southern companies, who for the most part were able to forge ahead, cross the river onto the north bank of the Thames, and serve both the City and the West End, effectively breaching the Commissioners' ban on termini on the north bank. The one exception was the London & South Western, which had to remain at Waterloo, relatively isolated until relieved by the completion of the Waterloo and City Line in 1898 and, as far as access to the West End was concerned, by the opening of the Bakerloo Line in 1906, followed by what was then known as the Hampstead Tube, now the Northern Line, in 1926.

The next stage was the House of Commons Parliamentary Select Committee on Metropolitan Communications in 1855. This worthy body had all sorts of ideas thrown at it, many of which reflected the now unbounded confidence of the Victorians. Joseph Paxton, the genius behind the Crystal Palace, had one of the grander visions. His Crystal

Palace had by now been moved happily from Kensington to Sydenham. Indeed, very happily for the fortunes of the London Brighton & South Coast Railway, that had been behind the choice of a new location so well suited to generate considerable volumes of off-peak suburban traffic. For his next great achievement Paxton favoured an inner circle railway, the Great Victorian Way, incorporating a shopping arcade no less than 72ft wide stretching all the way from Regent Street to the City, all of it under glass! Within this arcade communication would be enhanced by a railway running 24ft above the pavement. 'We do not want to raise our citizens under forcing-frames and grow aldermen like cucumbers,' thundered the *Daily Telegraph*. 'We must protest against being disturbed in our slumbers by a whistle and a roar overhead, as if the powers of darkness were engaged in a tournament.'

The newspaper went on to propose that instead of putting shopping arcades under railways, the railways themselves should be put underground. This was the same conclusion that the members of the Select Committee reached, also proposing that the main London termini should be connected with each other, with the River Thames, which still carried passengers at the time, with the docks and with the Post Office, at the time taken to mean the main establishment at St Martins-le-Grand. One point overlooked by all concerned was, of course, that many of the lines from the south into London were in reality already overhead railways, being carried on broad viaducts in an attempt both to ease disruption and to avoid gradients. Waterloo station itself is built on top of supports and the opportunity was taken to produce under-station storage there, while the viaducts carrying the lines from Kent and from the south-west provided within their arches much-appreciated business premises for many small concerns.

Its work over, the Select Committee on Metropolitan Communications lapsed, and it was left to the House of Lords to return to the subject in 1863, at the height of a renewed, and very short-lived, railway boom. The House of Lords Select Committee on Metropolitan Railway Communications looked once again at the concept of a large central terminus for all of the railways, and once again reported against it. The Committee was again of the opinion that any new lines within the central area would have to be underground, with the limits placed by the original Royal Commission of 1846 being extended still further out. As already seen, there were some exceptions to this extension of the 1846 limits, with the main one being that the Great Eastern was to be allowed to reach Liverpool Street, probably because this was reached by tunnel. Less significant, the London & North Western encouraged the North London Railway to edge across the boundary to build a station next door at Broad Street, while the London Chatham & Dover even opened a line, partly on viaduct, partly underground, between Blackfriars and King's Cross, with a very blatant bridge at the bottom of Ludgate Hill, obscuring the view of St Paul's Cathedral from Fleet Street, of all places! The concept of an 'inner circle' north of the Thames to link the termini was first mooted, and this was endorsed the following year by the Parliamentary Joint Committee on Railway Schemes (Metropolis). Thus the basis of the Circle Line was laid and assured of political support. It might have been even better if the line had managed to touch Euston rather than simply dump passengers with heavy luggage nearby, and also stray south of the Thames to include Waterloo, whose passengers at the time were the most inconvenienced since those arriving at London Bridge could transfer to a Charing Cross or Cannon Street train, or even, if coming off the Brighton line, could have opted for Victoria instead.

Opinions on the sometimes haphazard way in which the railways arrived vary. There is no doubt that there is a school of opinion that would have favoured central direction, as in Europe, but this would have resulted in a far less dense network than was the end result. Others see the whole chaotic system as being the result of having been the first country to have had railways, and there is some truth in this. The real point, of course, is that the British way of doing things meant that at least the railways followed the money. It was also easier to persuade people, usually local landowners and business people, to invest in a line that showed a tangible and immediate local benefit. After all, why tax the population as a whole, which might not see the point in providing a railway to link two provincial towns, when some people are ready and willing to put their own money into the venture?

More to the point, there is an enormous and often overlooked difference between the British way of doing things and that of mainland Europe, with the British approach usually being closer to that of the USA. While the various parliamentary committees struggled to see a way forward for the railways in London, their deliberations were not always pointless, for they foresaw the need for the Circle Line and also the problems of a single central railway terminus, and their work was made much more difficult by the fact that London was already Europe's largest city. This was due to a combination of factors, with the railways, with their scope for spreading the population into the suburbs, undoubtedly playing a part, but it was also because London was not just a capital city; it was also the country's largest port. The British had, moreover, been far more involved in overseas trading ventures than their European counterparts, partly, but not entirely, because of the size of the British Empire. After all, Hudson at one stage was interested in a plan to build a railway in Spain, while more successful were those British entrepreneurs who ensured that many South American cities received urban tram systems, or who built the line across the Andes linking Argentina and Chile and, in doing so, the Atlantic with the Pacific. The result of all this activity lay in the City of London, that tightly packed 'Square Mile' with its Stock Exchange, Lloyd's and the Bank of England. No one can really doubt that the politicians, asked to pronounce on the future shape of London's transport system when it might have been still viable to develop some of the grander schemes, had an impossible task.

## THE BUBBLE BURSTS

The railways were the fruits of capitalism. It has been pointed out that the entire canal construction programme, itself no small achievement and one that produced considerable benefits by slashing the costs of moving coal and other bulk commodities, required less than £20 million (£900 million today) to be raised on the stock market. Between 1820 and 1844 the new railway companies in England alone raised more than £40 million (around £2,000 million today), and six years later, in 1850, the share capital of Britain's railways totalled no less than £187 million (£12,492 million today), and they were still far from finished by that time, with less than a third of the eventual network built and many of the great termini and major bridges, viaducts and tunnels still to be started. The result of all of this frantic activity, as mentioned earlier, was that the railways themselves were as instrumental in creating the modern stock market as they were in establishing a transport network, and their misfortunes were as instrumental in establishing many of the rules of the market as their accidents were in building a solid foundation of rules on safety.

Today we are often reminded that the value of shares can go down as well as up. Not only did the end of the twentieth century and the dawn of the twenty-first see a speculative bubble burst in the shape of the so-called dot.com shares, but it also heralded a long fall in stock-market prices, with even some viable companies losing as much as 75 per cent of their peak value. This has always been the way, especially when prices have been boosted to unsustainable levels by too-frantic buying followed by an economic downturn.

In the case of the railways, the excitement, and the feeling that everyone who had any money to spare must invest in railways or miss a great opportunity, had two consequences. The first was the usual one: that in such a fevered atmosphere share prices often exceeded the true value of the assets and the potential for revenue and profits of the new railway companies. The second was that far too many schemes were brought forward, including many that were no-hopers and others that were simply premature, although they might have been viable given further expansion of the communities being served. The construction industry often became involved, seeing the promotion of railway lines as their own route to riches, so that the usual practice of a promoter of a business venture seeking a contractor was reversed, with many speculative 'contractors' lines' being built, usually with little real thought for the market that was to be served. All this meant that the new railways were vulnerable once reality set in.

Even though much time and money is spent in wooing the stock market and in briefing analysts, and financial institutions spend a great deal of time and money researching companies to make recommendations to investors or would-be investors, the whole question of the stock market in the UK as elsewhere is not so much one of research and logic but one of confidence and emotion.

The boom induced by the railway mania resulted in tightening credit in the mid-1860s. The inevitable happened, with the start of a line of bankruptcies, some of the first being two contractors involved in railway promotion and development – Watson & Overend and Thomas Savin. The latter had been involved in an ambitious plan for an Aberystwyth and Coast Railway, but had fallen out with his partner on the financial realities of the project while still struggling to complete the Newtown & Machynlleth Railway through mountainous, and hence expensive, terrain. Watson & Overend had been working on the Mid Wales Railway, again in difficult terrain without a substantial population or industry to serve. The completely unconnected banking firm of Overend, Gurney & Co. was a major investor in the Mid Wales, and had stretched itself beyond prudent limits on this and other railway ventures, so that when the High Court ruled that many of the railway company's shares had been issued illegally the banker collapsed on 10 May 1866 with liabilities of almost £20 million (£1,000 million today). In the ensuing panic, share prices fell and as an emergency measure the bank rate was increased to the then unprecedented level of 10 per cent. While the bankruptcies and the increased bank rate took the heat out of the market and resulted in many railway projects being cancelled or postponed, it also had more immediate consequences. The collapse of Overend, Gurney & Co. led to the collapse of yet another contractor, one of the largest, Peto & Betts, because of its liabilities to Overend, Gurney & Co., and this in turn forced the London Chatham & Dover Railway into receivership since it was depending on Peto & Betts to finance and build its line extensions. A railway company with work on its extensions halted was in great difficulty as the projected revenue simply could not happen, while it would have issued shares on the basis of the extension being built and earning within a reasonable period. The other significant receivership of this unhappy period was that of the Great Eastern Railway, which had been formed as recently as 1862 to end the scrabbling between five poverty-stricken companies attempting to serve East Anglia.

By this time many railway contractors and promoters were also heavily involved in similar projects overseas, and the consequences of their failure rippled around the globe. Other railways and other finance houses also fell in 1866, one of the most miserable years, if not the most miserable, for the railway industry. It was to take five years for the London Chatham & Dover to recover and emerge from receivership in 1871. The real way forward for this company was, of course, the ending of its ruinous competition with the South Eastern Railway. The first glimmerings of sanity did not occur until a merger was first proposed in 1890, but disagreements over the values of the respective companies meant that action was deferred until 1899.

As luck would have it the crisis of 1866 coincided with the sitting of yet another Royal Commission on Railways, the so-called Devon Commission, which sat from 1865 until 1867. The Devon Commission had a very broad remit, including an examination of the powers of the BoT, but in fact is far better remembered as another commission to consider nationalisation of the railways.

Greater state control of the railways had been proposed almost from the dawn of the railway age by those who were concerned about the impact of the new form of transport. In many ways some of the early 'regulators' can be dismissed, since they included those who objected to the speed of the new form of transport, or to the fact that the arrival of the railway made almost every other form of inland transport redundant. As early as 1836 one James Morrison wanted Parliament to revise the railway's tolls, this being the time when railways were seen as being rather like turnpike trusts with open access to anyone who wanted to put a carriage or wagon on the iron road. No less a person than the Duke of Wellington, in opposition in 1834, was to urge Lord Melbourne to protect the country against the mismanagement and monopoly of the railways. This, of course, shows an early divergence of opinion between those who saw the railways as a monopoly supplier and those who felt that the monopoly was nothing more than the superiority of the railways compared with all other forms of inland transport. Certainly, throughout the early years Parliament never intended any one railway to have a monopoly, and the authorisation of so many competing schemes underlines this.

Nevertheless, outright proposals for nationalisation had come as early as 1843 and 1844, when a certain William Galt wrote a series of four books on railway reform, and it was this that led Gladstone to include in his Railway Regulation Act 1844, a measure giving the government the power to acquire from 1865 onwards any company sanctioned following the 1844 Act. Galt was a solicitor and it is generally taken that in pressing for reform of the railways he was more concerned with what would be best for the country as a whole, seeing the railways as similar to the highways and the Post Office, than advocating state ownership as part of a political platform. He returned to his theme in 1864 when his book was revised and republished, providing a thorough survey of the state of the nation's railways at the time, and then went on to appear before the Royal Commission on the railways the following year. The members of the Devon Commission certainly considered nationalisation, but decided that nothing further should be done.

The economist Walter Bagehot was another advocate of nationalisation, writing in the *Economist*: 'It is easy to show that the transfer of the railways to the state would be very beneficial, if only it can be effected.' In other words, Bagehot was keen on nationalisation but unsure about just how it could be done. In fact advocates of nationalisation fell into several camps, and it was not until much later that this became part of a political platform, and one that contemplated state ownership far in excess of the railways. Many of the earlier advocates saw the railways as constituting a public service, rather like the Royal Mail, and their views were strengthened when, in 1868, the first nationalisation appeared in the form of the government buying out the operators of the telegraph. This included the many telegraph lines operated by the railway companies, and the measure was not without benefit to many of them, with, for example, the London Chatham & Dover Railway, albeit still in receivership, using the £100,000 (around £5 million today) paid by the Post Office for its telegraph system towards the building of a much-needed new station in the City of London at Holborn Viaduct to relieve the congestion at Ludgate Hill. It is not surprising, therefore, that Sir Rowland Hill, the Postmaster General, was among those keen on nationalising the railways, but more surprising to find that he was joined by, for example, a shipowner who was also a director of the London & North Western Railway. The BoT inspector, Henry Tyler, was also pro-nationalisation, although this did not stop him from later becoming a director of the Grand Trunk Railway of Canada and a Conservative MP.

Arguments against nationalisation largely centred on the powers of patronage that it would put in the hands of politicians, as was allegedly the case in Belgium. Quite why people interested in the fate of the railways in the UK kept looking across the English Channel at this little country, itself a creation of the Victorian age, and with little in common with their own, remains a mystery.

For the believers in private enterprise, the trouble was, of course, that state ownership of the telegraph system was an almost instant success. It created a single unified telegraph system where before it had been fragmented. This strengthened the argument of those advocating similar treatment for the railways. On the other hand, a railway is not a telegraph system. Inter-operability is far easier to ensure between railways even within different ownership, and there are even opportunities for competition that can benefit the consumer and even hasten technical progress. It is also true that the railways were not guaranteed their predominant position in inland transport forever, although this could not be foreseen at a time when even the future shape of the railways was unclear. Once again, though, we come back to another argument, which is that the railway network would have been far sparser were it not for the boom of speculation. The lines in the far north of Scotland were built with public money or relief from rates, and it would seem fair to speculate that, had the railways been nationalised earlier, many uneconomic lines might have been built for social and strategic purposes, while the development of lines in the heavily industrialised and densely populated areas might have been relatively neglected. The shape and the deficiencies of today's highway network provide some idea of what might have happened. One can surmise that there would have been too few lines, with many cross-country routes not built and the trunk network having fewer sections with multiple track (i.e. more than two lines).

Nationalisation finally became a political issue in 1894, when the Amalgamated Society of Railway Servants, predecessor of the National Union of Railwaymen, declared in favour of state ownership. In 1899 Sir George Findlay, a director of the London & North Western Railway, looked at the problem and, while opposed to nationalisation, worked out a system which could allow it to work. The new Labour Party made nationalisation one of its core policies early in the twentieth century.

Many advocates of nationalisation saw the railways becoming a department of state, rather like the Post Office, and one wonders just how many, especially in the trade unions, would have been so keen had they realised that it would eventually be state ownership at arm's length in what would be effectively a state corporation.

A further Royal Commission was appointed in 1913 by the then Liberal government to consider the question of nationalisation of the railways, but its deliberations were overtaken by the outbreak of the First World War. Wartime saw the railways under state control, and in 1919 the question of nationalisation was raised again, but it was decided instead to amalgamate the railway companies into four strong geographically based groups, as we will see later.

CHAPTER SEVEN

# Not a Great War
# for the Railways

It was clear that the railways would be vital for the conduct of war, both in moving troops and supplies to the front and in keeping industry operating under wartime pressures. The role that railways could play had been brought home to the British during the Boer War, when Southampton became the main port of embarkation. Even earlier the wartime potential of the railways had been seen in another far-off conflict, the American Civil War. The conflict between Unionists and Confederates was the most bloody in American history, not only because American was fighting American, or because of the appearance of such innovations as the machine gun, trench warfare and barbed wire, but also because the railways meant that generals for the first time could command that adequate numbers of troops and their supplies could be where they were needed when they were needed, and soldiers could arrive fit to fight.

In the First World War, once the western front settled down into fixed positions, the military even built railways behind the front line to support the armies, with narrow gauge railways bringing men and supplies to wherever they might be needed.

Both the Admiralty and the War Office were anxious to ensure that the new railways could be of use in wartime, and were never backward in protecting their own interests. They were anxious from the outset that smooth and efficient railway communication should not be hampered by a break of gauge, for example. Nevertheless, their initial attitude to the railways was one of suspicion. It took some time before the London & South Western Railway and the London Brighton & South Coast Railway were allowed by the Admiralty to reach the waterfront at Portsmouth, so that at first travellers to and from the Isle of Wight had to travel between Portsmouth Harbour and the town station by horse-drawn carriages.

The initial rejection of the railway at Portsmouth was not unique. The private bills authorising some lines were amended at government insistence so that defence requirements would be taken into account, as with the alignment proposed for the South Eastern Railway's line from Hastings to Ashford, before Parliament in 1850. As at Portsmouth, the London Tilbury & Southend Railway's extension to Shoeburyness was opposed by the War Office in 1877, anxious to protect the Army's gunnery school, but in a complete about turn the War Office accepted the extension in 1882.

Concerns with the 1842 legislation that first linked the railways with defence control around internal security rather than warfare. There had been a prolonged spell of peace, for with the final defeat of Napoleon in 1815 some decades were to follow before the outbreak of war in the Crimea. The government's emergency powers over the railways were further extended in 1844 and 1867, and again by the Regulation of the Forces Act 1871, which gave the government complete state control of the railways in wartime. This was not nationalisation as such, for the government would direct how the railways would be used, but operational control would remain in the hands of the individual companies.

Despite the growing interest of the Admiralty and the War Office in railways, the only railways actually built for the armed forces were those running within defence establishments, as at Portsmouth and, inland, the Longmoor Military Railway covering the extensive training grounds near Bordon. Invasion fears rose again in 1859, and these lent urgency to considerations of the use of the railways in wartime, and even led to a proposal for a circular line around London for armoured trains containing artillery to defend the capital, though nothing came of this 'iron road M25', which might have been useful in peacetime. Railwaymen were present in the reserve forces, as were those from other walks of life, but their special importance was emphasised with the creation of the Engineer & Railway Staff Volunteer Corps in 1865, while in 1896 an Army Railway Council was established, later being renamed the War Railway Council.

The London & South Western Railway (LSWR) and its terminus at Waterloo experienced the demands of wartime traffic first of all, as all of the troops sent to the Boer War between 1899 and 1902 passed through the port of Southampton. The majority of them also went through Waterloo, while the cavalry and their horses used Nine Elms. Over three years no fewer than 528,000 troops and a substantial number of horses passed over the LSWR's metals and through its recently acquired port at Southampton. Nevertheless, the LSWR remained under the control of its management throughout and no attempt was made to interfere with its running.

With the Boer War experience in mind, extensive changes were made to the railways so that links with the training and rear concentration areas near Salisbury Plain were improved between the turn of the twentieth century and the outbreak of war in 1914.

The widely anticipated start of hostilities in 1914 saw the railways almost immediately pass into state control for the first time, still under the overall control of the BoT, whose president was nominally chairman of the Railway Executive Committee (REC), which had been formed to run the railways on behalf of the government and whose members included the general managers of the eleven most important railway companies. Possibly it was because of the LSWR's Boer War experience, albeit at a much lower level of conflict, that its general manager, Herbert Walker, one of the youngest to hold such a post, effectively ran the REC on behalf of the President of the BoT, although officially described as acting chairman of the REC, and his valuable work was recognised by a knighthood in 1917.

As in the Boer War, Southampton was to be used extensively by the military during the First World War, but this time considerable pressure was also to fall on the Channel ports, with first Dover and then Folkestone closed to civilian traffic. In the First World War it was the South Eastern & Chatham Railway (SECR) that became Britain's frontline railway, with the heaviest responsibility for the movement of men and materials to the coast. Charing Cross also had the role of being Westminster's local station, and a special train, code-named 'Imperial A', was held ready at all times for VIP journeys to the coast, being used for 283 journeys during the war years. This was a short-formed but luxurious operation, usually consisting of just a Pullman car and a brake composite. A military staff officers' train operated daily from Charing Cross to Folkestone, leaving at 12.20. Less happily, but still an incredible achievement, after the start of the Battle of Messines at dawn on 7 June 1917 the first wounded arrived at Charing Cross at 14.15 on the same day.

The SECR displayed some considerable foresight during the war years. The concept of aerial warfare was completely new, although there had been some use of aircraft for offensive operations during the Balkan Wars, but as early as late October 1914 a lookout was posted on

Hungerford Bridge watching for Zeppelin raids, and if an air raid seemed possible no trains were allowed on to the bridge.

In wartime many ordinary services were cut in order to free men and equipment for military use, while a substantial number of railwaymen volunteered for the armed forces, with no fewer than 184,475, 45 per cent of those of military age, enlisting. What had not been foreseen at the outset was that the role of coastal shipping, in peacetime so important for the movement of bulk commodities such as coal, was severely restricted by enemy activity in the North Sea and the English Channel. Few warships were fuelled by oil at this stage in the Royal Navy's history, because of fears that sufficient oil might not be available in wartime. The Grand Fleet had moved to its forward wartime base at Scapa Flow in Orkney, not the most convenient location for supply by railway, but coal had to be carried from South Wales to Grangemouth, where it was transferred to coastal shipping, on the so-called 'Jellicoe Specials', named after the admiral commanding the Grand Fleet. All in all no fewer than 13,630 coal trains were run for this purpose alone between August 1914 and March 1919, with Pontypool Road on the Great Western Railway being the main loading point. Grangemouth had to be the main transhipment point because further north the railways, with most of the route mileage single track, could not have coped, and there were insufficient port facilities in the far north of Scotland. Naval manpower was moved further north by rail, putting the Highland Railway under great strain between Perth and Inverness and then north to Thurso. Even so, 'naval specials' were operated every night, covering the 717 miles from Euston to Thurso in 21½ hours.

Such was the volume of traffic across the Channel that a new port had to be built at Richborough, close to Sandwich in Kent, despite the closure to civilian traffic of both Dover and Folkestone. Train ferries were introduced to carry war material across the Channel, and also to help move locomotives and rolling stock across as well. More than 600 locomotives were pressed into military service overseas as the ½ inch or so difference between British and French track gauges mattered little. Routine operations were severely affected as railway workshops were converted to help with the war effort, including the manufacture of armaments, while rolling stock was converted to provide ambulance trains. Some minor railway lines, as far apart as near Dumfries in the south-west of Scotland and at Southsea on the south coast, were closed in wartime never to reopen, but the creation of new manufacturing plant, such as an ordnance factory near Gretna close to the border between Scotland and England, also meant that additional facilities had to be created quickly.

Much was made by the pro-nationalisers of the integrated nature of the railways under REC control. In fact, the pre-war railways had generally managed very well despite being fragmented, otherwise many longer-distance routes, and the Anglo-Scottish trunk routes in particular, would simply not have worked. The real point was that, to ensure the system could cope both with the pressure of heavily increased wartime traffic and sudden demands from the military for troop trains and ambulance trains, integration was necessary, so that resources could be diverted to the point of need without undue waste of time in negotiations between companies.

The big difference between the two world wars was that during the First World War the railways suffered relatively little from bombing. They were not completely immune, of course, since railways were from the beginning recognised as an important target. The most significant incident occurred in London during an air raid on 13 June 1917, when the City of London was the target, including Liverpool Street station. Three bombs landed on the station, one of which was a dud, another exploded on a platform, and the third hit a King's Lynn and Hunstanton express, setting the dining car alight.

Sadly, as we have seen, the war years also saw the worst accident in British railway history, on 22 May 1915 at Quintinshill, near Gretna on the Caledonian Railway. Although the accident was caused by the irregular working practices adopted by the signalmen, a contributory factor was the extreme pressure on the section of track at the time.

State control of the railways may have been an operational success as the railwaymen and the many temporary staff recruited to fill wartime gaps in the personnel numbers did their best, but financially it was a disaster for the railway companies. Postwar, one general manager noted that the combined profits for the railway companies in 1913 had totalled £45m, but that by 1920 these had dropped to less than £7m, owing to improved rates of pay during the First World War when the railways were under direct government control. By 1921, immediately prior to government control ceasing, the railways were running at a loss overall of around £9 million. Part of the reason was almost certainly the cost of manpower. Railway wages in 1913 had totalled £47m, but by 1920 had risen to £160m. This was a clear example of the state having power without responsibility! It is also possible that this poor financial position was one reason for nationalisation being dropped.

There was one final measure as the war ended. It was recognised that the railways had outgrown the BoT, and in 1919 a new department of state, the Ministry of Transport (MoT), was created, with Sir Eric Geddes its first minister. In many ways he should have been the ideal choice, having joined the North Eastern Railway in 1904 at the age of twenty-nine, becoming deputy general manager of the company by 1914. Geddes had grand ideas for reorganising and streamlining Britain's transport system, including the railways, and indeed his ideas even extended to the supply of electricity; so grand indeed that he did not even bother to consult the railway companies about their future. Nationalisation was one of the options considered, but in pushing through the Railways Act 1921 that authorised the grouping Geddes must already have known that he would not remain to see the scheme through to fulfilment in 1923. In 1922 he left to join the board of Dunlop, the tyre and rubber products manufacturer, becoming its chairman, and in 1924 he became part-time chairman of the new Imperial Airways. The cynics who define a 'whizz kid' as someone who moves on before his mistakes catch up with him would see in Geddes a prime example for, after all, he not only left the new MoT, but he positively abandoned railways by moving to firms with interests in road transport and aviation!

CHAPTER EIGHT

# Grouping and
# Road Competition

It is said that the new Ministry of Transport did not foresee the extent to which the railways would be affected by road competition, and indeed it was to be eleven years before any measure to control this reached the statute book, but given Geddes's experience of the railways and his subsequent career moves, one cannot help but question this. The ministry might not have foreseen the future, but Geddes surely must have done, driving through the Railways Act 1921 to the Statute Book.

As mentioned earlier, the grouping was seen as an alternative to nationalisation. Wartime coordination of the railways had been viewed by many as a success, and the mood of the time was in favour of coordination rather than competition. Despite the growing losses of the railways at the end of government control, it still seems that memories of the high rates of return earned at one time by many railway companies remained strong among politicians. The feeling was that the railways needed firm regulation to avoid making excessive profits, and the mood of the time did not trust competition to do this. This again mirrors Bagehot's description of the railways as 'competing monopolies', but inevitably grouping was to extend the size and depth of the monopolies and reduce the opportunities for competition at the fringes.

In wartime the state had failed to keep its promise of maintaining revenues at 1913 levels and of protecting the equity of the railway companies, who were no longer seen as desirable stocks by many investors. A sum of £60 million (£1,164 million today) was eventually offered to the railway companies in compensation for the impact of wartime and state control on their finances. The problem was that Parliament would neither set the postwar railways free nor nationalise them. Not content with enforcing the grouping, it was also considered necessary to apply other controls as well. The grouping was intended to ensure that the railway shareholders would receive what was described as the 'standard' revenue of £51.4 million (£997.2 million today) annually spread across all four companies and based on the 1913 figure, which, fortunately, had been a remarkably good year for the railways. Despite the efforts of a Railway Rates Tribunal this figure was never realised in practice because of the changes that occurred postwar and in particular the depressed state of the economy for most of the time. It seems limiting enough, given the economic conditions prevailing between the wars, although deflation meant that costs actually fell, but it would have been impossible given the often high levels of inflation encountered in the four decades following the end of the Second World War.

## GROUPING

The Railways Act 1921 forced 120 companies of varying size, listed in the Appendix, into four large main-line groups. Not every railway was included and a number of independent railways did survive, including a number of narrow-gauge and light railways. Ireland was left alone, as Home Rule had occurred the year before the grouping, and of the two railways operating entirely within the new political entity of Northern Ireland, one, the Belfast & Northern Counties, was a subsidiary of the Midland Railway, so became part of the new London Midland & Scottish, while there were three railways in Northern Ireland which all had cross-border operations, leaving just the small Belfast & County Down as independent and operating solely within Northern Ireland. Even so, two of the new 'grouped' railway companies, the Southern and the Great Western, each found itself with a narrow-gauge railway, the Lynton & Barnstaple and the Welshpool & Llanfair respectively.

The grouping legislation did not pass through Parliament without some controversy. In the Isle of Wight, for example, a plan was moved to allow the three island railways to become a small independent group on their own, which superficially made sense, except that they could not have updated (modernisation would be far too strong a word for it) their locomotives and rolling stock without the benevolent oversight of the Southern Railway, which made it clear that the island lines were an extension of its main lines to Portsmouth and Southampton, and invested accordingly, especially in new ships.

Yet, when viewed with hindsight and the post-nationalisation structures of British Railways, the grouping did seem slightly illogical. If competition was to be removed, why leave such great opportunities for competition on the Anglo-Scottish routes? There were two routes between London and Birmingham, with the Great Western and the London Midland & Scottish catering for this important traffic, and two routes to Exeter as well, with Southern and Great Western rivalry. To some extent these situations were inevitable and the alternative, as we will see later post-nationalisation, was far worse. On the other hand, defying logic and most unexpected was the decision to leave the London Tilbury & Southend line with the London Midland & Scottish as successor to the Midland Railway rather than transfer it along with the services from Liverpool Street to the London & North Eastern Railway (LNER), leaving two companies operating between Southend and the City of London. The Southern and Great Western did, nevertheless, cooperate on their shipping services to the Channel Islands, extending an arrangement that had preceded the grouping. That an element of competition remained is also borne out by the fact that the French investigated operating the overnight through-sleeping car 'Night Ferry' from an east coast port when they thought that the Southern Railway, faced with a downturn in its continental traffic, was dragging its heels on this ambitious, prestigious and, almost certainly, hopelessly uneconomic project.

Would a grouping based on the post-nationalisation regions of British Railways have worked better? There would have been, no doubt, a Southern Railway and a Great Western Railway, an Eastern, or even a Great Eastern Railway, a London Midland Railway and a North Eastern Railway as well as a Scottish Railway. This would have left the Anglo-Scottish expresses running through two or three companies' areas, and little improvement on pre-grouping.

Certainly the grouping was not without its defects. The most obvious one was the failure to separate out the LNER services from London's Liverpool Street and Marylebone termini from those from King's Cross. Its boat trains to Harwich and its services through sparsely populated East Anglia to King's Lynn and Norwich notwithstanding, there is no doubt that Liverpool Street was primarily a commuter railway with a secondary continental traffic and agricultural traffic, while King's Cross was at the end of a number of longer-distance main-line services in addition to serving the large industrial and mining areas of South Yorkshire and the north-east of England, as well as the Scottish lowlands. This mattered for another reason. The London & North Eastern (LNER) soon became a railway very much along the lines of the old SNCF in France, at least until comparatively recently, in that it cared very much for its prestigious main-line traffic and produced fine expresses with motive power and carriages to be proud of, but it didn't care much for its suburban and branch-line services, which were often slow, drab and dirty. Despite promises it never introduced electrification to its suburban network, confining itself to some electrification of its freight lines in the north-east. No doubt, confined to King's Cross, the LNER, which was extremely short of money and had to struggle to finance modernisation from revenue since an approach to the shareholders would have been a miserable failure, could have been a more affluent railway, although it was severely affected by the 1926 miners' strike and by the downturn in the coal trade that followed it. The survival of a possible Great Eastern (GER) at Liverpool Street and Great Central at Marylebone could have meant continued struggle, but even so, there is the sneaking suspicion that the London suburban network would have been accorded a much higher priority had the Great Eastern remained independent. On the other hand, we should not forget that, while the old GER had been among the first to suffer from electric tramway competition as early as 1901, it had failed to electrify, although historians accord it great praise for its successful and very efficient operation of a completely steam-hauled high-density suburban service. Compared to this, leaving the London Tilbury & Southend line in different hands was a small matter indeed.

It is not just the combining of such disparate operations into one company that suggests that the grouping was a merger or two too far. The evidence suggests that between the wars managements struggled to make the grouping work. The Great Western fared best of all, as the only company to emerge intact from the grouping by simply bolting on the smaller companies to its own well-established structures, so that it was able to boast in 1937 of being the first and only British railway company to celebrate its centenary. The London Midland & Scottish was almost rent asunder by factional infighting between the old Midland Railway and the old London & North Western, with Euston versus St Pancras, to which the answer was seen as introducing a highly centralised structure. The London & North Eastern decentralised, which may have done much for local community relations, but one feels that opportunities were missed. As for the Southern, it almost immediately perpetuated the old pre-grouping set-up by having Eastern, Central and Western sections almost equating to the former South Eastern & Chatham (SECR), London Brighton & South Coast (LBSCR) and London & South Western (LSWR) railways.

In fact, with the exception of the Great Western and its unashamed takeover of the smaller companies, it seems that many opportunities to rationalise the network and operations were missed. It took the Southern some time to open up passageways between the Brighton and South Eastern sides of Victoria station, which did not occur until 1924, while it took until 1928 for similar improvements to take place at London Bridge. There was delay too in appointing a single stationmaster for Victoria. There was some rationalisation of lines in the Thanet area to improve operations, but these should have been carried out by the SECR when it had been formed in 1899. One of the two stations at Midhurst was closed and traffic concentrated on the old LBSCR station. Stations were renamed to avoid confusion throughout Britain, but even so old definitions were allowed to continue, such as Bedford Midland. The main rationalisation came with the rundown of some locomotive and carriage works, with the main activities concentrated on the major works.

The grouping did not silence demands for nationalisation, but it did push the question into the background between the wars, largely because most of the inter-war governments were Conservative and opposed to nationalisation in principle. The Labour government of 1924 lasted but briefly, while that of 1929 came at a time of financial crisis, and in 1931 was eventually forced to seek a coalition of national unity. Many Labour Party supporters saw this almost as an act of treason, but it really simply underlined the fact that the governments of the day had so much more to worry about, and with large-scale unemployment the demands on the exchequer were huge at a time when tax revenues were adversely affected by recession. It was soon clear that the railways were themselves not an inviting prospect for any government, as the revenues predicted on grouping were not being realised, and even in the relatively prosperous south of England the Southern Railway saw its continental traffic not simply fall but plummet after the sterling crisis of 1931 and the subsequent devaluation. It was to take a devaluation of the French franc later for traffic to stage a partial recovery. Even at this time the Southern was to report that it was beginning to feel the impact of competition from air services on its cross-Channel traffic, and, no surprise, airline competition hit its premium traffic hardest.

## END OF THE LEVY

There were four major political moves between the wars that were of significance to the railways. The first of these was the abolition of the tax on passenger travel, followed soon afterwards by the first steps in the regulation of road transport and then by the creation of the London Passenger Transport Board as the first transport nationalisation, while the Guarantees and Loans Act 1934 was a further stimulus to modernisation.

In his budget of 1929 the Chancellor of the Exchequer in Baldwin's Conservative administration, the then Mr Winston Churchill, announced the abolition of the Railway Passenger Duty that had first been introduced in 1832 and by the late 1920s was levied on all passenger fares above 1*d* per mile, on condition that the sums realised were capitalised and used for railway modernisation. While this was one of the few occasions when political interference with the railways proved beneficial, it is only fair to add that Churchill had not the interests of the long-suffering passenger in mind, but instead was concerned to reduce unemployment by encouraging investment through this form of 'pump-priming'. The measure didn't work politically as in the ensuing general election a Labour government was elected. No doubt the measure was widely overlooked by the electorate, and certainly the election was held before its benefits could be assessed.

On the Southern Railway it was easy to draw a direct connection between ending the duty and further expansion of electrification. The Southern's share of the capitalised duty was £2 million (around £100–120 million today), and it was estimated that extending electrification to Brighton and West Worthing would cost £2.7 million, including the provision of a much-enhanced train frequency, with the number of departures more than doubled. To achieve a satisfactory return an increase in revenue of 6 per cent would be needed. The company was not to be disappointed.

The postwar period also saw unprecedented competition from road transport. Before the war this renaissance in road transport had really resulted in competition for the electric tramways, which had been confined to the urban areas and their suburbs, and to railway passenger traffic, but competition from the motor vehicle seemed to know no bounds. Rural branch lines faced competition from the country bus, able to handle comfortably and profitably passenger loads that would not have filled more than a couple of compartments on the local train, and without the massive overhead costs of the railway. The main lines faced competition from the motor coach, and both branch and main lines found themselves competing with the motor lorry. It was not just a case of the greater flexibility and economy of the motor vehicle; their routes could be more direct. Nowhere was this more important than in the handling of goods traffic, which could be safely overseen by the lorry driver from departure to destination instead of getting lost in some siding. Worse still for the railway, in many cases goods had to be taken to the goods station and collected from it, so even when the railways provided this service, often free within a limited radius of a station, time was spent in transhipment between road and rail. In addition it was, and it remains true, that transhipment is usually the stage at which most damage to goods is done.

It was also the case that, while road haulage contractors could pick and choose their traffic and even specialise in a particular commodity, the railways were saddled with the burden of the common carrier obligation, a throw-back to the days when their rule of inland transport was unchallenged.

Just as many railway lines had been built that could have no future given a renaissance of passenger road transport, the small sidings nestling alongside many country and suburban stations required the railways to operate so-called 'stopping goods', with trains running at between 5 and 10mph, and the overall journey time extended at the smaller stations when the goods train's locomotive would have to be detached to do its own shunting. The sidings worked best when run by the local coal or timber merchant, but even then the quantities of coal delivered by railway were scarcely economic.

The seeming reluctance of many of the managers in the big four grouped companies to address the questions of integration and rationalisation had its counterpart in the reluctance of many railwaymen to countenance shedding uneconomic lines and uneconomic traffic. Even postwar one company envisaged electric traction for most of its lines, including through goods trains, with diesel for the less busy lines and for stopping goods trains.

## REGULATION OF ROAD TRANSPORT

Faced with a serious challenge from road transport, the railway companies tried to assess just how much business they were losing and lobbied for the government to do something about it. They were being tightly regulated themselves, so 'why shouldn't road transport be tightly regulated?' seems to have been the attitude. There was no question of 'setting the railways free'; instead the lobby was for a 'fair deal for the railways'. The result was the first of a succession of road traffic acts, the first being the Road Traffic Act 1930, which established a system of licensing bus services. It was to be another three years before a further Act of 1933 regulated road haulage.

It is debatable whether the restrictions on freight or passenger transport were the more burdensome. The passenger operator would be tied to certain routes with either a general 'stage' road service licence or an 'express' road service licence with a minimum adult single fare, or, in the case of excursions and tours, certain departure points. Woe betide any coach operator who charged separate fares in the guise of private hire. This gave many organisations, such as churches and clubs, considerable problems. Initially, bus and coach operators had what might be termed 'grandfather rights', enabling them to register their existing services, but new routes had to face the traffic commissioners, where the railways had a right to object to the granting of a road service licence. Potential customers had to be dragged off to the commissioners to testify that existing services did not meet their needs, although the bus operator could also seek support for its case from a local authority or a local employer who could also attend the hearing to support the bus or coach operator in his application.

In 1933 restrictions were extended to road haulage, with operators limited to a specified number of vehicles of a certain tonnage, with the only exception to overall control being for those operating vehicles under a contract licence. In one sense one could argue that in freight transport it was not so much a question of licensing but of rationing. Businesses could easily enough gain a 'C' licence to deliver their own goods to their own customers, but this was really seen as a means of helping the butcher and baker, the grocer and greengrocer. Far more difficult to gain was the 'A' licence, which was meant for a general haulier to operate for hire and reward. For this he had to show that there was a demand not being met by other hauliers, and once again prospective customers were often put to the bother of a visit to the traffic commissioners to testify on the haulier's behalf! In between there was the 'B' licence, usually meant for those businesses delivering their own goods, but also hoping to collect a return load for which they would be paid, perhaps blurring the distinction between commercial 'A' licence haulage and private 'C' licence delivery by picking up deliveries from suppliers, but naturally adjusting the price paid to reflect this. There was no attempt to control prices in the industry.

To be fair, there was some need for legislation in the interests of the road transport industry and of its customers as much as anything else. Safety was one issue, with annual inspections of vehicles, and in the case of passenger vehicles the imposition of certain minimum standards through a certificate of fitness. Reliability of service was another point, and bus and coach operators had to abide by the timetable attached to the road service licence for each route. There was also the case that some operators had made a point of undercutting rival operators and forcing them out of business, after which fares were increased, so fares were also controlled, with operators having to seek permission to raise fares. All of this indicated that some legislation was necessary to protect both the honest and reliable operator and the customer, but what emerged was little short of rationing.

The main-line railways retained their own lines within London when on 1 July 1933 the London Passenger Transport Board (LPTB) came into existence under its own legislation promoted by the government earlier that year. Bus operators were not so fortunate and many, including Thames Valley and Aldershot & District, had to transfer depots, vehicles and routes to the new organisation, while those operating entirely within the 2,000 square-mile area of the LPTB were taken over completely, including a number of municipal operators. The new LPTB acquired the entire London underground network, including the District Line that used some of the Southern Railway's metals, while the Bakerloo and the District used those of the London Midland & Scottish (LMS) to reach Watford and Barking respectively. There were a few exceptions to the takeover by London Transport, with the Hammersmith & City Line operated jointly with the Great Western until it passed completely to London Transport in 1948, while the Southern Railway was able to hang on to the Waterloo & City Line, the 'Drain', until nationalisation, after which it remained with British Railways until 1994. It also seems strange that the lines of the North London Railway, at least those between Richmond and Broad Street, remained in railway company hands.

Intended from the outset as an integrated road and rail transport organisation for London, the London Passenger Transport Area stretched out as far as Windsor, Guildford, Horsham, Gravesend, Tilbury, Hertford, Luton and Dunstable. Within this area all suburban railway services were to be coordinated by a Standing Joint Committee consisting of four LPTB members and the four main-line railway general managers, and all receipts from the area, less operating costs, were to be apportioned between the LPTB and the railways. The Southern Railway's share of these receipts was fixed at 25.5 per cent, a tribute to the traffic growth generated by its investment in suburban electrification, by this time completed, but hardly an incentive to further modernisation.

Worst of all, in the London Passenger Transport Area no one could operate a bus service without the permission of the London Passenger Transport Board (LPTB), or London Transport as it chose to call itself, so that a monopoly could perpetuate itself for all time. Even when some local authorities petitioned for the right to operate services, London Transport asked them to pay for buses which it then operated.

The Guarantees and Loans Act 1934 was also intended to provide work, easing unemployment and lifting the country out of recession in what would today be regarded as an example of Keynesian economics and 'pump priming'. Regardless of how one feels about Keynes and his ideas, in practice here was yet another new incentive for the railways to modernise. In November 1935 the government agreed with the four main-line railway companies to provide funds for major improvement schemes at an interest rate of 2.5 per cent, lower than that generally available on the money markets at the time, through a Railway Finance Corporation that would have its initial capital of £30m (£1,800 million today) guaranteed by the Treasury. Once again we find the Southern, despite being by far the smallest of the railway companies, taking an ambitious approach, with a loan of £6 million to fund further electrification and improvements at a number of stations, as well as construction of a new branch line.

## PROFITABILITY

The failure of the railway companies to reach their standard revenues between the wars has already been mentioned. The reasons were varied, and included the recession that struck manufacturing industry within a few years of the end of the First World War and, although attention always focuses on the years of the great depression, British industry remained in recession for far longer. The country certainly was not helped by the General Strike of 1926 and the miners' strike that accompanied it and continued for long after the former ended. A consequence of the strike by mineworkers was that, inevitably, many markets for British coal, including export markets, were lost for good, resulting in lower traffic levels for the railways and for the ports, many of which were in railway ownership. There was also a Railways Rates Tribunal that existed to authorise any change in rates, although the railways, facing intense road competition, were free to charge 'exceptional rates' to retain traffic of as much as 40 per cent below the standard rate. They also tried to stimulate passenger traffic, or at least win some of this back from the coach operators – with the Southern, for example, introducing special 'summer fares' of 1*d* a mile.

Of course there are those complete 'free market' supporters who would argue that transport shouldn't be regulated in this way. But the bus company or railway, or even the airline, is not like the butcher, baker or candlestick-maker. Nothing is more perishable than the seat on any form of transport, for once it departs, if not sold it is lost forever. The baker has a few hours in which to sell his bread, the butcher somewhat longer if his meat is kept in good cool conditions, and the candlestick-maker has all the time in the world, and may even re-price his wares upwards if given time! Shipping companies have generally avoided this kind of legislation by opting for self-regulation through what was known as the 'liner conference system', under which shipping lines trading on the same route coordinated tariffs and sailings to provide a more frequent service.

Of course the railways also adopted another means of countering road transport competition, for they were soon allowed to operate bus services due to a change in legislation in 1929. Later they were to be allowed to operate air services as well. The railways soon acquired shareholdings in bus companies, and in many cases also bought some of them outright. They extended their own collection and delivery road transport interests by acquiring hauliers, and between them the four grouped companies took over parcels carrier Carter Paterson, and removals company Pickfords, as well as acquiring the travel agency Thomas Cook. Coordination between road and rail did occur on a local basis, but it was patchy. To some extent this was understandable, since the railway passenger, especially the first-class railway passenger, was not always amenable to being carried by bus, and the cost per mile of bus travel, especially in the towns, was less than that of railway travel.

Despite the effects of the Road Traffic Act 1930 the railways continued to suffer during the rest of the decade. In 1938 a 'Square Deal' campaign was launched to ease the restrictions under which they operated, but it received a poor press and aroused public hostility, the latter largely due to fears of increased fares and other charges. The road transport lobby that had done so well from the restrictions on the railways happily played on the fears of the public. Yet, a look at the results for the main railway companies in 1912 and for the big four during the mid to late 1930s tells its own story.

Taking the Southern Railway as an example, in 1912 the four companies that were to make up the Southern were mainly in profit, with the London & South Western paying a dividend of 5.62 per cent on its ordinary shares, while the London Brighton & South Coast paid 5 per cent, and of the two companies operated by the South Eastern & Chatham Managing Committee, the South Eastern paid 3.87 per cent, leaving just the poor London Chatham & Dover to pay nothing. Yet after extensive investment in successful electrification schemes the Southern Railway could only pay 4 per cent on its preference stock while the ordinary, or deferred, shares received nothing in 1935. In 1936 the preference shares continued to attract 4 per cent and the ordinary stock received just 0.5 per cent. In 1937 the preference shares received 3 per cent and the ordinary 1.5 per cent, but this was a high point, because in 1938, although the preference shares received 4 per cent, once again the ordinary shares received nothing. Modernisation came at a high price if you were a holder of ordinary shares!

The Great Western Railway had also managed to pay 5.62 per cent in 1912, but the railway that gave the world what was for a short period the world's fastest scheduled daily service, 'The Cheltenham Flyer', could only pay 2.75 per cent by 1935. This was maintained in 1936, and then rose to 3.5 per cent the following year, before collapsing to 0.5 per cent in 1938. For the ordinary railway shareholder a Post Office savings account must have seemed very attractive at times like this.

Of the companies that combined to form the London & North Eastern Railway (LNER), in 1912 the Great Eastern managed to pay 2.5 per cent and the Great Northern 4.37 per cent, with 6 per cent on the North Eastern, but the North British had struggled to pay 3 per cent on its preference stock and 1 per cent on its deferred stock, while the Great Central paid nothing. At least the latter's shareholders were prepared for what happened in the years 1935–8, when the LNER could not pay a dividend.

On the other side of the Pennines, of the companies that amalgamated to form the giant London Midland & Scottish Railway (LMSR), in 1912 the London & North Western paid a healthy 6.5 per cent, and even in

Scotland there were dividends, with the Glasgow & South Western leading the way with 4.87 per cent, followed by the Caledonian at 3.75 per cent and the Highland at 2.25 per cent, while the Midland, famous for the comfort of its trains, was not too well rewarded for its care, with just 2.5 per cent on its preference stock and 3.87 per cent on its deferred stock. The LMSR was renowned for its adoption of modern American management practices, and it also sorted out some of the sillier practices of its predecessor companies, among which the Midland, for example, had tended to build only smaller locomotives, so that double-heading was frequently required, which, lacking the means of remote control usual on electric and diesel double- or multiple-headed locomotives, also doubled labour costs and did not make the best use of coal. Despite this, the LMSR failed to pay a dividend in 1935, could only manage 1.25 per cent in 1936, and although this rose to 1.5 per cent in 1937 it disappeared once again in 1938!

The Great War had been anything but 'great' for the railways and their shareholders, something that became all too apparent because for most of the companies mentioned the dividends for 1913 were either the same as for 1912 or even better, with two exceptions, the London Chatham & Dover (LCDR) and the Great Central. How the LCDR shareholders must have wished that their company had been taken over by the South Eastern in 1891, and how they must have cursed their ancestors for their ambition in creating a rival to the SER all those years earlier, when it had seemed so important for Chatham to have its own railway while the South Eastern had seemed so keen on developing its railway south of the Weald. As for the Great Central, its management had been ambitious, too ambitious, and its shareholders must have resented the refusal of Parliament to allow its original planned merger with the Great Northern.

It would be unfair to describe railway stock in 1938 as junk bonds, but it took an act of faith, even of blind optimism, for anyone to consider investing in the railways. The directors and managers of the grouped companies had maintained their railways to the best of their abilities, and had invested as heavily as they could, especially after the incentives of 1929 and later. This was most obvious on the Southern Railway, although to some extent the introduction of more powerful steam locomotives necessary for the longer-distance services had taken second place to electrification. Even so, the Southern had tried its best to spread modernisation around its system. The Great Western as well had not simply been content to concentrate on its expresses, but had thought about the problems of rural branch lines with its diesel railcars. Given the picture of poor returns, one can have some sympathy for the other two companies, running a limited number of fine expresses but not doing much for the rural and suburban lines. The LMSR did at least have a substantial number of fine mixed-traffic locomotives, the handsome and rightly famous Stanier 4–6–0s, or 'Black Fives', which were to be largely copied by the postwar nationalised railway, and which were equally happy on the lighter expresses, suburban trains or on goods work.

Could the companies have done more for their shareholders without sacrificing their service to the public and to industry? Possibly. The Southern had squandered money on its prestigious continental trains. The 'Night Ferry' had just twelve *Wagons Lits* sleeping cars built for its overnight through-service between London and Paris, which in itself tells the story of a service that was costly to operate and yet served a market that was not simply small but by railway standards minute. The famous 'Golden Arrow' day Pullman service on the same route was little better, for it had its own dedicated ferry when the simple expedient of providing a first-class lounge and dining-room on other ferries would have sufficed. The 'Atlantic Coast Express' was a rolling stock programmer's nightmare. At a time when the Southern, and before it the London Brighton & South Coast, had eased shunting and standardised the make-up of even steam-hauled trains through arranging carriages in sets, the 'Atlantic Coast Express' demanded six or more composite brake carriages, which would be detached along its route and shunted on to local trains so that North Devon and North Cornwall could have a through train each day to and from Waterloo. This was inefficient, and costly. The passengers would have been as well served by changing on to well-timed connections, and it would have been quicker, especially for those further down the line.

## THE FAILURE TO RATIONALISE

The railway companies had also been slow to rationalise, other than in their locomotive and carriage works, which many would suggest should have concentrated on overall and heavy maintenance and abandoned new construction in favour of using independent builders and competitive bidding. This was the practice on the continent, and it was also the practice of almost every other mode of transport. In the United States aircraft manufacturers had been barred from running airlines at an early stage under anti-trust legislation, and in the UK this had ended when Imperial Airways was formed, taking over, among others, Handley Page Air Transport. In the UK the only other instances of a transport operator building its own equipment was Bristol Tramways, which built its own 'Bristol' branded buses and sold them to many other operators, and the Birmingham & Midland Motor Omnibus Company (BMMO), 'Midland Red'. Earlier, the London General Omnibus Company had distanced itself from bus manufacture by keeping the Associated Equipment Company (AEC) at arm's length. London Transport did not build its own underground trains.

There was also a very real reluctance to consider closing stations or branch lines. The Southern Railway's main closure was that of the Lynton & Barnstaple, which the London & Southern Western had bought before grouping from its unhappy shareholders for far less than the cost of construction, but many other lines survived, even after the acquisition of bus companies serving the area. On the Isle of Wight it was better to take the bus between Ryde and Bembridge than take the train, changing at Brading, or a through bus between Newport and Ventnor rather than changing either at Merstone Junction on to the Ventnor West branch, or at Sandown for Ventnor itself. The branch to Freshwater and Yarmouth had been a small and ailing railway before grouping, but even after it could not support a Sunday service in winter: was it really worth keeping it open for the summer through train, 'The Tourist', from Ventnor and Shanklin?

The same story was repeated throughout the country. Did Peebles in the Scottish borders really need two railway lines, one running from the West Coast main line and the other from Edinburgh? The latter possibly, even though Peebles was yet to become a dormitory for Edinburgh. Could short branches such as that to Moffat be justified, when the bus from Dumfries could link the town to the railway by calling at Beattock?

Most thought was given to the problems of rural branch lines by the Great Western. For a long time many railways had attempted to run such lines with what was sometimes called a 'railmotor' service, effectively a very small steam locomotive sharing the same underframe as a single passenger carriage and looking very much a hybrid between a locomotive and a carriage rather than having any resemblance to, for example, a steam-powered bus. As the motor bus gained both maturity and reliability, helped by wartime provision of many more men with mechanical and driving skills, eventually this concept extended to the railways, and so the 'railbus' was born. At first these really were buses adapted to run on rails, while in France a variation on this concept was the 'Micheline', a petrol-engined bus with solid rubber tyres and steel-flanged wheels to enable it to run on rails, but with the passenger saloon, lightweight and low-slung, and separate from the cab which also contained the engine in a similar format to an articulated lorry. After trials in France in 1932, Armstrong Siddeley expressed an interest in production and built two examples under licence for the LMS; these entered service in 1936, but were withdrawn in 1939 when more urgent matters were pressing. The LMS had earlier, in 1934, bought three 40-seat four-wheeled diesel railbuses from Leyland. These were usually described as lightweight although this was only in railway terms, since the seating capacity was greater than that of the contemporary single-deck motor bus, which was limited to 35 seats at most when using two axles.

During the 1920s, railcars, slightly heavier than railbuses, were used on the light railways operated by Colonel Stephens which had escaped the grouping, as well as for the narrow-gauge County Donegal network running from Londonderry across the border. The first consistent and serious application of the diesel engine in Britain was on railcars intended for use on lightly used lines and initiated by the Great Western in 1934, building a total of thirty-eight before 1942. The GWR favoured diesel mechanical propulsion for its railcars, although English Electric had developed diesel-electric versions that offered a better performance and actually exported a number of these before the outbreak of the Second World War. The diesel-mechanical railcars were probably slightly more difficult to drive, and were slower in acceleration than the diesel-electrics, but offered a lower axle weight and probably lower fuel consumption, so were better suited to the lines which the GWR had in mind. In any case, they could still provide a faster service on a branch with many stations and halts than could a steam locomotive.

*George Hudson, the Railway King, responsible at one time for a third of the country's railway network.* (Illustrated London News)

*Hudson worked largely on his own, but one important associate was the great engineer George Stephenson, at a time when one engineer handled track, signalling and major structures such as bridges as well as locomotives and rolling stock.* (NRM BTC 643/56)

*Later, Stephenson's son Robert continued the family tradition by working with Hudson.* (NRM BTC 255/69)

*The great statesman Gladstone was one of the first politicians to take a close interest in the railways, doubtless because of his family connections, and even considered nationalisation for a future date.* (Illustrated London News)

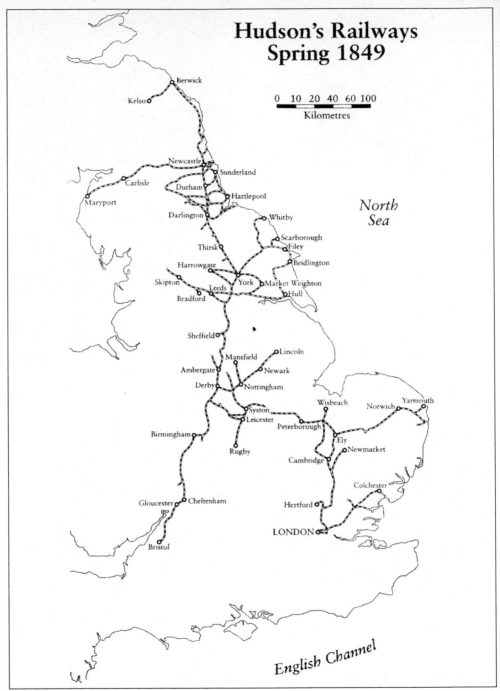

# Hudson's Railways
# Spring 1849

0  10  20  40  60  100
Kilometres

North
Sea

Berwick
Kelso

Newcastle
Sunderland
Carlisle
Durham
Maryport
Hartlepool
Darlington
Whitby
Scarborough
Thirsk
Filey
Harrowgate
Bridlington
Skipton
York
Market Weighton
Leeds
Hull
Bradford

Sheffield

Lincoln
Mansfield
Ambergate
Newark
Derby
Nottingham

Wisbeach
Norwich
Yarmouth
Syston
Leicester
Birmingham
Peterborough
Rugby
Ely
Newmarket
Cambridge

Colchester
Gloucester
Cheltenham
Hertford

LONDON

Bristol

English Channel

*Even on its own, Hudson's railways resembled a network of sorts, although direct routes were not always apparent. It is notable that the network provided many important cross-country links.*

# EASTERN GROUP OF RAILWAYS.

# EAST COAST ROUTE.

# ENGLAND & SCOTLAND

### Via Forth and Tay Bridges.

*FOR TRAIN SERVICE, SEE PAGES 332, 728, 734, 776, and 782:*

## THE ONLY ACTUAL "COAST" ROUTE.

---

## Quickest Route

# LONDON & EDINBURGH

(KING'S CROSS)      (WAVERLEY)

### IN $8\frac{1}{2}$ HOURS.

---

## RESTAURANT CARS attached to Day Trains,
## SLEEPING CARS attached to Night Trains

### between

LONDON (King's Cross) and... {
EDINBURGH,
GLASGOW,
FORT WILLIAM,
DUNDEE,
ABERDEEN,
PERTH,
INVERNESS.

*A fragmented railway did not mean a localised railway, as companies worked together to provide an 'East Coast' and a 'West Coast' route, and later a third route from St Pancras. This is a 1922 advertisement, on the eve of grouping. (Bradshaw)*

**COMMENCING JULY 10th, 1922.    Week Days.    Sun. ngt & Mon. mrn.**

| STATIONS. | h | | | g | | a | a | b | b | | | b | d | b | a | | | | |
|---|---|---|---|---|---|---|---|---|---|---|---|---|---|---|---|---|---|---|---|
| | mrn | mrn | mrn | mrn | aft | aft | aft | aft | aft | aft | mrn | aft | aft | aft | aft | aft | aft | aft | aft |
| London (Euston) ......dep | .... | 5 0 | 6 45 | 10 0 | .... | 1 30 | .... | 7 30 | .... | 9 20 | .... | 11 0 | 11 0 | 1140 | 11 45 | 7 40 | 9 30 | 11 0 | 1140 |
| Birmingham (New St.). " | 3 j 0 | 7 15 | 9 10 | 11 0 | 12 15 | 2 50 | .... | 8 20 | .... | 10 50 | .... | .... | .... | .... | 12 25 | 6 50 | 10 15 | .... | .... |
| Liverpool { Lime Street " | .... | .... | h | .... | .... | .... | .... | .... | .... | 1040 | .... | 12 45 | 12 45 | 1245 | .... | 9 V 0 | 12 45 | .... | .... |
| { Exchange.. " | 9 47 | 9 47 | 12 40 | .... | 3 20 | .... | 5 8 | .... | .... | .... | 1750 | 1 50 | .... | .... | 1 40 | .... | 1 50 | .... | .... |
| Manchester { Exchange " | .... | .... | .... | .... | .... | .... | 5 0 | .... | 1035 | .... | 1 10 | 1 10 | 1 10 | .... | .... | 1115 | 1 10 | .... | .... |
| { Victoria.. " | 9 40 | 9 40 | 12 30 | aft | aft | 3 0 | .... | .... | mrn | mrn | .... | .... | .... | mrn | 2 55 | .... | .... | mrn | mrn |
| Carlisle.............. arr. | 1245 | 1 19 | 3 25 | 3 58 | 4 9 | 6 25 | 7 44 | 8 27 | 1 40 | 2 14 | 4 0 5 | 5 16 | 5 33 | 6 40 | 6 20 | 2 14 | 4 46 | 5 16 | 6 40 |
| | aft | | | | | | | | | | | | | | | | | | |
| Edinburgh (Princes St.)arr. | 3 20 | 4 5 | 6 0 | .... | 6 30 | 9X18 | 10 10 | 11 0 | .... | .... | .... | 8 0 | 8 15 | .... | 9 0 | .... | .... | 8 0 | .... |
| Glasgow (Central)..... " | 3 20 | 4 22 | 6 5 | 6 30 | .... | 9X15 | 10 10 | 11 0 | .... | 6 55 | 7 40 | 8 0 | 9 35 | 9 0 | .... | 7 16 | .... | 9 35 |
| Greenock (Central)..... " | 4Q35 | 5 28 | 7 25 | 7 25 | .... | 10 37 | 11Y31 | .... | .... | 7R55 | 8R48 | .... | 9 15 | 1030 | .... | 8 48 | .... | 1030 |
| Gourock .............. " | 4Q52 | 5 41 | 7 39 | 7 39 | .... | 10 51 | 11Y45 | .... | .... | 8R10 | 9R 0 | .... | 9 29 | 1042 | .... | 9 0 | .... | 1042 |
| Oban ................. " | 9 55 | .... | .... | .... | .... | 4 44 | 4 44 | 9 55 | 9 55 | .... | 2 50 | .... | .... | 9 55 | .... | 2 50 | .... |
| Perth ................. " | 5 37 | .... | 8 10 | .... | 12 35 | 1235 | 5 5 | 5 35 | .... | 9 12 | 9 37 | .... | 5 35 | .... | 9 12 | .... |
| Dundee (West)........ " | 7 22 | .... | 8 58 | .... | .... | 6 50 | 6 50 | .... | 10 5 | 1022 | .... | 6 50 | .... | 10 5 | .... |
| Dunkeld ........... " | 8 6 | .... | .... | .... | 2F4 | 2F4 | 6 21 | 6 21 | .... | 10 6 | .... | 6 21 | .... | 10 6 | .... |
| Inverness via Dunk'ld " | .... | .... | .... | 6F0 | 6F0 | 9 25 | 1015 | .... | 4 42 | .... | 9 40 | .... | 4 42 | .... |
| ABERDEEN ............ " | 9 5 | .... | 10 35 | .... | 3 0 | 3 0 | 7 40 | 7 40 | .... | 11 50 | 1155 | .... | 7 40 | .... | 11 50 | .... |
| Ballater............... " | .... | .... | .... | .... | .... | 9 45 | 9 45 | .... | 5 0 | .... | 9 45 | .... | 5 0 | .... |
| Inverness via Aberd'n " | .... | .... | .... | 8F56 | 8F5f | .... | 1155 | 1155 | .... | 6 21 | .... | 1155 | .... | 6 21 | .... |

**Week Days.    Sun. from Scotland.**

| | mrn | mrn | mrn | mrn | | a | aft | aft | | | | aft | aft | b | d | aft | mrn | aft | | aft |
|---|---|---|---|---|---|---|---|---|---|---|---|---|---|---|---|---|---|---|---|---|
| Inverness via Aberd'ndep. | .... | .... | .... | .... | a | .... | 7 40 | .... | b | b | .... | 1250 | 1250 | b | d | .... | .... | .... | | .... |
| Ballater............... " | .... | .... | 6 50 | .... | .... | 9 55 | .... | .... | .... | 3 35 | 3 35 | .... | .... | .... | | .... |
| ABERDEEN ............ " | .... | .... | 6 30 | 9 30 | .... | 12 30 | aft | .... | .... | 7 30 | 7 45 | .... | .... | 1 10 | | .... |
| Inverness via Dunk'ld " | h | h | h | 1120 | aft | 8 10 | a | a | 10 30 | mrn | 4 30 | .... | 4 30 | .... | a | .... | | .... |
| Dunkeld ........... " | .... | .... | 7 51 | mrn | 10 6 | .... | 1 10 | aft | .... | T | .... | T | .... | .... | | .... |
| Dundee (West)........ " | .... | .... | 8 0 | mrn | 1110 | .... | 2 25 | .... | 9 10 | .... | 9 45 | 10 0 | .... | 3 0 | | .... |
| Perth ................. " | .... | .... | 9 5 | mrn | 1150 | .... | 3 25 | .... | 9 30 | .... | .... | 5 30 | .... | 3 50 | | .... |
| Oban ................. " | .... | .... | 5 40 | mrn | 8 45 | .... | 11 45 | mrn | .... | 5 30 | .... | 5 30 | .... | .... | | .... |
| Gourock .............. " | 8 20 | 8 20 | .... | 1145 | 2 50 | 3 50 | aft | 8 0 | .... | 9 5 | .... | 9 59 | 59 5 | .... | 3 15 | | .... |
| Greenock (Central) " | 8 32 | 8 32 | .... | 1155 | 2 59 | 4 1 | .... | 8 11 | .... | 9 15 | .... | 9 15 | 9 15 | 9 15 | .... | 3 24 | | .... |
| Glasgow (Central) " | 10 0 | 1010 | .... | .... | 1 30 | 4 10 | 5 30 | .... | 9 30 | .... | 1030 | .... | 1110 | 1110 | 1110 | 10 0 | 5 30 | | 1030 |
| Edinburgh (Princes St.) " | 10 0 | .... | .... | 1010 | .... | 4 10 | 5 30 | .... | 9 20 | .... | 1030 | .... | .... | 10 0 | 5 40 | | 1030 |
| Carlisle............. arr. | 12 0 | 12 14 | 1232 | 1252 | .... | 3 38 | 3 48 | 6 50 | 8 23 | .... | 12 5 | 1 10 | 1 0 | 1 25 | 1 56 | 1 50 | 2 8 | 1235 | 8 20 | | 1 0 |
| | aft | | aft | a | | aft | aft | aft | | | | | mrn | mrn | mrn | | mrn | | mrn |
| Manchester { Exchange arr. | .... | .... | .... | .... | 7 27 | 7 27 | 1036 | .... | .... | .... | .... | .... | | .... |
| { Victoria.. " | 3 35 | .... | 3 50 | 4 35 | 7 2 | .... | 1035 | 12 18 | .... | .... | 5 50 | 6 5 | .... | | .... |
| Liverpool { Lime St.... " | .... | .... | .... | .... | 12 45 | .... | .... | .... | 4 15 | .... | | .... |
| { Exchange.. " | 3 25 | .... | 3 45 | 4 43 | 5 7 | 5 | 1025 | .... | .... | .... | 6 0 | 6 15 | .... | 12 25 | | .... |
| Birmingham (New St.). " | 5 17 | .... | 6 40 | .... | 9 45 | .... | 2 15 | .... | 6 52 | 7 10 | .... | 4 22 | | .... |
| London (Euston) ...... " | 6 30 | .... | 7 30 | .... | 1030 | .... | 5 0 | .... | 6 55 | 7 40 | 7 30 8 | 0 8 20 | .... | 7 23 | 2 15 | | 6 13 |
| | | | | | | | | | | | | | | 7 30 | 5 0 | | 7 30 |

### SLEEPING SALOONS ON NIGHT TRAINS.

**a** CORRIDOR, DINING, AND REFRESHMENT CAR EXPRESS.   **b** Not on Saturday nights.   **d** Saturday night and Sunday morning.   **F** No connecting Trains to these Stations on Sunday mornings.   **g** Corridor, Luncheon, and Tea Car Express.   **h** Luncheon Car Express.   **j** Leaves Birmingham 3 10 mrn. on Mondays.   **q** On Saturdays arrives Greenock 5 31 aft. and Gourock 5 45 aft.   **R** On Sundays arrives Greenock 9 15 and Gourock 9 29 mrn.   **s** Saturdays only.   **T** Calls at Dunkeld when required to pick up passengers. Notice to be given at the Station.   **V** Via Newton-le-Willows.   **X** On Saturdays arrives Edinburgh 9 23 aft., and Glasgow 9 20 aft.   **Y** On Wednesdays and Saturdays arrives Greenock 11 42 aft. and Gourock 11 56 aft.   **Z** Sunday mornings excepted.

**ARTHUR WATSON, General Manager, L. & N. W. Railway.**

**DONALD A. MATHESON, General Manager, Caledonian Railway.**

*July, 1922.*

---

*Although one could travel to Edinburgh and Glasgow from Euston, King's Cross and St Pancras, the companies preferred to promote their strengths, so the West Coast route concentrated on Glasgow.* (Bradshaw)

## SCOTLAND and CORNWALL

calling at
**Principal Towns**
in the
**NORTH, MIDLANDS**
and
**SOUTH WEST.**

*RESTAURANT AND
SLEEPING CARS.*

|  | Page |  | a.m. | p.m. |
|---|---|---|---|---|
| ABERDEEN | 784 dep. |  | 9 45 | 12 50 |
| Dundee | 784 " |  | 11 41 | 2 53 |
|  |  |  | noon |  |
| Glasgow (Queen St.) | 791 " | 12 0 | 4 0 |  |
| Edinburgh | 778, 779 " | 1 30 | 5 15 |  |
| Newcastle | 782 " | 4 20 | 8 3 |  |
| Sunderland | 782 " | 3 30 | 7 ‡ 0 |  |
| West Hartlepool | 782 " | 3 20 | 6 50 |  |
| Middlesboro' | 782 " | 4 33 | 8 13 |  |
| Darlington | 782 " | 5 15 | 8 59 |  |
| Scarboro' | 758 " | 4 50 | 8 5 |  |
| York | 669 " | 6 25 | 10 3 |  |
| Hull | 698, 700 " | 5 3 | 8*49 |  |
| Sheffield (G.C.) | 698, 700 " | 7 36 | 10§25 |  |
| Nottingham (Vic.) | 698, 700 " | 8 31 | 12 33 |  |
| Leicester (Cen.) | 698, 700 " | 9 4 | 1 28 |  |
| Rugby | 698, 700 " | 9 29 | 1 56 |  |
| Banbury | 699, 701 arr. | 10 0 | 2 33 |  |
| Oxford | 82, 80 " | 10 33 | 3 25 |  |
| Swindon | 15, 12 " | 11 30 | 4 35 |  |
|  |  | a.m. |  |  |
| Bath | 15, 12 " | 12 35 | 5 26 |  |
| Bristol (Temple M.) | 15, 12 " | 12 57 | 5 52 |  |
| Taunton | 15, 12 " | 2 0 | 7 ‡ 42 |  |
| Exeter (St. David's) | 22 " | 2 46 | 8 ‖ 38 |  |
| Newton Abbot | 22 " | 3 23 | 9 ‖ 52 |  |
| Plymouth (North Rd.) | 22 " | 4 25 | 10 ‖ 0 |  |
| Par | 22 " | 5 40 | 11 ‖ 27 |  |
| Truro | 22 " | 6 18 | 12 ‖ 3 |  |
| PENZANCE | 22 " | 7 40 | 1 ‖ 20 |  |

|  |  |  | a.m. |
|---|---|---|---|
| PENZANCE | dep. |  | 11 0 |
|  |  |  | p.m. |
| Truro | " |  | 12 6 |
| Par | " |  | 12 47 |
| Plymouth (North Rd.) | " |  | 2 0 |
| Newton Abbot | " |  | 2 55 |
| Exeter (St. David's) | " |  | 3 27 |
| Taunton | " |  | 4 12 |
| Bristol (Temple M'ds) | " |  | 5 00 |
| Swindon | " |  | 6 15 |
| Oxford | " |  | 7 7 |
| Banbury | " |  | 7 42 |
| Rugby | arr. |  | 8 15 |
| Leicester (Cen.) | " |  | 8 38 |
| Nottingham (Vic.) | " |  | 9 11 |
| Sheffield (G.C.) | " |  | 10 4 |
| Hull | " |  | 1 36 |
| York | " |  | 11 13 |

|  |  | a.m. | a.m. |
|---|---|---|---|
| Scarboro' | " | 5 55 | 10 7 |
| Darlington | " | 2 3 | 2 3 |
| Middlesboro' | " | 5 45 | 5 49 |
| West Hartlepool | " | 5 35 | 5 35 |
| Sunderland | " | 5 26 | 6 11 |
| Newcastle | " | 1 9 | 3 5 |
| Edinburgh | " | 5 30 | 6 6 |
| Glasgow (Queen St.) | " | 5 30 | 9 35 |
| Dundee | " | 5 31 | 9 18 |
| ABERDEEN | " | 7 30 | 11 22 |

A Arrives later on Sundays.  B Sundays excepted.  D By slip carriage to Swindon.
* Via Selby and Pontefract.  ‡ Via Newcastle.  § Via Rotherham and Masboro.

## EDINBURGH & NEWCASTLE AND SOUTHAMPTON & BOURNEMOUTH

*RESTAURANT CAR
SERVICE.*

|  | Page |  | a.m. | a.m. |
|---|---|---|---|---|
| EDINBURGH | 778 dep. |  | .... | 10 15 |
| Newcastle | 731 " |  | 8 0 | 1 6 |
| Sunderland | 731 " |  | 7 20 | 12 30 |
| Durham | 731 " |  | 8 24 | 12 37 |
| West Hartlepool | 731 " |  | 7 40 | 12 5 |
| Middlesboro' | 781 " |  | 7 52 | 12 22 |
| Darlington | 731 " |  | 9 0 | 1 38 |
| Scarboro' | 758 " |  | 8 20 | 1 55 |
| York | 669 " |  | 10 13 | 3 0 |
| Hull | 696, 698 " |  | 9 0 | 1 55 |
| Sheffield (G.C.) | 696, 698 " |  | 11 45 | 4 17 |
| Nottingham (Vic.) | 696, 698 " |  | 12 39 | 5 15 |
| Leicester (Cen.) | 696, 698 " |  | 1 16 | 5 58 |
| Rugby | 696, 698 " |  | 1 41 | 6 35 |
| Banbury | 697, 699 arr. |  | 2 12 | 7 24 |
| Oxford | 81, 82 " |  | 2 48 | 8 0 |
| Winchester (LSW) | 127, 128 " |  | 4 39 | 10 7 |
| Eastleigh | 127, 128 " |  | 4 52 | 10 23 |
| Southampton (West) | 127 " |  | 5 10 | .... |
| " (Town) | 128 " |  | .... | 10 46 |
| BOURNEMOUTH (C.) | 135,136 " |  | 6 13 | 2 0 |

|  |  | e | a.m. |
|---|---|---|---|
| BOURNEMOUTH (W.) | dep. | a.m. | 11 50 |
| " (Cen.) | " | .... | 12 3 |
| Southampton (Town) | " | 7 35 | p.m. |
| " (West) | " | .... | 12 53 |
| Eastleigh | " | 7 54 | 1 8 |
| Winchester (L.&S.W.) | " | 8F16 | 1 24 |
| Oxford | " | 10 50 | 3 15 |
| Banbury | " | 11 25 | 3 48 |
| Rugby | arr. | 11 57 | 4 23 |
| Leicester (Cen.) | " | 12 21 | 4 45 |
| Nottingham (Vic.) | " | 12 57 | 5 19 |
| Sheffield (G.C.) | " | 1 51 | 6 13 |
| Hull | " | 3 50 | 8 11 |
| York | " | 3 24 | 7 45 |
| Scarboro' | " | 4 37 | 9 2 |
| Darlington | " | 4 32 | 9 3 |
| Middlesboro' | " | 5 10 | 9 40 |
| West Hartlepool | " | 6 20 | 10 4 |
| Durham | " | 5 9 | 9 39 |
| Sunderland | " | 6 5 | 10 21 |
| Newcastle | " | 5 35 | 10 5 |
| EDINBURGH | " | 8 45 |  |

C In connection at Southampton with Steamers to Havre and Channel Islands.
e Through Carriage, Southampton and Glasgow. Restaurant Car Express, Oxford and Scarborough.
F Winchester (Cheesehill).

## NEWCASTLE, &c., AND CARDIFF, SWANSEA AND PRINCIPAL TOWNS IN MIDLANDS AND WEST OF ENGLAND.

*RESTAURANT CAR
SERVICE.*

|  |  | a.m. |
|---|---|---|
| NEWCASTLE | Page 731 dep. | 9 30 a.m. |
| Sunderland | 731 " | 9 13 " |
| Durham | 731 " | 9 57 " |
| West Hartlepool | 731 " | 9 25 " |
| Middlesboro' | 731 " | 9 48 " |
| Darlington | 731 " | 10 35 " |
| York | 669 " | 11 45 " |
| Hull | 696 " | 10 50 " |
| Sheffield (G.C.) | 696 " | 1 0 p.m. |
| Nottingham (Vic.) | 696 " | 1 55 " |
| Leicester (Cen.) | 696 " | 2 28 " |
| Rugby | 696 " | 2 53 " |
| Banbury | 697 arr. | 3 26 " |
| Cheltenham (South) | 104 " | 4 53 " |
| Gloucester | 104 " | 5 4 " |
| Chepstow | 70 " | 5 50 " |
| Newport | 70 " | 6 16 " |
| Cardiff (General) | 70 " | 6 40 " |
| Barry Docks | 113 " | 7 15 " |
| Bridgend | 62 " | 7 55 " |
| PortTalbot & Aberavon | 62 " | 8 16 " |
| Neath | 62 " | 8 28 " |
| SWANSEA (High St.) | 62 " | 8 45 " |

|  |  | a.m. |
|---|---|---|
| SWANSEA (High St.) | dep. | 7 30 a.m. |
| Neath | " | 7 48 " |
| PortTalbot & Aberavon | " | 7 59 " |
| Bridgend | " | 8 23 " |
| Barry Docks | " | 9 2 " |
| Cardiff (General) | " | 9 35 " |
| Newport | " | 9 55 " |
| Chepstow | " | 10 24 " |
| Gloucester | " | 11 2 " |
| Cheltenham (South) | " | 11 16 " |
| Banbury | " | 12 43 p.m. |
| Rugby | arr. | 1 16 " |
| Leicester (Cen.) | " | 1 33 " |
| Nottingham (Vic.) | " | 2 9 " |
| Sheffield (G.C.) | " | 4 15 " |
| Hull | " | 5 31 " |
| York | " | 4 15 " |
| Darlington | " | 5 45 " |
| Middlesboro' | " | 6 34 " |
| West Hartlepool | " | 7 46 " |
| Durham | " | 6 20 " |
| Sunderland | " | 7 39 " |
| NEWCASTLE | " | 6 45 " |

*The pre-grouping railway cooperation meant through services across country avoiding London as
well as the trunk routes. Aberdeen–Penzance was the longest through service on Britain's railways,
and already well established by 1922. (Bradshaw)*

*The grouping saw a number of changes, but the companies varied greatly in their approach. The Southern Railway pressed ahead and by the end of the 1930s had virtually completed electrification of its suburban network, and then started on main line electrification. This is Guildford in August 1939, with (left to right) a suburban train for London, an Up Portsmouth express and a train taking the tortuous route to London via Aldershot and Ascot. (NRM Box 512)*

*On the other hand, the London & North Eastern favoured prestige trains for its main routes but at the cost of its suburban and branch-line services. Here is an Anglo-Scottish express hauled by none other than the famous locomotive* Mallard, *which still holds the world speed record for steam of 126mph set in 1937. (HMRS AAH707)*

*The Great Western's expresses were worthy of the appellation, but the company was also anxious to improve the economics of branch-line operation and compete with the motor bus, so here is one of its early railcars.* (NMRS M20002)

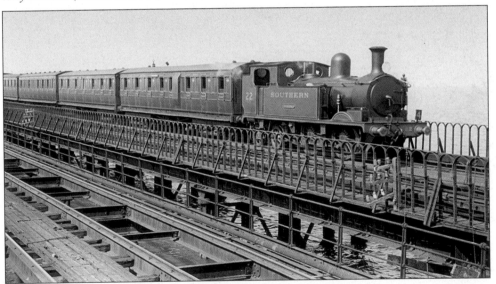

*After nationalisation a modernisation plan was put in hand under a Conservative administration, but even so, even up to the end of the steam age in 1967, not just pre-nationalisation but also pre-grouping rolling locomotives and rolling stock remained in daily use.* (HMRS AEP312)

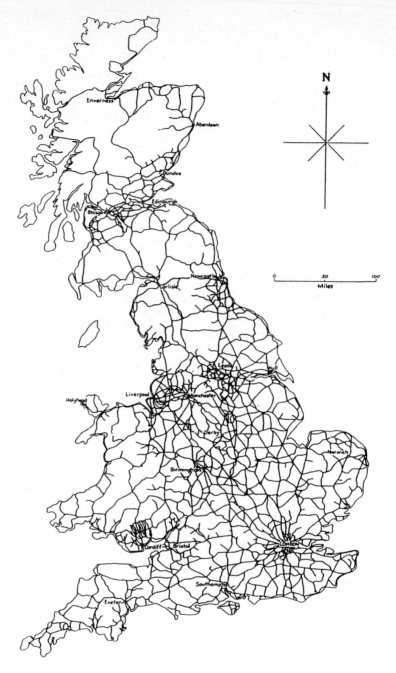

The railway network peaked in 1930 at more than 20,000 route miles and has been halved since, although some new lines were opened even during the 1930s. This was the network in 1952, only just past its peak, but with the bulk of the cuts still to come.

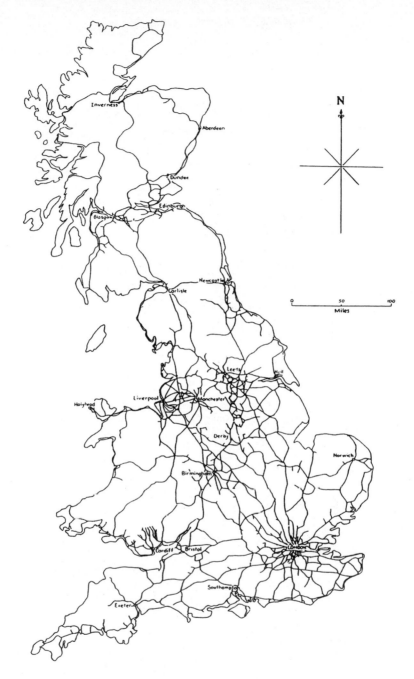

*The railway network in 1985 after Beeching but before even more drastic cuts were considered by Serpell.*

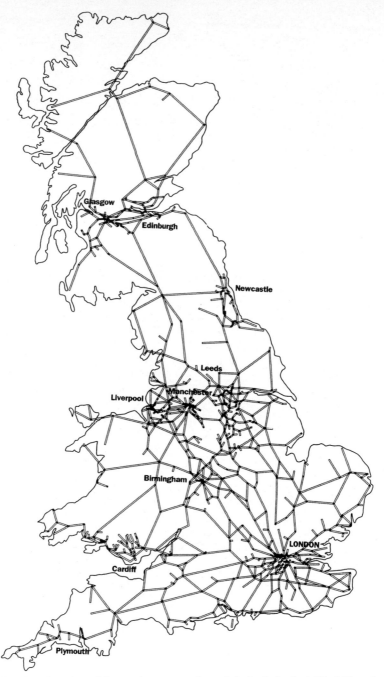

*This slightly reduced version of the previous system formed the basis for Serpell's deliberations.*

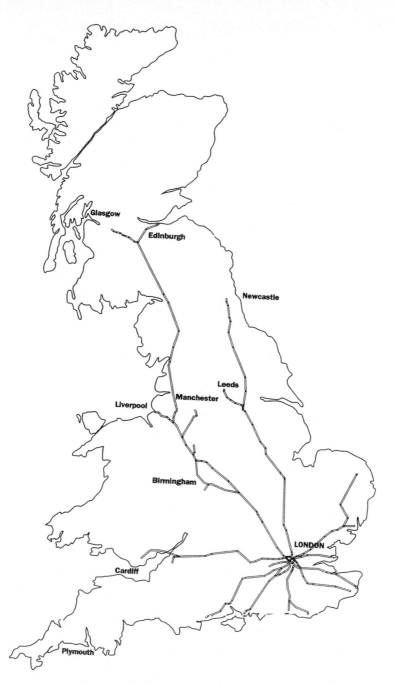

*This is what Serpell considered to be a commercial network – is your nearest station on it? No one seems to have wondered just how viable Portsmouth to Waterloo would be with the line actually starting just outside the city, or Newcastle–London without traffic from north of the border.*

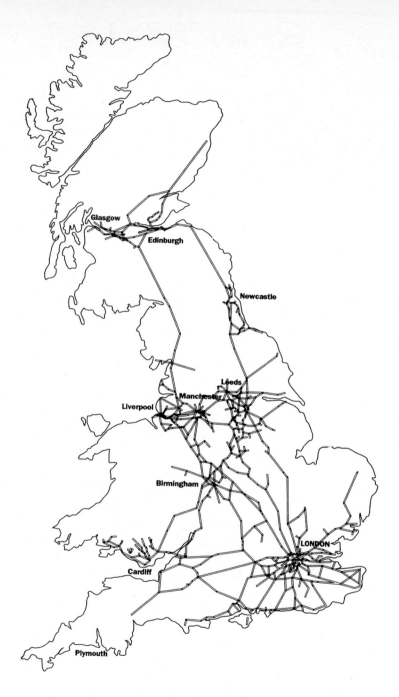

*Possibly recognising that the truly commercial network was politically unacceptable, Serpell also looked at a network that would require a lower level of public funding. Surely, however, much of the traffic from Exeter to Paddington starts from Plymouth, or even further west?*

*The nationalised railway had its successes, of which surely the best had to be the HST or InterCity 125, the high speed train that caught the public imagination, but whose specification was reduced by constraints on public spending. Even so, it still holds the world speed record for a diesel.* (GNER/Rail Images)

*Better still, but not able to display their full potential on the congested lines and relatively poor track of southern England is the 'Wessex Express', a third rail version of the HST with the power-operated doors that might have saved so many lives on the original trains.* (South West Trains)

*The Isle of Wight ended the steam age with Victorian trains, and has entered the twenty-first century with pre-Second World War ex-London tube trains!* (Island Line)

*Modernisation on the cheap meant that the next stage in railway development, the so-called InterCity 225 (for 225kph, or 140mph) for London–Edinburgh had the supports for the overheads spaced too far apart, making them vulnerable to high wind, a not uncommon phenomenon on the east coast of England and Scotland! In practice, the trains are limited to 125mph owing to track condition. No less serious, a design unique to this route and a limited production run gave the post-privatisation operator difficulty when traffic demand or accident losses meant more trains were needed.* (GNER/Rail Images)

*A desire to provide more but shorter trains on the cross-country routes led to excessive congestion – so Operation Princess had to be scrapped. This is a Virgin Voyager. (Virgin Trains/Milepost 92½)*

*The West Coast main line is the preserve of the 'Pendolino', an Italian tilting train for services from London Euston to Birmingham, Liverpool, Manchester and Glasgow, but like the GNER trains, a failure to provide track and signalling of the required quality means that they are unlikely to run at more than 125mph, although capable of more. (Virgin Trains/Milepost 92½)*

*Crux of the reliability problems on many cross-country routes is congestion at Birmingham New Street, used by most cross-country services. Here a Voyager makes its way through the West Midlands. (Virgin Trains/Milepost 92½)*

# CHAPTER NINE

# The State Becomes
# a War Profiteer

'There comes a time when locomotives are more important than guns,' declared Erich von Ludendorff, the German general and strategist, in 1918, and it remained true during the Second World War. When referring to the record of the railways in 1944 Sir Alan Mount, the Chief Inspecting Officer of Railways, was able to say that it represented 'an eloquent tribute, to their efficiency, standard of maintenance, and on the high factor of safety attained, all of which reflects the greatest credit on every railwayman and woman for the part they played in this historic year'. As we will see in the next chapter, these comments late in the war by an impartial public servant were ignored by the politicians.

That the railways played such an important role so successfully in wartime was by no means a happy accident. Experience of the demands of wartime was still fresh in the memories of many working railwaymen; they had had almost two decades when their priority had been the preservation and improvement of the railway despite severe economic hardships, and they had their plans. There was also a sense of foreboding. With their experience of the First World War recent enough still to be much to the forefront as war loomed yet again in Europe, the directors of the railway companies were pessimistic about the prospects for their companies and their shareholders. In the earlier conflict the fact that the railways had been guaranteed their 1913 revenues had been reassuring for, as explained earlier, this had been a good year. Not one of the years in between the two wars had been nearly so good, and shareholders had had to accept scarce money being devoted to keeping the system up to date, and even extensively modernised, rather than being devoted to dividends. They had in short shown a remarkable degree of public spirit that would be hard to find today, and given their eventual reward the fair-minded can only say 'Small wonder'. Even so, the financial situation of the railways had deteriorated miserably during the previous period of state control, largely because of a complete failure by the state to control costs. On grouping there was a backlog of maintenance and renewals left over from the war years.

Fresh concerns about war were coupled with the realisation that much would be different this time. Between the wars the belief had spread that 'the bomber will always get through', so the railways would be prime targets in a way that had not happened during the First World War. Anyone with the remotest interest in the affairs of the world had seen what bombers had achieved during the Spanish Civil War, only just ended at the beginning of 1939, and what they were achieving in China.

The other big difference was that before the earlier conflict the railways were still the supreme mover of goods and people inland, although this had been dented somewhat in the larger urban areas by the success of the electric tramways, especially when railways had been slow to electrify their suburban lines. Between the two wars road transport had undermined the railways, almost entirely owing to the spread of road haulage, bus and coach services, for the private car was still a rarity. It was clear that wartime would be accompanied by stringent fuel rationing, and that much of the traffic carried by road would come back to the railways. This was not a matter for rejoicing, as the railways would be expected to take on the extra burden without having benefited from its revenues for some twenty years. Once again we come back to the basis on which railway revenues would be protected.

## UNDER STATE CONTROL AGAIN

Meanwhile the Ministry of Transport, later to become the Ministry of War Transport, moved quickly to seize control of the railways on 1 September 1939, before the outbreak of war, using powers granted under the Defence Regulations Act 1939. Once again the minister operated through a Railway Executive Committee, which included the general managers of the four main-line railways and of London Transport. The London termini were obvious targets, so the railways evacuated many of their administrative personnel to the outskirts and to the provinces. The Railways Executive Committee itself found safety in an abandoned underground station on the Piccadilly Line at Down Street, between Green Park and Hyde Park Corner stations, with office accommodation and dormitories provided.

The haste to grab control of the railways was in contrast to the tardiness in finalising the arrangements. State control made the railways contractors to the government, with all revenue passing to the government, which then allocated shares from a pool, initially set at a guaranteed £40 million (around £2,152 million today). The Southern share of the pool was fixed at 16 per cent, the same as for the GWR, while the LPTB received 11 per cent, the LMS 34 per cent and the LNER 23 per cent. These percentages were based on the average net revenues for the companies and LPTB in the three years 1935–7, which the government took as each company's standard revenue. Once the guaranteed £40 million had been paid any balance was allocated to the five train operators on the same percentage terms up to a maximum of £3.5 million. After this, if there was a further balance, the revenue over £43.5 million would be divided equally between the government and the pool until the pool total reached £56 million. At this stage, if the revenue share allocated to any of the companies then exceeded its standard revenue, the excess would be shared out proportionately among the other companies.

Costs of maintenance and renewals had to be standardised, while the cost of restoring war damage would be met up to a total of £10 million in a full year. Privately owned wagons were also requisitioned by the Ministry of War Transport, and the individual companies had to meet the costs and revenue attributed to the wagon owners out of their share of the revenue pool.

This was a 'take it or leave it' type of agreement, with the government leaking threats of nationalisation if the companies failed to agree, although these were officially denied. While the years in question had been bad ones for the British economy, 1938 had been even worse and the railways had difficulty in getting the government to understand this. The railway companies never achieved the revenues anticipated by the Railways Act 1921. All that can be said for the deal was that the government was anxious to avoid inflationary pay claims from railway employees, but the inescapable fact was that the railways were having their revenues more or less fixed while costs were bound to rise as they struggled to meet the increased demands that wartime would place upon them. The upper limit on the costs of war damage was either political expediency to keep the unions quiet and retain the Labour Party in the wartime coalition government, or simple naivety since normal insurance measures were not available in wartime.

In addition to taking over the 'Big Four' and London Transport, the Railway Control Order also applied to joint committees of any two or more of these railways, and to other lines, including the East Kent, Kent & East Sussex, and Shropshire & Montgomery light railways, the King's Lynn Docks & Railway and the Mersey Railway. Anyone who has regarded the Romney Hythe & Dymchurch Railway as a 'toy railway', with its 15-in gauge and scaled-down locomotives based on standard-gauge designs, should be aware that this was requisitioned by the military, becoming a vital link in the defences of a low-lying, and therefore vulnerable to invasion, section of the Kent coast. The government had earlier warned the railways that as many as 800 locomotives might be required for service overseas, but as the war did not follow the pattern of 1914–18 not all were required.

While the railways were expected to give up manpower and equipment for the armed forces, the impact was less than during the First World War, in which 184,475 men were conscripted. Some 110,000 men had to be given up for national service, with more than 100,000 actually conscripted into the armed forces, while 298 steam and 45 of the still rare diesel locomotives, mainly shunting engines, were also taken for service overseas. These figures were in addition to the use of railway workshops for war work, which naturally moved a further substantial number of personnel away from railway work.

## EMERGENCY MEASURES

Wartime meant that the railways had to economise in the provision of their services, saving fuel and making locomotive power and rolling stock available for the many specials required by the armed forces. For the first time the railways had to participate in a massive evacuation programme, moving children and expectant and nursing mothers away from areas judged to be at risk from enemy bombing. Evacuation was to be a problem that recurred during the war. Many first-wave evacuees drifted back home during the long months of the so-called 'phoney war', the period between the outbreak of war and the start of the German advance, first northwards into Denmark and Norway and then westwards through the Low Countries and into France. As France fell, a further evacuation moved many evacuees away from what had now become an endangered zone, the coastal and country districts in the south-east and south of England as far west as Southampton, as well as evacuating many of the residents of those areas. A further evacuation later in the war was caused as the V-weapons took their toll on London and the south-east.

Before the war, preparations had been made by the railway companies, although these were not helped by threatened industrial action which was only averted at the last moment. Evacuation was ordered on 31 August. In London alone 5,895 buses were required to move 345,812 passengers to the stations. The Southern Railway was not unique in handling this traffic, but did account for much of it, although not every parent sent their child away and some made their own arrangements. The pressure on the railways in and around the main industrial conurbations and other likely target areas, such as the Medway towns, Portsmouth, Gosport and Southampton, was such that during the four days of the operation, from 1 to 4 September 1939, only a skeleton service could be provided for the public outside the rush hours.

Even while the evacuation from London was in full swing 27 trains a day were moving children, including the young occupants of Borstal prison near Rochester, from the Medway towns to safer parts of Kent. Another 127 trains took some 30,000 people from Southampton and Gosport to the more remote parts of Hampshire and to adjoining Dorset and Wiltshire, and later in September a further 18 trains were run from these two towns and also from Portsmouth.

The railways also had to arrange 34 ambulance trains for the partial evacuation of hospitals in these areas, while later all hospitals within 20 miles of the South Coast were also partially evacuated. These measures were not just to move patients to places of greater safety but to free beds for the bombing when it came, and also to empty hospitals near the coast in case of an invasion.

Other preparations included air-raid notices displayed in the compartments of trains on the Southern Railway's Eastern Section, judged most likely to be affected because of its proximity to Europe, and at Victoria the station lights were replaced by blue lights. On the eve of war, 2 September, blackout was enforced.

Initially, excursion and cheap-day tickets were withdrawn, but day tickets were reintroduced on 9 October, although with tighter conditions that meant that they were not available before 10.00 and could not be used on trains departing from London between 16.00 and 19.00 Monday to Friday.

There had been much rehearsal over the previous year or so. Railwaymen had practised working in blackout conditions, which meant that no lights could be shown externally, with all windows screened, while station platforms could only be lit by blue lights or, as there were still many lit by gas, specially shaded gas lamps. Drivers had to pull up their trains beside oil lamps placed on the platform as markers. Steam locomotives had canvas draped between the engine cab and tender to hide the light of their fires, while the side windows on the more modern locomotives were blanked out. Colour light signals which had improved railway safety were now a danger because they were so visible, and long hoods had to be fitted over them so that they could not be seen from the air. At first trains ran at night without lights, but later shaded lights were introduced.

Wartime acted as a spur to extending loudspeaker announcements to stations, and while initially station name signs were no longer lit, those under station canopies were allowed to be illuminated later, provided that they were swung round at right angles to the platform. Stations that had had their names painted on the canopies to help airmen with their navigation had them blanked out. Two final safety measures were the removal of glass from roofs and canopies, essential since even a small bomb could create so many shards of broken glass as to be an effective anti-personnel weapon, and at major city stations air-raid shelters were prepared for the often large numbers of passengers who might be caught on an exposed platform or concourse during an air raid.

After the evacuation was over services returned to normal but briefly, for on 11 September government-inspired cuts were imposed, inflicting hardship on passengers as normal commuter traffic remained virtually at pre-war levels. Some large companies had dispersed, especially those with strategic importance such as the shipping lines, but it was not possible for everyone to do so. The usual 20-minute suburban frequencies were cut to half-hourly, while off-peak and Sunday services became hourly. Some suburban services were cancelled completely. Not only did this lead to unacceptable levels of overcrowding, with many passengers left behind, but it also meant that station dwell times were extended as passengers struggled to alight from trains or climb aboard. After the uproar that followed normal services were reinstated on weekdays from 18 September.

Nevertheless, this was simply a temporary reinstatement and indicated that the blanket reductions of 11 September had not been properly thought through. Wartime meant that services had to be reduced. Reductions in passenger services followed on 25 September for both the Great Western and London Midland & Scottish, with the London & North Eastern following on 2 October, and the Southern Railway, with its extensive commuter network, on 16 October, but this time with better allowances for peak-period travel. Off-peak, most main-line services lost their hourly trains, to be replaced by a service every two hours, often on extended timings as trains called at more stations. Off-peak suburban services were hourly. On some lines services were curtailed late in the evening, but others had special late services after midnight for the benefit of shift workers.

Catering arrangements were reduced. Pullman and buffet cars were withdrawn and restaurant car service ceased on most routes. These cutbacks must once again have aroused some public reaction and been regarded as too severe, for on 1 January 1940 Pullman cars reappeared, as did pantry cars and more buffet cars.

Some idea of the impact of the cuts and extended journey times can be gathered from a comparison between October 1938 and the same month a year later. On the Great Western between London and Bristol, for example, the number of daily trains fell from 20 to 14, while the average journey time for the 118 miles increased from 135 minutes to 178 minutes, which disguises the fact that pre-war journeys included a fastest time of just 105 minutes. Its importance to the Royal Navy notwithstanding, Plymouth suffered even worse, since all trains were routed via Bristol, so that the pre-war best time of 245 minutes and average of 284 minutes for 225 miles stretched to 386 minutes for a journey of 246 miles, while the number of trains fell from 12 to 9 daily.

Services between London and Glasgow on the London Midland & Scottish were halved from 12 trains daily to 6, with the fastest time for the 401 miles stretched from 390 minutes to an average of 604 minutes, compared with the pre-war average of 486 minutes. Trains to Manchester were cut from 22 to 14 daily, while the 188 miles were covered in an average of 292 minutes compared with a 1938 average of 223 minutes and a best of 195 minutes. Inverness became a tedious 986 minutes compared with a best 780 minutes and an average 870 minutes for the 568 miles pre-war, while the number of trains was halved from 4 to 2, about the same as today if sleepers are included.

On the London & North Eastern the Edinburgh service saw the number of trains cut from 15 to just 8, while the journey times for the 393 miles increased from a pre-war best of 390 minutes and an average of 466 minutes to 608 minutes. The Norwich service was cut from 18 trains daily to 12, and the 115 miles were covered in 206 minutes compared with a pre-war best of 130 minutes and an average of 170 minutes.

On the Southern Railway the service to Southampton was cut from 28 to 20 trains daily and the timing for the 79 miles was stretched from a pre-war best of 85 minutes and a 1938 average of 110 minutes to 123 minutes. Portsmouth, doubtless because of the Royal Navy and the heavy commuter traffic on this line, saw its services cut slightly from 45 to 40 daily, while the journey took an average of 118 minutes in 1939 compared to a 1938 best of 90 minutes and an average of 98 minutes. Commuter traffic on its own wasn't enough to save a service, for the Brighton line suffered one of the heaviest reductions in the number of trains, more than halved from 100 trains daily to 46.

There were many reasons for the extended journey times. Wartime shortages of materials and the disruption of the normal renewals and maintenance programme would take its toll, with many 'temporary' speed limits, while war damage became extensive, especially in the London area and along the south and east coasts. Trains had extra stops and extra carriages. Long-distance trains from some London termini would have to be divided in two to fit the platforms, with the first half pulled out of the station, and then backed on to the second half to be coupled, before the journey could start. At intermediate stations such over-long trains had to make two stops so that passengers could board and alight.

Limiting a railway service has many disadvantages beyond the inconvenience to travellers, especially during bad weather when the frequent passage of trains and movement of signals and points can help to stop icing. Late January 1940 saw exceptionally severe weather that froze the conductor rails on the electrified lines and, having started on a Sunday when only a limited service was operating, froze many trains in the sidings. Communications were further disrupted as telegraph wires were brought down. On the more exposed electrified routes steam locomotives had to assist the electric multiple units through the worst-affected lengths of track. Passengers suffered the worst disruption many had seen.

## MOVING THE TROOPS

Meanwhile, in addition to evacuation and providing support for the British Expeditionary Force in France, a taste of future traffic demands arose when in December 1939 the first Canadian troops arrived in the UK and had to be moved from the docks to their new camps and training grounds. In May 1942 there was a repeat of this performance when the first significant numbers of US personnel started to arrive, part of a steady build-up first in anticipation of the North African landings, and then, later, for the invasion of Europe.

The 1940 Whitsun holiday was cancelled by the government since the Germans were sweeping through the Low Countries and into France. This ultimately led to the evacuation of the British Expeditionary Force from Dunkirk, along with many French troops and some from Belgium as well.

By the time of Dunkirk many railway ships had been requisitioned by the government, but as the situation in France began to spiral out of control the signal was received that 'all available railway steamers of 1,000 tons gross with a range of 150 miles are required for immediate Government service'. Closest to the emergency the Southern Railway immediately handed over nine ships. The railways had already lost ships to enemy action by this time, including a number clearly marked as hospital ships and crowded with wounded soldiers.

At 17.00 on 26 May the code-word 'Dynamo' was sent to the railways, warning them that the evacuation was due to start. The operation ran from 27 May to 4 June, and the difficulty of organising it was made worse by the sudden realisation on the part of the authorities that a second evacuation was needed of many children moved from London, but who were now too close for comfort to German airfields. Neither the railways nor the military knew how many men to expect from Dunkirk; in the end more than 338,000 were carried. This of necessity meant massive disruption to ordinary services, with even the slimmed-down wartime timetable suspended in many cases. Worst affected were services between Tonbridge and Redhill, and between Redhill, Guildford and Reading. This was an important cross-country route bypassing the London area for those troops being taken to Wales, the West Country and the Midlands. The usual passenger trains along the Tonbridge–Reading lines were suspended and replacement bus services provided, resulting in greatly extended journey times along the narrow and meandering A27.

While in many ways the whole exercise has been seen since as a masterpiece of organisation and improvisation it took place amid chaos. No one knew how many troops would arrive, when or where, with no idea of how many were fit and how many were wounded, and still less of where to send them. Trains were turned round at Dover and sent off before the authorities had any idea of a destination, so often drivers were instructed to 'Stop at Guildford and ask where you are going to'.

Exceptional circumstances demand exceptional measures, and the railway companies quickly agreed among themselves to provide a large pool of carriages. The GWR provided sufficient for 40 trains, the LMS 44, the LNER 47 and the Southern 55, a total of 186 trains comprising almost 2,000 carriages, with the Southern's total concealing great hardship for passengers on the non-electrified routes as the electric trains could not reach the Channel ports. Dover filled 327 trains, Ramsgate 82 and Margate 75 troop trains plus another 25 ambulance trains, while Folkestone had the surprisingly low figure of 64 trains. Sheerness handled 17 trains, while there was also a small number of men landed at Newhaven and even a few at Southampton, some distance from the main evacuation scene. The busiest days were 1 June and 4 June, with as many as sixty vessels alongside at Dover at any one time on the latter day. The entire operation was achieved by having holding points for empty trains at Faversham, Margate, Queenborough and Ramsgate, although at one time the system became so congested that four trains had to be held as far away as Willesden. Possibly the railways managed so well because they were used to the demand for special trains caused by major sporting events, but one general was heard to wish that the army 'could operate with as few written instructions as the Southern Railway does!'

## FURTHER EVACUATION

The rapid German advance westwards changed everything. At the outset many had believed that the Second World War would see the same long-drawn-out tussle on French soil that had marked the First World War. The embarrassing further evacuation, moving children from Kent (and for that matter Essex and Suffolk as well) westwards, started as early as 19 May 1940, using 16 special trains to carry 8,000 children from the three most threatened counties. On 2 June, in the midst of the Dunkirk evacuation, 48,000 children were moved from towns on the east coast in 70 trains. Ten days later, on 12 June, the move of 100,000 London children to Berkshire, Somerset, the south-west and Wales started, and continued until 18 June.

As the Battle of Britain raged hop-pickers in Kent were offered the opportunity to travel westwards rather than return to London, and this required another 15 trains for 8,000 people. In the autumn a further evacuation was organised from London for 13,500 women and children using 23 trains. As the length of journey increased and the winter weather set in the authorities asked the railways if they could provide hot meals on the trains – a tall order since, with the exception of Pullman trains, normally only a fraction of the usual number of travellers required hot food – but this was done on condition that the escorts for the children helped with serving and washing up, and all for a shilling.

Some idea of the effect of the war on the civilian population was that the pre-war population of Dover was around 40,000, but reduced to around 23,000 after Dunkirk. Some of these moved because the ending of the cross-Channel ferries would have meant that many jobs were no longer available and the labour would have been directed elsewhere, while the crews of the Channel packets would often have followed their ships' war work.

As the Battle of Britain turned to the Blitz, with London bombed every night bar one for 67 nights, a scheme was drawn up to evacuate 746,000 people from certain parts of the south coast and east coast during early summer, 1941. The plans were prepared in great secrecy to avoid panic, but they called for 988 trains to be used and for the operation to be completed in just four days. Fortunately the evacuation was not necessary.

The threat of invasion faded away and the Blitz also eased after the German invasion of the Soviet Union. Yet even after D-Day there were other threats with which to contend. The appearance of the flying bombs meant yet another evacuation. Many civilians left on ordinary services, but the authorities sanctioned an official evacuation of children and mothers with young children, and 200,000 people were moved from London and the south coast on special trains. This was a more difficult evacuation than the earlier ones, actually carried out under attack, while the railways were busy moving reinforcements and supplies to support the fighting in France, and over a system that had already suffered five years of wartime attack and neglect.

Throughout the war years there was an almost constant trimming of services to reduce fuel consumption. At the same time the changing traffic patterns created by wartime saw new stations opened and some new lengths of track to meet the needs of war workers and the military. The Elham Valley line was one of a number taken over completely by the military. In addition, as the war progressed other restrictions were applied. On 6 October 1941, under the directions of the Minister of War Transport, all suburban trains became third class only. The reasons for the move were practical, to make the best use of all accommodation on the reduced number of trains, and recognising the difficulty in finding the right class of accommodation during the blackout. To drive the point home, carpets were removed from first-class compartments and the first-class indications on the compartment doors painted out, while timetables and departure indicators described trains as 'Third Class Only'. Blackout or not, regular travellers seemed to be able to find their way to the most comfortable part of the train and gravitated towards the superior room, and plusher upholstery, of the former first-class compartments, so that these soon became shabby. While main-line trains retained first-class accommodation, on 22 May 1942 many lost all catering facilities, although some service was maintained on the longer-distance routes.

It now became important to discourage unnecessary travel. The lack of sporting events and the fact that the coastal resorts had their beaches wrapped in barbed wire meant that normal leisure pursuits were not available. Again on the instructions of the Minister of War Transport, on 5 October 1942 off-peak cheap returns were finally scrapped, leaving seasons as the only discounted tickets.

The pre-war system of switching on full heat on main-line trains between October and April when the temperature fell below 48°F at any one of a number of monitoring points, and half-heat when the temperature fell below 55°F, was reduced to full heat when the temperature fell below 45°F and half-heat when it fell below 50°F between November and March.

Shortages of skilled staff in the workshops and the conversion of many of these to war production, as well as shortages of materials, meant that the intervals between routine overhauls were extended. The railway companies were also severely restricted in the type of steam locomotive that they could build, but new building was allowed both to replace locomotives lost to enemy action and also to ensure that sufficient power was available for the many military specials. In theory just two standard types were allowed, but on the Southern Railway, where there was a dire shortage of large locomotives, the wily chief mechanical engineer Oliver Bulleid introduced his famous 'air-smoothed', as opposed to streamlined, Pacifics, or so-called 'spam cans' because of their shape, by convincing the authorities that these were really mixed-traffic locomotives! He compensated by also introducing a utility design of unsurpassed ugliness.

## PLACATING THE UNIONS

The threat of war had not changed the turbulent nature of the British industrial relations scene. The period between the two world wars had been one of stable prices, indeed of deflation, and the railways had ensured that track and rolling stock were kept in good condition, and wherever possible modernised and improved, hoping for an eventual upturn in the economy to bring its rewards. All of this was done at the expense of paying dividends to the shareholders, many of whom were not necessarily wealthy, and some of whom may well have inherited their stock. There was little money to meet improved pay awards, although there were some changes to conditions of service, including shorter hours, much to the dismay of at least one general manager who argued that applying the same hours to the signalman or crossing keeper on a quiet country branch as to their counterparts on a busy main line was nonsense.

As war loomed the vastly increased defence budgets, with an all-out arms race that threatened to bankrupt the country, resulted in improved traffic although not, it seems, improved profits in 1938. The railway unions noted the improved traffic and started to agitate for a pay increase, doubtless spurred on by Nazi propaganda that mocked the conditions for British workers, since this seems to have upset the then general secretary of the National Union of Railwaymen (NUR) when addressing his audience at their AGM at Abergavenny in mid-August 1939. The result was a pay claim demanding a minimum £2 10s (around £134.50 today) for adults, to which the railway companies responded with an offer of £2 5s. For the sake of comparison, the best-paid skilled workers at this time earned about £3 10s per week, and the sums mentioned for railway workers would have been for unskilled staff. A new recruit to the armed forces would have received just 14s per week, and a corporal would have earned around £1–£1 5s a week, although accommodation and food would have been provided free, and for married servicemen there would have been an additional allowance.

In the resulting impasse between the railway companies, the NUR decided to put its claim to the Railway Staff National Tribunal, but the Associated Society of Locomotive Engineers & Firemen (ASLEF) opted instead to bring out its members on strike from midnight on Saturday, 26 August. Not all footplate staff belonged to ASLEF, but they were the overwhelming majority, although naturally not the lowest paid.

The strike decision appalled politicians and the media. Ernest Brown, the Minister of Labour, met the ASLEF executive on 24 August, and at first the two sides went through a ritual recital of the basis of the claim, but then the Minister played his strong hand, emphasising that with war almost certain and evacuation plans already laid, 'We may need you to get the children away to safety.' This struck a chord, and later that day ASLEF called off the strike and agreed to follow the NUR in referring the claim to the Railway Staff National Tribunal. This was just as well, with the evacuation starting on 1 September, and the numbers involved being far beyond the abilities of any other form of public transport: at the time a typical single-deck bus would have carried no more than 35 passengers, and a double-deck bus on two axles, as most motor buses were, 52 or 56. Trolleybuses, larger in many, but not all, towns, could carry up to 70 passengers, but could not have ventured beyond the limits of their urban systems.

The unions' claim was based on a working day at a time when most public transport workers worked a six-day week. The difference between ASLEF members and those of the NUR showed in the claim, with the latter seeking the £2 10s minimum while ASLEF looked for a £2 14s minimum for engine cleaners over the age of twenty-two, plus the guarantee of a fireman's minimum rate and uniform if such a cleaner was not promoted to fireman after 313 firing turns. The minimum rate claimed for a fireman was £3 3s per week, rising to £3 12s with the guarantee of the driver's minimum after 313 driving turns. For drivers and motormen a minimum of £3 18s was sought, rising to £4 16s. These claimed rates were augmented by extra payments for Sunday working, amounting in theory to time and a half, but boosted further by the claim demanding an 8-hour minimum both for Sunday working and any roster that extended from Sunday into Monday. Two weeks', that is twelve working days', annual paid holiday was also demanded. The Railway Clerks Association also made a claim, largely along the lines of the other unions but with the additional proviso that continuous night duty should attract one night off in ten in addition to normal rest days.

In total the unions' claims amounted to an extra £4.8 million annually for the railway companies, at a time when their income was fixed by the government. The country went to war while the claims were being pursued, and the tribunal reported on them in late October, succeeding in recommending a compromise that would increase the wage costs of the railway companies by £1 million. Minimum rates were raised to £2 7s for railwaymen in rural areas, with an extra for those in industrialised areas, while those in London were to receive the £2 10s demanded by the NUR. A sign of the times, women were to be paid around 12s less than men, and possibly the substitution of female labour for male as men joined the armed forces eased the burden on the railway companies. The Railway Companies Association representative, Mr H.E. Parkes, produced a minority report proposing a lower settlement, generally some 2s less for adult males, but he accepted the tribunal recommendations for women's pay. There were also some changes to minimum payments so that any Sunday roster would attract a minimum of four hours' pay for shifts of up to three hours, and for longer shifts, or if there were two short shifts eight hours' pay would be given, but footplatemen were granted their Sunday claim of a minimum of eight hours' pay.

The unions accepted the offer, but by 1 December the NUR was back for more, asking the Railway Executive Committee for an all-round 10s a week cost of living increase. It is true that prices were beginning to rise and this was later to be a factor in the introduction of rationing, but for those on the minimum adult wage for the London area this represented a pay increase of at least 20 per cent, and even more for those in the provinces and for women.

Meanwhile, the shareholders were still waiting to learn what compensation they would receive for what effectively amounted to the requisition of their property. In 1914 agreement had been reached quickly, in September, using the Regulation of the Forces Act 1871, but in 1939, using the new Emergency Powers (Defence) Act 1939, the government was dragging its feet. Encouraged by the delay in reaching agreement, the Labour MP for Bristol South asked Captain Euan Wallace, Minister for Transport, on 22 November whether he would consider nationalising the railways. The Minister rejected this at the time, assuring the House that he was confident that agreement would be reached shortly, and also reminding them that unified control had already been achieved through the Railway Executive Committee (REC). Another month passed and the question of nationalisation was becoming more serious, as rumours that could only have been officially inspired that nationalisation was being considered began to circulate, obviously intended to apply pressure to the railway companies. 'It cannot be for the good of the community that such a monopoly as a main line should be controlled by any group of individuals, however public spirited', ran one statement on the matter, completely ignoring the fact that the railways were no longer controlled by the companies but instead by the REC. Many writers on railway matters saw opportunism in these threats, arguing that those in favour of nationalisation would find their arguments less convincing in a period when policy could be considered at leisure. Even so, it was not until 7 February 1940 that the Minister was able to give the House of Commons the news that agreement had been reached over the terms under which the state would control the railways.

## BATTLING AGAINST THE GERMANS AND THE TREASURY

The financial basis of state control of the railways in wartime had been agreed or, depending on one's viewpoint, imposed. Nevertheless, it was soon clear that the original scheme had many deficiencies, and as early as December 1940, a short Act of Parliament allowed those railways under the control of the Minister of Transport to make agreements with the Minister to cover financial matters arising from the period of control. The railway companies were given the freedom to enter into arrangements provided that the Minister laid an order. In fact the position of Minister of Transport had fallen prey to revolving door syndrome. The ailing Euan Wallace was replaced by Sir John Reith when Winston Churchill took over as prime minister, and was replaced in turn by Lt-Col J.T.C. Moore-Brabazon before the end of the year. But he lasted just six months or so before the Ministry became the Ministry of War Transport under Lord Leathers of Purfleet, and the 'new' department absorbed the Ministry of Shipping. These changes meant that transport was in turn looked after by a man, although originally a civil engineer, whose reputation was based on the creation of the British Broadcasting Corporation and then by one of the great pioneers of flight, before finally passing in May 1941 to Lord Leathers, a businessman with extensive interests in coal, who was ennobled for the purpose rather than have the government wait for a Parliamentary by-election. When the railways lost the humourless Reith they gained Moore-Brabazon, who as a young man had taken up a pig in a balloon to show that 'pigs could fly'. Lord Leathers' suitability for his new role was being questioned by the railway press as further negotiations between the railways and the Treasury were in hand. The fear was that the pursuit of the public interest would become too one-sided.

Part of the problem was that no one in government really understood, or perhaps even cared about, the problems encountered by the pre-war railways, let alone the difficulties facing them in this new conflict. As before, coastal shipping was badly affected by wartime conditions, but the seriousness of the situation was far worse than in the First World War. Now German forces controlled Europe from the North Cape almost to Bordeaux, and occupied the Channel Islands. The North Sea and the English Channel were effectively out of bounds to merchant shipping, regardless of the strength of the convoys, although further west shipments of Welsh coal to the South Coast ports, including railway-owned Southampton, had more than trebled.

The Treasury was its usual unsympathetic and unrealistic self. The Chancellor of the Exchequer, Sir Kingsley Wood, decided that war damage would not be treated as an element within working expenses which could be offset against the guaranteed sums paid by the government, but instead was to be charged to the capital account, transferring this uninsurable cost from the government to the railways. On 7 April 1941, in his budget speech, the Chancellor announced that its policy was to combat inflation and restrict price increases as far as possible, and that included railway fares and rates for goods traffic. This was important news but it took more than a week for Moore-Brabazon to write to Lord Stamp of the LMS, as chairman of the Railway Companies Association, who unfortunately was killed that night, 16 April, in an air raid.

Moore-Brabazon moved on, and so it was left to his successor, Lord Leathers, to explain to the railway companies the bad news about pricing and war damage, and even then, in June 1941, the advice was oral, almost as if the government was ashamed to commit itself to paper. Instead of the original agreement of a £40 million guarantee and a share in net revenue in excess of that amount up to £56 million, there would be a fixed annual guarantee. The railway companies were in an impossible situation. With the nation expecting German invasion and having come through the Blitz, no one was to know that salvation would come, in the short term, through German attention being diverted to the invasion of the Soviet Union. To argue would be construed as being unpatriotic, and many would have had memories of how war profiteers had been vilified by the press and politicians in the First World War, although no one had ever suggested that such charges applied to the railways. The railway companies were negotiating under duress, and the government had clearly already settled on the fixed figure of £43 million, eventually referring to the changes in the light of the previous year's legislation permitting an amendment. The government promised to make good any deficiency in the fixed figure, but would also take any surplus. Division of the £43 million and the relative shares were to be:

| | | |
|---|---|---|
| Great Western | £6,670,603 | 15.5% |
| Southern | £6,607,639 | 15.4% |
| London Midland & Scottish | £14,749,698 | 34.3% |
| London & North Eastern | £10,136,355 | 23.6% |
| London Transport | £4,835,705 | 11.2% |

Clearly there were winners and losers, although the variation in percentage terms was marginal. The Southern and Great Western were both slightly worse off in percentage terms, the former the more so, while the LMS, LNER and LPTB all made marginal gains. Shareholder protests that the deal was mean in the extreme were countered by socialists claiming that the deal was far too generous.

'Certain sections of the community, always vocal in these matters, have not disguised their disappointment that the Government has decided not to adopt the advice they have given so freely and with so little practical knowledge, to nationalise the transport system of the country', thundered the *Railway Gazette*. It continued:

The new agreement, which provides for renting the railways by the State, has also been criticised on the grounds that its terms are unduly generous to the transport system. How little substance there is in these protestations is easy to see if one is prepared to delve far enough into the facts of the case, to divest one's mind of prejudice, and to approach the problem from the basis of equity. On this basis, the original agreement can by no means be judged generous to the proprietors of the railways; nor can the second. At best it provides a very meagre return upon the capital which has been invested in the undertakings and without which, allied to the patience which, perforce, has been exercised by a long-suffering body of stockholders, the railways of this country could not have reached their present high standard of efficiency, which has contributed so greatly to the successful prosecution of the war. . . .

Of recent years there has been all too prevalent an idea that the standard revenue which was fixed by the Railways Act, 1921, as fair and reasonable and in the public interest is beyond the possibility of attainment – that the £51,359,000 at which it now stands has become but a mythical figure. It should be remembered that Parliament considered the attainment of that standard revenue was so expedient in the public interest that it placed a duty on the Railway Rates Tribunal to fix charges so as to enable a company to earn its standard revenue. Although it is a fact that Parliament's object was not attained . . . this has been due very largely to acute and unregulated competition by road interests. There can be no doubt that in present circumstances the railway companies could earn their standard revenues. . . . Moreover, the use now made of the capital provided by the railways is much greater than in the period before the war, and includes the use of assets that were then operated at a loss, but were continued in use to meet conditions which now exist. Taking into consideration . . . the London Passenger Transport Board, a total of £56,853,000 would be required as the total standard revenue of the whole of the undertakings, and it is this figure that should be borne in mind when comparisons are made with the fixed annual revenue of the five major parties in the revised arrangements which provide for a rental of £43,000,000 in addition to the net revenue from certain excluded items.

The excluded items were the railways, revenue from associated businesses such as road haulage and bus operations. The *Railway Gazette* continued to emphasise that the railways had made considerable sacrifices in accepting the deal, but were obviously influenced by two factors – the national interest, and that while the earnings even for 1941 were far in excess of the sums provided by the deal there could be developments that would reverse this situation, such as invasion. It went on to remind its readers that the railways would now have to pay for restoring their own war damage, and that there could be no grounds for suggesting that the £43 million annually was a subsidy to the railways, but instead it was clear that the railways were subsidising the government. Gross expenditure by the five railway undertakings controlled by the REC during 1940 had amounted to £203.5 million, of which more than £150 million was accounted for by labour costs, while the capital cost of the five undertakings amounted to £130 million. The £43 million included the revenue from ancillary businesses, and amounted to a return of less than 3.5 per cent on the capital. The one item that the railways could charge for was the manufacturing work carried out in railway workshops, which over the war totalled £38,999,000.

Further adjustments were not made in the later stages of the war when it was clear that the invasion threat was long past, even though the net earnings of the railways were by this time well in excess of their fixed annual payments by upwards of 100 per cent for three years running. In fact, the surplus profits taken by the government for 1943, 1944 and 1945, reached a total of £155 million. By this time, the railways were not simply serving the British armed forces, but they were also playing their part in supporting the build-up of men and equipment for the invasion of Europe. And there were also the leave specials, and not just for British servicemen, who wanted to get home to see their families, but for Americans whose idea of a good time off-duty meant heading for London.

## RAILWAYS UNDER PRESSURE

It is hard to judge just how much railway passenger traffic was affected by the war since the available statistics do not show the average length of journey, which was likely to have increased considerably. The number of originating passenger journeys on the GWR in 1938 was 129 million, but by 1944 this had increased to 190 million. On the LMS the figures showed a smaller rate of increase, from 421 million to 456 million, itself down 2 million on 1943, and were static on the LNER at 281 million, but again down on 1943. The big exception was on the Southern, where passenger journeys fell from 361 million to 347 million, owing in no small part to the loss of the holiday and excursion traffic. For all of the railway companies, the number of coaching train miles fell between 1938 and 1944, including empty stock workings.

Freight increased overall by 46 per cent between 1938 and 1943, with the biggest increase, 86 per cent, in merchandise, which doubtless included manufactured items such as munitions. While coal and coke traffic rose only by 13 per cent, the length of haul rose by no less than 30 per cent. There must have been a great deal of one-way traffic because of the war effort since loaded goods train miles rose by 11 per cent between 1938 and 1944, yet empty miles rose even more, by 51 per cent.

The statistics are inadequate since they consist of totals provided by each company, not by the Railway Executive Committee, so that, for example, a train from Portsmouth to Rosyth could count as four trains, running over the Southern, GWR, LMS and finally the LNER. Nevertheless, passenger specials for the government rose from 24,241 in

1940, doubtless boosted by the Dunkirk evacuation, and after a drop in 1941, to 47,381 in 1943. Freight specials showed a steady increase, from 20,888 in 1940 to 45,583 in 1943.

Naturally enough, throughout the war the hostilities took their toll on railway staff, many of whom continued to work under conditions that many would regard as incredible today. Not only was serious damage repaired as quickly as possible, sometimes with military help, to maintain services, but locomotives and trains were moved to safety at the height of air raids, and many continued to work amid burning buildings. In one celebrated case a signalman remained at duty in his box despite a naval mine clearance team working on an unexploded landmine outside! The worst incident occurred at Soham in Cambridgeshire, on the LNER, on 1 June 1944, when a fire on a train of ammunition wagons raged out of control and led to an explosion.

For the railways' other businesses, including the docks, the picture was mixed, with shipments at many ports falling dramatically between 1938 and 1943, especially for those on the east coast of Scotland and England. They also fell at the South Wales ports. Coal shipments at Southampton increased, but overall traffic was down – Liverpool and Glasgow were safer alternatives for the convoys and the troopships – and, of course, the cross-Channel and Channel Islands ferry traffic from Southampton, with the latter also from Weymouth, had disappeared.

Overall, in 1935–37 the five railway undertakings had average annual total operating receipts of £195,236,000 and expenditure of £158,500,000, which gave them net operating receipts of £36,727,000 and net revenue of £39,903,000. By 1944 the annual figures had risen to total operating receipts of £394,360,000 and expenditure of £301,200,000, giving net operating receipts of £93,193,000 and net revenue of £90,256,000, but, of course, of the last figure they were only allowed to keep £43,469,000, with the rest going to the government. Overall, for 1941–44 the railways received a total of £173,876,000 and the government received £176,199,000.

CHAPTER TEN

# *Nationalisation*

'Do they think that the public will have a better and a cheaper service? Do they think that the wage earning and the salaried staffs of the Main Line Railway Companies will be better off? . . . I challenge the nationalisers to prove their case. I accept the challenge to prove that public interest can best be served by private ownership of the Southern Railway.' This was fighting talk. Colonel Gore-Browne was angry and indignant. He was speaking at the 1946 annual general meeting of the Southern Railway, of which he was chairman. After putting up such a robust defence of the railways under private enterprise, in hindsight it seems ironic that just a year later he found himself defending his actions in the face of criticism from the shareholders, whose turn it was to be angry. 'Now may I turn to the record of last year and to the plans which we have in view,' Gore-Browne told his audience. 'Some . . . have asked "Why, as things are now, have you made any plans? Is not your only duty to protect your stockholders' interests?" We feel it necessary to take a wider view. We have always regarded your undertaking as a service to the public . . . the Chancellor of the Exchequer who described the railways as "a very poor bag of physical assets" will in our case be agreeably surprised.'

Facing nationalisation from a Labour government with a massive majority, the Southern Railway's directors and senior management had continued to plan as if nothing was going to change. Possibly, seeing that the country had other priorities after a long and financially debilitating war, the Southern's directors and senior management were hoping for a last-minute change of heart. Either way, their enthusiasm for renewed planning and investment had angered many shareholders, and it is hard not to have sympathy with them, for they had stuck with the company through the lean years of the 1920s and 1930s, when it had developed the world's largest electric suburban network and electrified the main lines to the Sussex coast and to Portsmouth, as well as vastly extending the docks at Southampton and becoming involved in domestic air transport, only to see the state profit from the Herculean efforts made by the railways in wartime. Every penny spent on modernisation could have been paid in dividends, instead of being invested in new trains, track and signals and thus a gift to the future owner of the railways.

'This railway system of ours is a very poor bag of assets,' Hugh Dalton, Chancellor of the Exchequer, had told the House of Commons during the second reading of the Transport Bill on 17 December 1946. 'The permanent way is badly worn. The rolling stock is in a state of great dilapidation. The railways are a disgrace to the country. The railway stations and their equipment are a disgrace to the country.'

If Britain's railways were such a poor bag of assets indeed in 1947, one might wonder why it was that the lines on the Isle of Wight continued to operate Victorian locomotives and rolling stock right up until 1966, which were then replaced by elderly rolling stock dating from the 1930s that had been withdrawn from the London Underground? The Southern Railway's plans to pick up where it had left off in 1939 and extend electrification as far as possible, with diesel traction for the less economic lines and for what were then known as stopping goods trains, serving small stations that at the time still had their own sidings, were to come to nothing. The Treasury would see to that.

At the time MPs were discussing the terms of compensation to be paid to the shareholders, and the Chancellor had been pressed to justify the appalling compensation that was proposed. He managed to avoid mentioning the strains of war, but by the time the measure became law the *Financial Times* was moved to point out that the claim that the railways were a 'poor bag of assets' had been disproved. Indeed, among those with an open mind it could be seen that the railways were truly war-battered and exhausted. Not only had the system been worked to the limits, not only had it endured heavy enemy aerial attack, but it had also seen its locomotives and rolling stock taken as far away as Persia, present-day Iraq, and at home hastily trained labour had taken the place of the skilled men who had either volunteered to join the armed forces or had been conscripted. In addition to the shortage of materials and manpower, the workshops had in many cases been given over to war production and, faced with the need to repair bomb damage, the priority was repairing and rebuilding while routine track and rolling stock maintenance had to be neglected.

## GREY DAYS

These were grey days for the country as a whole. Much has been made of the return of the bright lights by VE Day with the end of restrictions enforcing the blackout, but the population had to continue with rationing of almost everything, except one or two items such as fresh fish. Bread, which had not been rationed during the war years, was rationed postwar!

People had to use public transport. Even if one could get hold of a car it would be old since, with the exception of a few models for military use, car production had stopped for the duration, and petrol was difficult to obtain. Buses, including those of London Transport which had come to pride itself on the condition of its fleet and its overhaul arrangements, now included many with holes in their bodywork; others had chassis that sagged alarmingly in the middle. In just under six years of total war the country had been so battered and its circumstances so reduced that it resembled what would today be described as a third-world state, with little that worked. Large areas of many towns and cities had been razed to the ground, or had the remains of gutted buildings standing bleakly against the sky.

Just how much of the public enthusiasm for nationalisation resulted from onerous wartime travel restrictions and the controls that left the timetable often halved or worse, when additional traffic had to be handled, or journey times extended by a third or more, is hard to say in retrospect. On the other hand, the vote for Labour may not have been a vote for nationalisation but a vote against what many had come to see as the unfairness and inequality of some aspects of British life.

The service restrictions early in the war led the then Mayor of Brighton to accuse publicly the Southern Railway of always having treated his town badly! This despite the fact that it had not only been the first beneficiary of the Southern's main-line electrification plans, but had also enjoyed a more than doubled frequency of trains in the process! He withdrew his accusations when the Southern's directors produced a vigorous response. This was a clear example of how the railways were blamed for government policy.

There were other factors at work. The full evil of the Soviet system had still to be revealed and postwar Communism was even respectable. Few people were shareholders, and few understood, or even cared, how the system worked.

Apart from enthusiasts, the railways never enjoyed great popularity. The errors and shortcomings of the worst obscured the achievements of the best. This still happens today. In 2003 a reader of *Modern Railways* wrote a letter, tongue in cheek, claiming that he had been cheated of his quota of cancellations, delays and overcrowding on his daily journeys across Yorkshire. At a time when the author commuted daily on the Portsmouth line there was certainly a spell when the original electrification stock, well past its working life and often showing signs of neglect, created many problems and delays, but once it was replaced 'on time' arrivals occurred on 90 per cent of journeys, and 'on time' in this case meant bang on time, not within five minutes as with today's punctuality figures! Despite this people still grumbled and few were appreciative. Part of the problem is, of course, that public expectations of the railways are often unobtainable and unrealistic. One MoT civil servant once told the author that the by then nationalised railways were making vast profits out of suburban commuters because the trains were so overcrowded, and refused to believe that if the train then spent the whole day idle in a siding it was losing money. Most of its peak-hour passengers were enjoying heavily discounted fares anyway, with savings on annual season tickets amounting to 40 per cent on suburban journeys and up to 60 per cent on longer-distance services. The real problem over the nationalisation debate was simply that the public, the electorate and taxpayers, didn't care.

Who did care then? The railway shareholders were outnumbered by the railway workers. Nationalisation in the UK was driven by the workers in particular industries. Labour was committed to the nationalisation of almost everything, although in later years some prominent ministers would deny that they would nationalise 'down to the last corner shop'. Railwaymen, coal miners, steel workers, all wanted to control their own industries, a series of 'soviets'. Labour also decided that air transport should be run by the state. How shipping managed to remain off limits is a mystery, although even this was in the sights of later Labour administrations. The docks belonging to the railways were nationalised, but the remainder were left untouched simply because so many of them were in local authority control, or run by public bodies, later leading one Conservative rebel, Enoch Powell, to propose that the ports should first be nationalised so that the situation could be sorted out, and then all be denationalised again!

There can be no doubt that the attitude of the workers postwar was very much that the railway would soon be 'theirs'. This is not an unreasonable assessment of their attitudes since the establishment of the

Railway Executive disappointed many trade unionists because it was dominated by railway managers.

Public attitudes may have been strongly influenced by the wartime restrictions on railway operation, failing to fully appreciate that these were imposed on the railways by the REC, which in turn was instructed by the Ministry of War Transport and, before it, the MoT. In wartime the railways were for the first time victims of diktat by the Treasury. This would not be the last time either; the three separate service ministries all had frequent demands on the railways, as did the Ministry of Supply. In fact, the paying public, the regular traveller, the voter, the customer, all really just one category, came bottom of the heap. But it was not the fault of the railways.

The neglect of suburban and branch-line travellers on the mighty London Midland & Scottish and the not-quite-so-mighty and poverty-stricken London & North Eastern must have affected the image of the railways. It was not enough to have the fine expresses streaking across the countryside, outside the experience of the vast majority of travellers. It was the day-in, day-out slog on a slow and dirty, if not downright dilapidated, branch-line train or an overcrowded suburban train that stuck in the memory. There is general accord that the LNER achieved much with its suburban services, and with steam locomotives that could, in the case of one class, match the performance of electric trains for acceleration, and perhaps even outperform them when the rails were wet or slippery. But electrification had been promised and electric trains were cleaner and, most of all, they were *modern* – the buzzword between the wars. Times were changing; they not only had electric trams, but they had electric buses with the silent efficiency of the trolleybus, while the first electric household implements were finding their way into the more affluent homes. For many the radio had arrived, and for the few the television made an appearance almost on the eve of war. Not only that, but the passenger enjoying first class on the 'Coronation Scot' or the 'Flying Scotsman' could well have a connection with one of the grimy branch or suburban trains, or might have travelled on the gleaming new electric trains of the Hampstead tube, now renamed the Northern Line, or on Circle Line 1938 stock – all part of the *nationalised* London Transport. Perceptions are all. Even the Great Western, by now treating both classes of passengers decently and with its diesel railcars on the branches, still depended on steam for its admittedly small London commuter business.

The undereducated and unthinking masses had the vote and intended to use it. The affluent liberal-minded were attracted by the efficiency between the wars of the nationalised European railways. It mattered not at all to them that Mussolini had made the trains run on time in Italy by demanding realistic timetables, and not by improvements in efficiency. In Germany, where things were efficient and becoming more so, Britain's railways were shown up when the Great Western's 'Cheltenham Flyer', at one time the fastest regular train in the world, lost its crown to the Berlin–Hamburg express. Meanwhile, in the USA steam was fast losing its crown to the advance of the diesel, and it didn't occur to the educated elite that in that country of vast distances and infrequent long-distance trains the railways were already losing the battle for not just long- but intermediate-distance travellers to the airlines. The Douglas DC-3 or C-47, known in the UK as the Dakota, transport had originally emerged as the 'Douglas Sleeper Transport', or DST, to carry passengers overnight across the USA.

Nationalisation of the railways overnight gave the state control of the main ports, plus the railway hotels, haulage firms such as Carter Peterson and Pickfords, and the travel agency Thomas Cook. It provided a substantial ferry and coastal shipping fleet, and a substantial number of bus companies, especially when the state also managed to absorb the bus interests of Thomas Tilling, Scottish Motor Traction and the British Automobile Traction Group. The government's priority was nationalisation, greater state control and a cradle-to-the-grave welfare state, rather than reconstruction and improvement of the manufacturing base and infrastructure. These assets were all acquired cheaply, but they had been neglected out of dire necessity during the war. In the immediate postwar period the railway companies could not even obtain their usual peacetime allocation of materials for routine maintenance and renewals, let alone make significant inroads into the massive backlog.

## BTC AND BRITISH RAILWAYS

The way in which the state viewed transport was made clear in nationalisation. A massive new body, the British Transport Commission (BTC), was formed under the chairmanship of Sir Cyril Hurcomb, a civil servant. The five full-time board members also included John Benstead of the National Union of Railwaymen and Lord Rusholme from the Co-operative Movement, although Lord Ashfield, who had been chairman of the Underground Group and then of London Transport, had considerable experience of urban and suburban road and rail transport, as did Sir William Wood, who had considerable experience of railways in Ireland and with the LMS, before working on the Railway Executive Committee during the Second World War. Lord Ashfield died that year.

The BTC was given a massive remit, including the coordination of transport, and was also given the powers to influence traffic movement through charging schemes to allow the different costs of the individual modes of transport to be used to direct freight and passenger traffic to the most economic and efficient mode for the particular traffic. The environment was ignored. Bus services were intended to be integrated through a series of area schemes that emphasised local monopolies and which allowed the newly nationalised bus companies to make local acquisitions to strengthen their hold on the network. Even so, there were many local pockets of resistance, sometimes in towns such as Winchester, where the Chisnell family kept King Alfred Buses independent, and Gosport and Fareham, where the Provincial Traction Company reigned supreme on local services and became the last British bus operator to charge a penny fare. Companies such as Bere Regis & District, with a sprawling rural network that cannot have made its three owners a fortune, also remained independent. The British Electric Traction bus companies, only two of which employed electric traction (Mexborough & Swinton and the Hastings Tramways network of Maidstone & District), also remained independent, even though some had railway, and now BTC, shareholdings. Independent road hauliers were in turn also purchased.

The BTC in effect became a massive interfering bureaucracy sitting between the Ministry of Transport, which was responsible for government policy on transport and for its regulation, including the operation of the traffic commissioners for road passenger transport and the licensing authorities for road freight transport, and the individual modes of transport, which were in turn administered by 'executives', of which the Railway Executive, commonly known as British Railways (BR), and the London Transport Executive were but two. The title British Railways had originally been coined during the war years and used in publicity then and immediately afterwards, usually to discourage the public from travelling at holiday periods, especially after the Normandy landings led the civilian population to believe that they could resume their old holiday habits.

Squeezed between the operators and the Ministry, the BTC was unpopular. For its part the BTC saw the different executives as unwilling to modernise and embrace new ideas. The executives saw the BTC as including not just bureaucrats, but often politically motivated idealists wishing to test their new ideas on the businesses.

From the start, despite being run by a civil servant, it was the intention that the BTC should pay its own way as a business.

The new British Railways started life on 1 January 1948, with 19,639 route miles of track, a small fall in route mileage since 1930 due partly to some minor pre-war trimming of the network and wartime closures of unnecessary routes. BR inherited 20,023 steam locomotives, 36,033 passenger carriages, plus a further 4,184 carriages contained within electric multiple units, and 1,223,634 goods wagons, of which half had been privately owned prior to nationalisation and with which, as already mentioned, the outgoing railway companies had been compelled to share their compensation, even though many belonged to the soon-to-be-nationalised coal mines and steel works! There were small numbers of diesel railcars and shunting engines. The executive was to be criticised for foot-dragging and a reluctance to modernise, but it was also subject to direction by the BTC, which can hardly have encouraged initiative. Enterprise must also have been inhibited by the very scale of the undertaking, as a solution that would be acceptable in the south-east might not work so well in the north-west and could be completely wrong for Scotland or Wales.

At the grouping the companies found themselves with a system that had been strained by the First World War and had suffered from neglect as necessary materials and manpower had been directed elsewhere. The new British Railways found itself with a system that had suffered from all of this, but for longer, as well as from enemy action. BR also had to standardise the operating practices of the former railway companies. Although it included the Irish Sea ferries operated by the old LMS and GWR, it did not have control of railway services in Northern Ireland, apart from the LMS-owned Belfast & Northern Counties Railway. Nationalisation was delayed on the other side of the Irish Sea because three out of the five railway companies operating within Northern Ireland had cross-border operations, and it was not worth nationalising the small Belfast & County Down Railway, the other purely 'internal' operator, on its own.

At first, the boundaries of the old Southern Railway and the Great Western approximated to those of the new Southern Region and the Western Region. There was some tidying up, with Fenchurch Street transferred to the new Eastern Region, while joint lines were each allocated to the most appropriate region. The LNER was divided between the Eastern, North Eastern and Scottish regions, and the LMS between the London Midland and Scottish regions. In effect, the east coast and west coast main lines in many ways reverted to what was almost a pre-grouping structure. On the Southern Region, the old pre-grouping structure continued in the three divisions, Eastern, Central and Western, that perpetuated the areas of the South Eastern & Chatham, London Brighton & South Coast and London & South Western railways.

After his opposite number at the Great Western turned the job down Sir Eustace Missenden, the last general manager of the Southern Railway, chaired the BR executive. It was to be an unhappy end to his career on the railways. Beneath the chairman, the executive comprised functional officers who issued directions to their counterparts in the regions, each of which had a chief regional officer to act as a representative of the executive on the one hand, and a coordinator of the departmental or functional officers on the other.

Early priorities included a new corporate identity. Members of the executive stood and watched as a succession of steam locomotives each wearing different liveries steamed slowly past, all with railway carriages again displaying different liveries. In the end blue was selected for express locomotives and black for goods and mixed traffic, while carmine and cream became the new passenger rolling-stock livery, variously known as 'strawberries and cream' or, to the cynics, 'blood and custard'. Exceptions were the Southern electric multiple units with a simplified green livery, Pullmans retaining their traditional brown and cream, and, of course, the 'Night Ferry' *Wagons Lits* blue stock. Later all-over red was used for local and suburban stock outside the Southern region, while diesel and electric multiple units were painted green. Standardisation also meant new uniforms and new designs.

While many of Bulleid's initiatives on the Southern Railway's Pacific locomotives were appreciated, the main focus of attention was on Stanier's mixed-traffic locomotives, and this design was modified slightly, most noticeably by the design of the tender, and returned to production both in tender and tank engine form. The new standard Pacific, the 'Britannia' class, owed much to Stanier, but incorporated some Bulleid features, while the rebuilding of the Bulleid Pacifics led Bulleid to resign. The 'Britannia' class, while more reliable than the Bulleid 'Merchant Navy', 'West Country' and 'Battle of Britain' classes, was markedly less economical. The author recalls a railway manager who had earlier in his career been a fireman telling him that when a train was hauled by a 'Merchant Navy' he could probably relax before it cleared London Bridge, but that he had to continue firing almost all the way to Charing Cross on a 'Britannia'!

A new standard British Railways carriage appeared as the Mark I, available as a corridor carriage for main-line use and as a non-gangway carriage for suburban and other services. There were kitchen, buffet and restaurant car variants, as well as overnight sleepers and a variant for parcels use that could double up as a guard's vehicle, although second-class and composite brakes were also available. Later the Mk1 design was also made available for both diesel and electric multiple units, and both suburban and main-line versions were available with corridors or as open stock with gangways. It is worth noting, however, that Southern independence asserted itself with the first versions of the new EPB suburban electric multiple units, retaining the old Bulleid 'wide-bodied' design of the last 4 SUB units. However, conformity was all and eventually the standard carriage held sway; indeed, it remained in production for Southern use well after the Mark II design had been adopted elsewhere. The standard designs for locomotives and carriages were generally pleasing in appearance, and the use of special wood, to which the attention of the passenger was drawn by a descriptive label, in first class ended utility. The main-line Mark I's large windows were an attractive feature, especially appreciated by small children who could have a good view from the window seat – not possible with the high sills of later rolling stock.

The selection of a standard design did not mean any great rationalisation of railway manufacturing and production plant, while construction of new steam locomotives continued despite BTC objections, instead of electrification and the introduction of diesel power on the less busy routes. Just one major electrification programme was put in hand by the new British Railways, the Manchester–Sheffield–Wath line across the Pennines, completed in 1954 and mainly for freight, although an electrically hauled Manchester–Sheffield service was provided. Exactly why steam locomotive construction continued is something of a mystery, but continue it did until 1960, by which time diesel traction was already predominant on many routes and electrification had resumed. The stupidity of building steam locomotives was all too apparent in 1968, when steam finally disappeared from Britain's railways just eight years after production ceased! Indeed, at the end of steam many pre-grouping locomotives were still in service.

A new Conservative government passed the Transport Act 1953, abolishing the Railway Executive and establishing area boards under the British Transport Commission, with the new chairman of the BTC, General Sir Brian Robertson, becoming chief executive of the railways. The BTC moved out of the London Transport Executive (LTE) head office at 55 Broadway and into those of the Railway Executive at 222 Marylebone Road, the old Great Central Hotel. This was certainly a way of removing one layer of management and of control, but it is questionable whether it was the right layer to remove. The other executives survived, including the LTE, and it would have seemed wiser to have disbanded the BTC itself and given the executives greater freedom, reporting direct to the relative departments of the MoT. Many layers of control remained, with the British Railways regions including divisions, sections and areas.

The newly nationalised railways had an operating surplus of £19 million (£356 million today) in 1948, small enough given the size and turnover of the undertaking, but by 1955 this had become a deficit of £17 million (around £238 million today). The deterioration was blamed on rising costs and renewed road competition as well as an industrial dispute that seriously affected the railways throughout a substantial part of 1955, and doubtless gave a shot in the arm both to the road competition and to the expanding internal air services. With the railways firmly in its control, the BTC acted decisively. Construction of steam locomotives was phased out, but it still took another five years. In 1955 a modernisation plan was published.

SUBSIDIES

The move from a minuscule profit to growing losses brought with it an unforeseen problem: what to do with a loss-making state industry. Many nationalisers had greedily anticipated the profits going to the state, and some even argued that this was the purpose of nationalisation, so that profits did not go to shareholders. It was a pretty futile argument since before the Second World War there often hadn't been much profit to go anywhere. No doubt the argument was helped by the wartime experience, since during the war the more people and goods moved on the railways the more the state had benefited. Postwar the railways were in the happy position after nationalisation of having continued heavy traffic to carry, with the demand for raw materials for reconstruction and most households dependent on coal for their domestic heating needs. Cars were still few and far between. The armed forces had been cut once hostilities had ceased, but not very quickly, and the target figure was for them to have almost 900,000 men and women, more than four times the number today, so forces leave and weekend traffic remained substantial.

The question of losses became one of the major issues from the mid-1950s onwards. As we will see in the next chapter it was to be a combination of writing off losses and subsidy, of cutting the number of lines and of removing duplication, while looking for other ways of cutting costs, such as unstaffed stations or removing ticket inspections.

The question of state subsidies dates from as early as 1817, when the Exchequer Loan Commission was established to provide low-cost loans for major public works. Initially it was intended to support town councils, but between 1830 and 1844 five English railway companies, including the Liverpool & Manchester, and four Irish companies benefited from loans provided by the Commission. These could have been seen as an early form of pump priming, for afterwards few English railway companies were in need of state support as money for their construction flowed in from anxious investors, eager to share in the great boom.

Even when £1 million was set aside for the construction of light railways under the terms of the Light Railways Act 1896, only a fifth of the sum was actually used.

The two significant exceptions to subsidy came in the later years of the railway age, and reflected the need to ensure that some of the remoter parts of the country were served. Thus in the 1890s the North British Railway was guaranteed interest and also enjoyed alleviation of local rates for its new line to Mallaig, while the Highland Railway was actually given a subsidy for its extension to Kyle of Lochalsh, the terminus for those travelling on to the Isle of Skye.

A more generous approach to providing low-cost loans had been the spur to modernisation and employment creation of the Guarantees and Loans Act 1934.

# CHAPTER ELEVEN

# Modernisation and Beeching

The 1955 modernisation plan was the most ambitious programme ever prepared for the railways, but applied solely to Great Britain and Northern Ireland, where the bankruptcy of the Great Northern Railway of Ireland, operator of the Belfast–Dublin, Dublin–Londonderry and one of the two lines between Belfast and Londonderry, had finally tipped the governments on both sides of the border to nationalise the railways and road passenger transport.* The initial plan called for investment of £1,240 million (around £14,880, million today) but this was later increased to £1,500 million, which was, ignoring inflation, three times the cost to the British taxpayer of the Concorde supersonic airliner project in the early 1970s, and rather more if the inflation-prone 1950s, '60s and '70s are included!

The plan was the scheme that should have been introduced following nationalisation, and was the brainchild of a Conservative government. It was meant to dispense with the Victorian and Edwardian railway, of which so much was still in evidence, and create a truly modern railway. In addition to replacing steam with diesel and electric traction, it called for an end to loose-coupled and hand-braked goods wagons and for their

---

* The contrast in the treatment of the railways between the two 'Irelands' could not have been more marked. In the Irish Republic the railways survived, although it was to be some time before any substantial investment in modernisation was to be seen, including new rolling stock and the Dublin Area Rapid Transit (DART), with a name doubtless influenced by the American Bay Area Rapid Transit (BART). In Northern Ireland the policy was one of closing the railways. The lines of the Belfast & County Down virtually disappeared, with the exception of the line to Bangor, as did the Great Northern Railway of Ireland, with the exception of the line between Dublin and Belfast. The two narrow-gauge companies lost their tracks altogether in favour of running buses, but the old Belfast & Northern Counties remained with its main routes to Larne, Portadown and Londonderry largely intact, and eventually the surviving lines found themselves with a single Belfast terminus.

replacement by larger wagons with continuous braking, allowing higher speeds and greater safety as well as an improvement in productivity. The many small sidings would be replaced by a smaller number of purpose-built and mechanised goods yards, while passenger and goods stations would be modernised.

Electrification not only embraced the Southern Region, where the lines to the Kent coast excluding that to Hastings were to be electrified, but other regions as well. The suburban lines from Liverpool Street and King's Cross were to be electrified at last, while the other Eastern Region electrification was to be between King's Cross and Leeds, and possibly to York. On the London Midland Region the lines from Euston to Birmingham, Liverpool and Manchester were also to be electrified, as was the Scottish Region's Glasgow suburban network.

Rationalisation was to accompany the modernisation plan as an almost inevitable quid pro quo for its implementation. British Railways had already started a number of line closures by this time, including the hopeless line between Merstone Junction and Ventnor West on the Isle of Wight in 1952, joined the following year by the branch between Brading and Bembridge and by the line from Newport to Yarmouth and Freshwater, which had never been viable.

The plan meant the end of competition, which was not popular and did not always provide the savings expected. Birmingham was no longer to be served from both Paddington and Euston, and with electrification in mind for the main lines out of the latter, Paddington lost out. Given the bureaucratic mindset and the way in which politicians and even their civil servants see life as a series of politically motivated 'deals', this may also be why Paddington gained control over the entire south-west railway network. Plymouth was to be served entirely by trains from Paddington. This is where the economies failed to materialise. Concentrating all services from the south-west on under-used Paddington could have made sense but for two factors, the first of which was that Exeter had to continue to be served from Waterloo as well because of the number of important points on the line, including Salisbury, and because of the strategic and wartime needs of the British Army since the line ran through its main southern training grounds. The second was quite simply that the Waterloo route was the most direct, unlike the Hants & Berks line from Reading through Newbury. Indeed, for a while longer it remained possible to reach Weymouth from both Waterloo and by the roundabout route from Paddington. Had Waterloo become the terminus for trains from Devon and Cornwall, with those from Paddington routed via Bristol, the Hants & Berks could have been closed completely.

In any major project the wisest and most cost-effective course is to make all of the decisions before starting. On the London Midland electrification scheme initially the decision was taken to use the 1,500v DC overhead system. This offered the worst of all worlds, since unlike third rail, every overbridge and every tunnel, as well as a number of other structures intruding over the lineside, would have to be rebuilt, but like third rail, sub-stations would be required at frequent intervals. The scheme had already been delayed by many planning difficulties, again a consequence of overhead electrification. It should have been seen that the electrification system for the future was the modern 25,000v AC overhead system, which dispensed with many sub-stations and was the best for sustained high-speed operation. Yet it was not until part-way through the project that it was decided to switch to this system. This affected plans for both infrastructure and for traction.

In the process technical resources were found to be wholly inadequate for the full extent of the plan, so that only the Euston schemes could be progressed and plans for electrification out of King's Cross had to be delayed. This led to the next mistake for the cost-conscious railway management, the failure to create a long-term rolling programme so that skilled personnel moved on from one to the next, maintaining the most cost-effective pace rather than a series of stop-start schemes.

Meanwhile, such was the haste to make up for lost time and the desire to show that a modern railway was achievable not simply at breakneck speed but almost as an emergency programme, that common sense had gone out of the window. Diesel traction was not simply to be for those lines deemed uneconomic for electrification, such as the main lines out of Paddington to Bristol, Plymouth and South Wales, but it was seen as a stopgap measure for the routes being electrified out of Euston and, later, King's Cross, although, strangely enough, such an interim traction package was not considered for the lines from Victoria, Charing Cross and Cannon Street to the Kent coast on which a straight steam to electric switch occurred.

To replace steam on every branch line a whole series of diesel multiple units, diesel railcars and even diminutive diesel rail-buses derided as being 'too small, too underpowered and too late' were ordered from several manufacturers. The lack of experience on what might be described as 'dieselisation' led to too many different types of locomotive being ordered, usually without prototypes being built and tested, and not surprisingly many of them were found to be unsatisfactory. During the seven or eight years following nationalisation, no one had thought to copy the Southern Railway and visit the USA to learn from their experience. If a low-powered steam locomotive had to be replaced, a diesel of similar power output was sought. So underpowered and inadequate were many of the diesel locomotive classes that some spent almost all of their time from delivery to disposal rusting away in sidings. Insufficient thought was given to the design of main-line diesel multiple units, with few lines ever receiving these, despite work on the subject by the LMS before the war. The mistakes with the diesel locomotives were compounded by the failure to build not just prototypes but pre-production machines in limited but useful numbers for extensive service trials. In one case an unsatisfactory locomotive class was followed by an order for an up-rated version of the same class, further reducing reliability and availability. As they were introduced the new locomotives did not follow the Southern Railway's pre-war practice with its new electric trains and run from the factory to a purpose-built depot, but instead at first lodged alongside steam locomotives and were serviced in steam engine sheds, with all of the attendant dirt and filth that was the unfortunate disadvantage of the steam age. Once this found itself into the more delicate parts of the diesel locomotive reliability was still less likely. All of these problems were compounded by the failure to realise that, unlike the steam locomotive or the electric engine, a diesel could not be worked beyond its maximum power output without incurring mechanical damage. Too many classes, too little standardisation, too little preparation and too little experiment in too much haste were all problems with the diesels, but then the bill was being picked up by the taxpayer, not the shareholder!

On the London Midland diesel locomotives were introduced while electrification went ahead. The same happened not once but twice on the Eastern and North Eastern regions. First, steam was replaced by the massive Deltic diesel-electric locomotives, one of the best ever designs conceived for Britain's railways, which in turn were replaced by the even more brilliant, albeit flawed in some minor details, InterCity 125 high-speed train (HST). All this instead of thrusting forward with an electrification programme. The HST was a substitute for the failed advanced passenger train (APT), abandoned because of problems with its tilting mechanism that were not pursued long enough or diligently enough to be resolved. Unfortunately the HST was overshadowed by the glamorous French *Trains Grandes Vitesse*, the famous TGVs, and the Japanese 'Shinkansen' or 'bullet' trains. However, unlike these, which needed new lines, the HST could realise its full potential on standard track, always providing that the track was laid and maintained to a high standard and that someone somewhere remembered to upgrade the signal system for higher speeds at the same time. The TGV lost time when negotiating 'classic' track either on its way to and from the terminus or, as happened initially, on the route beyond Lyons.

There were other false starts as well. With such a substantial number of steam locomotives dominating the railway scene, and especially that for freight, it was perhaps not too surprising that the modernisation plan's ambitions for fully fitted goods trains should be based on the vacuum brake. But by this time the vacuum brake was out of date and the air brake was superior. Again, part way through the railways had to switch from building vacuum-braked stock to air-braked. More wasted money, but the taxpayer was still around!

Despite modernisation traffic continued to fall, and especially freight traffic. The plan failed to keep pace with changes in the market for rail travel and the movement of freight by rail, with the result that many of the impressive new marshalling yards were soon redundant.

Between the wars much had been made of conversion of relatively new steam-hauled rolling stock to electric operation, especially when the steam-hauled stock had in any case been made up into pre-formed sets for standardisation of train formations and ease of marshalling. The modernisation plan usually ignored such possibilities. Bulleid main-line rolling stock on the Southern was scrapped, all of it within twenty years of construction, while elsewhere on the same system older electric trains soldiered on for almost twice as long. The best of the old LMS carriages were not retained or converted. Even with the BR standard Mark I carriages the only time these were converted for an electrification scheme was with the Bournemouth electrification of 1967–8, and to some extent this may have been because the scheme itself was cut-price, with electrification running just beyond Bournemouth to the depot, and trains being operated on a 'pull–push' basis, with a single four-car-powered electric multiple unit pushing one or two unpowered sets as far as Bournemouth, where they were taken on to Poole, Dorchester and Weymouth by diesel electric traction – one of only two routes operated in this way, the other being between Edinburgh and Glasgow Queen Street.

For the most part the use of specially modified electric or diesel locomotive power for pull–push operations was ignored, even though this would have cut costs by extending the life of existing rolling stock and would have reduced turn-around times at termini.

The other major problem arose with single manning. The new electric and diesel traction did not need firemen, but these were retained as driver's assistants, and another advantage of the new forms of motive power was lost. The railways negotiated the assistant position as a separate productivity deal, a completely new and unnecessary extra cost and source of industrial conflict. When the Southern Railway had switched services from steam to electric no one had even dreamt of having a second man in the cab!

The so-called 'sparks effect' showed that electrification in particular was popular, but mostly with commuters. The spread of private car ownership has been blamed for the decline in the importance of public transport and for its worsened financial situation, but in 1959 the number of car owners was a sixth of that in 1999. The real culprit was television, taking theatre and to an even greater extent cinema trips in the evening from public transport. On Sundays coach trips to the seaside were cheaper and often more convenient than travel by railway. The growing gap between peak and off-peak loadings was another cause of the worsening financial situation on the railways.

Eventually the penny dropped. It was no use tinkering around with the executives under the British Transport Commission; it was the BTC itself that was to blame for much that was wrong. It had criticised the executives and especially British Railways for being insufficiently forward-looking, but it was itself large and unwieldy with too few people of any relevant experience at the top, and even these had experience confined at best to two modes of transport. The concept of inter-modal transport was still to come, and even when it was mooted it was mainly a combination of road and shipping or rail and shipping, and very seldom road-rail-ship. By the late 1950s the BTC was being criticised both for its size and for its lack of any commercial sense. It only managed to see through the electrification of the two Southern Region lines to the Kent coast in 1959 and 1961, leaving the residents of Hastings to be served by a distinctly ugly, noisy and rough-riding batch of diesel multiple units, costly because they were built exclusively for this line, and none of the synergies of using depots and crews for the electrified network could be realised.

There was a growing suspicion that the railway network was no longer in the shape that was necessary for British industry, and that it also included many lines that were no longer as sustainable as road hauliers and the passenger road transport operators gained authority for larger and more productive vehicles, and had the flexibility to adjust to changing market demands.

The lack of commercial sense could clearly be seen in one of the best-loved titled expresses inherited from the old railway companies, the 'Bournemouth Belle'. The shortage of passenger rolling stock and the train's pre-war popularity had encouraged the Southern Railway to re-introduce this all-Pullman train as early as 7 October 1946, with a full ten cars. Leaving Waterloo at 12.30, the train reached Southampton Central at 13.57 and Bournemouth Central at 14.35, before proceeding to Bournemouth West where it arrived at 14.46. This was a service for the business traveller, then not accustomed to leaving home very early and returning home very late, and on Sundays the schedule was ideal for the day tripper, with lunch out, an afternoon in Bournemouth, and then dinner on the return from Bournemouth West at 19.15 to reach Waterloo at 21.25. Many have ascribed the Southern's enthusiasm for reinstatement of its luxury trains to a desire to sweep away austerity and boost national morale, but bringing Pullman cars out of storage helped to ease the critical rolling stock shortage at a difficult time, while for the traveller opulent accommodation and a reserved seat were an attractive proposition at a time when far too many trains were overcrowded and still making extra stops. Perhaps too the Southern Railway's management was forward-looking enough to appreciate that unless something was done quickly to cater for the top end of its market many would be lured away by the motor car and the aeroplane as these became more widely available.

For reasons best known to itself, the evening departure was brought forward before nationalisation, giving passengers just two hours in Bournemouth and effectively ending the day tripper market, while the Bournemouth–London departure was far too early for dinner. After nationalisation five minutes was added to the schedules in 1948 and remained until 1963, before further decelerations were reintroduced to allow for delays due to engineering works as electrification of the Bournemouth line pressed ahead. As for the time spent in Bournemouth, it seems that it was more important to save wages with a two-hour lay-over at Bournemouth than to give passengers a reasonable period of time there and increase the market! It would have been far better to have scrapped this train with its uneconomic use of special rolling stock than keep it going in such circumstances, but nothing was done. Even weekly commuters would doubtless have preferred a later departure from Bournemouth.

Then, too, there was that other and even more notorious loss-leader, the 'Night Ferry', which enabled a small number of passengers to join the train in London and alight without changing in Paris. This was never a full train, with just eleven of its twelve *Wagons Lits* sleeping cars surviving the war. Its economics became even more doubtful when it was decided to serve Brussels as well as Paris, so that one short train became two very short trains in each direction. It was not until 1982, when demand for freight on the three train ferries forced the 'Night Ferry' to be withdrawn, that anything was done about it. At one time it could at least have been said that this was the one reliable way to attend an early morning meeting on the other side of the English Channel, but long before its withdrawal blind landing equipment had given such reliability to the airlines.

## ENTER LORD BEECHING

Mounting railway losses could not be allowed to continue. The Ministry of Transport had commissioned two reports on the future of the British Transport Commission (BTC), one of which was for public consumption, the other for its own internal use. Even so, it was not until the Transport Act 1962 that the Ministry grasped the nettle and broke up the BTC into its component parts, establishing the British Railways Board, the London Transport Board, the British Transport Docks Board, the British Waterways Board for canals, and British Road Services, which included Pickfords, formerly owned by the railways. Nationalised bus services were divided between the Transport Holding Company in England and Wales, and the Scottish Bus Group north of the border.

The 1962 Act also set the railways free from the common carrier obligation and the need to seek approval for freight rates. It could be said that this measure was thirty years too late. By ending the obligation to provide third-class accommodation it allowed the railways to 'upgrade' this by renaming it second class, later changing this to standard class.

Later other changes to the charging structure followed. Pre-nationalisation first-class fares had been around 60 per cent higher than those of third class, but the nationalised railway closed the gap to around

50 per cent. Originally any third-class (or later, second-class) fare was available as first class provided that accommodation was available, but in order to boost revenues British Rail abolished first-class day returns. It had the reverse effect, driving people to their cars or to second class, while the under-used off-peak accommodation became the haven of vandals, discouraging season-ticket holders and business travellers. First class on many routes was sacred, used not only by season-ticket holders but also by MPs and senior civil servants, as well as railway management and, at one time, members of the National Union of Journalists! The weakness of the measure was soon exposed on many services where the shortage of first-class travellers off-peak was countered by the concept of 'Weekend First' for which standard-class ticket holders paid a supplement, and which required the railways to differentiate between 'first-class' and 'weekend first-class' accommodation!

For the railways the new structure was preceded by a new chairman, with General Sir Brian Robertson, by now Lord Robertson, shunted out of office and replaced by a man from the private sector, Dr (later Sir) Richard Beeching. He had arrived at the BTC in 1961, before which he had been technical director of Imperial Chemical Industries (ICI), at that time regarded by economic historians as being one of the two truly internationally competitive British companies (the other was Rolls-Royce). ICI itself had been the creation of a kind of grouping of its own in the early 1920s, creating a new unified force in the chemicals industry.

Beeching felt that the new British Railways Board required a much simpler structure, and he also felt that it would benefit from an influx of senior managers from other industries whom he felt would be more familiar with developments in management techniques, and would also have a stronger market focus. Few of them stayed for more than a few years, but whether this was because they had difficulty in adapting to the realities of transport operation or whether they found life in a nationalised industry suffocating it is hard to say. They certainly got a difficult ride from some of the old school in the railway world, such as Gerald Fiennes, an ex-LNER man running the Eastern Region, who eventually resigned after writing a book, *I Tried to Run a Railway*, in which he argued that branch lines should be run more cheaply rather than close. Many believed Fiennes had a point.

Beeching was expected by the government to reduce at least the growing railway losses, and ideally eliminate these altogether. In fact his instinctive reaction was that of an accountant rather than a scientist, requiring and acquiring extensive statistics that showed just how much each section of line and each railway service earned, and how much each cost. He quickly came to the conclusion that many lines could be closed and so too could many stations which showed very poor receipts. There was also abundant evidence of poor utilisation of rolling stock, especially for trains such as summer holiday specials that spent most of the year rusting away in sidings. He published his findings in a report, 'The Re-Shaping of British Railways', proposing to close some 2,000 stations and end 250 train services. The media presented this to the public as a plan to cut Britain's railway network by a third.

Few have aroused such fierce passions as Beeching. Some would almost have him as the devil incarnate, while others point out that he merely accelerated a process that had already started. It is true that there were cuts well before Beeching. There are those who maintained that costs could have been cut on many railway lines and services retained. One big weakness of his method of analysis was that it concentrated too much on receipts from stations along a line and not enough on the earning potential of these stations. A good example of the way in which these figures can differ, and differ considerably, comes from stations in resort areas, where the local business, and hence receipts, could be very low, but the station would have considerable earning potential because of the large number of often long-distance journeys terminating there each summer. The weakness was one of traffic analysis, since the journeys mentioned would have been credited to the station of departure, which would have enjoyed a double boost to its income because almost every passenger would have purchased a return ticket. Insufficient attention was also paid to the impact of branch-line traffic on the main lines – what airline managers would describe as 'feeder traffic'. Ironically, shortly afterwards one of the London clearing banks produced an advertising campaign with the memorable slogan 'Our roots are our branches'.

Beeching maintained that main lines could be profitable, but branch lines couldn't. Specialised goods traffic could be profitable, while local or stopping goods using sidings at small stations were a major loss-maker. Commuter traffic was unprofitable by this time, but was socially and politically necessary.

If Beeching has been too severely criticised for his programme of cuts, he was also insufficiently recognised for the innovations he urged upon the railways, no doubt because the former obscured the latter in the perceptions of the media and politicians, and also of the public. It was Beeching who led the railways in the direction of the Freightliner concept, with what were initially known as 'Liner Trains' providing a regular fast service running to a tight timetable and carrying containers to ease problems of transhipment, both feeding the ports and, on internal routes, having road collection and delivery from major terminals. Another big innovation was 'merry-go-round' coal trains running constantly backwards and forwards between colliery and power station. Rail freight, Beeching found, was unlikely to be profitable or competitive with road haulage on distances of up to 200 miles, although given the high productivity of the merry-go-round concept, it could pay on shorter routes. In a further report, now little referred to, Beeching advocated continuing to invest heavily in the trunk routes.

In the end, while the innovations went ahead, Beeching started an accelerated programme of closures that saw many rural branch lines cut, and while those in the far north of Scotland remained for political and social reasons many other areas lost substantial local networks. Towns such as Hunstanton in Norfolk, once with a daily express from Liverpool Street, found itself cut off from the railway network, despite Royal patronage since the line also served Sandringham. The Settle and Carlisle line managed to survive, but lost its St Pancras to Scotland services, but one line across the Scottish borders, the so-called Waverley route, was closed. Cities such as Oxford found their railway service downgraded, as did Whitby, once so favoured by George Hudson, and Cheltenham found itself not just without the famous 'Cheltenham Flyer', but with very few direct trains at all. Even routes carrying boat trains were not immune, with the so-called Port Road from Dumfries to Stranraer closed, with Kirkcudbright losing its trains, and the boat trains from England to Stranraer for Larne being diverted via Glasgow, a route that entailed travelling two sides of a large triangle.

## POST-BEECHING

Before all of Beeching's proposals could be implemented there was a change of government, with Labour returning to power in 1963 after twelve years in opposition. Railway losses continued to rise, and it soon became clear that the closure programme would have to continue. Beeching retired in 1965 after the new government had settled in and was replaced by a railwayman, Stanley (later Sir Stanley) Raymond.

The Conservatives had been alarmed at the direction the railways had been taking, but had given the management a reasonable head, as well as having given the railways their single biggest dose of new investment ever. The new government had a much more interventionist approach, and while the railway losses continued to mount the new chairman had to suffer the indignity of the Minister of Transport, Barbara Castle, appointing a Joint Steering Group that reported to both of them. This was a recipe for disagreement and friction, as for the first time a government tried to run the railways directly. This might have pleased those who had foreseen nationalisation as the railways being run rather like the Post Office, but this was not how the railways had turned out. There were also many disagreements over the headquarters structure of the British Railways Board, perhaps not surprisingly because increasingly the Ministry and the steering group were usurping many of its functions. One of the few significant moves at the time was the merger of the North Eastern and Eastern regions, with the management moved out of London to York, effectively re-creating the territory of the old London & North Eastern Railway, and also leading to a greater role for divisional and area managements, again along the lines of the heavily decentralised LNER.

Raymond left office in late 1967 to be replaced by another railwayman, Henry (later Sir Henry) Johnson, who came from the London Midland Region and had just overseen the completion of the electrification project.

Having undermined one chairman, Barbara Castle at least helped his successor into office with the welcoming present of the Transport Act 1968, which at a stroke wiped out most of the accumulated deficit and for the first time recognised the existence of socially (and politically) necessary services that could never be remunerative by providing grants for their operation. It was not an entirely open-handed gesture, for some of the gains were balanced by losses. The best example of this came with the creation of the National Freight Corporation (NFC), a new nationalised industry, which released the railways from the burden of providing small consignment or sundries traffic, but also took the by now developing Freightliner service as well, plus the old British Road Services operations. The NFC allowed the railways to act as a contractor to Freightliner and forget about marketing and terminal operation, so while the railway's freight managers must have been bitterly disappointed this streamlining was on balance a massive benefit to the railway.

Another boost for the railways was the creation of passenger transport authorities for the major conurbations outside London, both to acquire the local bus services within their areas and to contract British Railways to provide socially necessary railway services. These were in effect mini-London Transports, probably too top heavy to provide local bus services economically, but the concept of providing an overall authority to ensure that services could be provided and coordinated was doubtless a step forward. The first PTAs were created in 1969 and 1970 for the West Midlands, Greater Manchester, Merseyside and Tyneside, joined in 1972 by Strathclyde, known initially as Greater Glasgow, and in 1974 by West and South Yorkshire, the year that the areas covered by the English PTAs underwent local government reform to become new metropolitan counties.

Not content with this, the 1968 Act also allowed for nationalisation of the remaining bus companies, and specifically those of the British Electric Traction (BET) Group, which included some of the biggest names in the industry, including Midland Red, Ribble and Southdown, as well as some smaller but highly regarded companies such as Aldershot & District. Despite a high-profile anti-nationalisation campaign the BET Group sold out suddenly, almost overnight, without waiting for the legislation. Bus company managements were supposed to have spent a frantic night stripping off the anti-nationalisation advertisements from their vehicles. The new acquisitions were not simply transferred to the old Transport Holding Company, but instead this and the former BET companies were taken over by a new National Bus Company. Ignoring the lessons that suggested that the law of diminishing returns sets in early with bus operation, at around 200 vehicles, many of the old companies were merged with previously nationalised companies to create larger units, with Aldershot & District and Thames Valley merged to produce Alder Valley, Southdown and Brighton Hove & District merged, and even some of the original nationalised companies merged to form larger units, as with Hants & Dorset and Wilts & Dorset. New liveries were introduced, with even a new standard bus, the unloved Leyland National. An express coach network, National Express, also emerged, although something similar had already existed in the form of Associated Motorways. National Express, despite its common all-over white livery and branding, continued the Associated tradition of operating through local companies. Many of the remaining privately owned bus companies were later taken over, including Chisnell's King Alfred in Winchester and the Provincial Traction Company, both of which passed into Hants & Dorset. This was the high summer for state-ownership of transport in the UK, although the weaknesses were already being increasingly exposed to the traveller in air transport, especially on the so-called domestic trunk routes where first British Eagle, then British Midland and British United (later British Caledonian), struggled eventually to find a toehold on services from London to Belfast, Edinburgh and Glasgow.

While the railways were at last being placed on a sound financial basis, there was also much else to give grounds for hope for the future. Almost twenty years after nationalisation a new generation of electrification programmes was finally reaching completion. This meant that electric trains could operate between Euston and Birmingham, Liverpool and Manchester, but third rail remained in use between London and Watford without any attempt to standardise on the new overhead system, while Merseyside also retained its own third-rail system.

Nevertheless, productivity was at last beginning to improve. Belatedly, the management was pressing for single manning of electric and diesel locomotives, while also looking to remove guards and, by definition, brake vans from fully fitted goods trains. However, there were other measures of productivity apart from staffing. When Johnson stood down at the end of 1971 to be succeeded by Lord Marsh, who as Richard Marsh had been a Labour Minister of Transport, the railway network's route mileage had been cut by 41 per cent since nationalisation, while passenger and goods stations had been cut by 67 per cent. The longest railway line to have escaped passenger station closures completely was that between London Waterloo and Portsmouth Harbour via Guildford, known as the 'Portsmouth Direct', but even on that line the goods stations had been closed and many of the sidings surfaced to provide much-needed car parking for commuters. The longest stretch of line in the country without a station closure was on the Waterloo to Weymouth line, where for more than 80 miles stations remained open until one reached the New Forest, to the west of Southampton. Many short spurs had been closed, including Bournemouth Central and the terminus in Southampton. It was soon no longer possible to use the line through Alton as an alternative if the main line to Southampton was blocked, or to reach Brighton via Uckfield and Lewes if the Brighton line was blocked. Elsewhere many lines had been singled, including large sections of the Waterloo to Exeter line west of Basingstoke. In the quest for further economy the number of points and cross-overs had been reduced, sometimes compromising flexibility of working during engineering works or following the failure of a train.

Bearing this in mind, it seems ironic that the new logo for the renamed British Rail was a double arrow symbol, which bore more than a passing resemblance to two lines joined by sets of points! The new name and new logo were matched by a new livery, with all-over blue for suburban and local trains, and blue and grey for main-line services, even replacing the Southern Region green, while elsewhere all-over maroon had earlier replaced carmine and cream. Electrification of the Glasgow suburban network had already seen the new overhead electrification EMUs painted blue and marketed as the 'Blue Trains'. The new corporate identity called for station name boards and signage to be in black lettering on a white background, marking a welcome advance in clarity.

As further evidence of improved productivity and especially the improved use of assets, the number of passenger carriages had fallen from more than 40,000 to just 17,000, and the 20,000 steam locomotives inherited on nationalisation had been replaced by 3,633 diesel and 317 electric locomotives. More doubtful, goods wagons had fallen by almost 80 per cent, but freight traffic had fallen most of all with no equivalent of the morning and evening commuter rush that had helped to keep passenger figures high.

While the system of subsidies for loss-making services had worked well, after a brief spell of Conservative government, Labour was back and the Railways Act 1974 tinkered with the system further, replacing the specific subsidies, or 'grants' in officialese, with an overall sum of money known as the Public Service Obligation. Ignoring the badly flawed German experience that pushed hundreds of millions of Deutschmarks into building private sidings, the Act also provided grants for industry to build private sidings in the forlorn hope that this would move freight from the roads to the railways. Even a Labour government had to bow to economic reality, however, and in 1975 already well-advanced plans for the construction of a high-speed link between London and the proposed Channel Tunnel, on which planning was also well advanced, were cancelled.

## HIGH-SPEED TRAINS

Of greater potential benefit, work on the advanced passenger train (APT) was not being adequately funded by the government, even though this train, with its tilt mechanism, was intended to lift the maximum speed on Britain's railways to 155mph, and to be able to take curves at speeds at least 20 per cent and as much as 40 per cent greater than could be managed by existing rolling stock. This meant that the train offered the chance of a high-speed railway without the need to build costly new high-speed lines, itself not just an economy but a saving of massive operational disruption and land use in a densely populated country. Despite the shortage of research funds a gas turbine-powered prototype had been authorised in 1969 and, after test runs, had given promising results. Three 25,000v AC electric trains, known as APT-P prototype, began trials in 1979, making their public debut in 1981, but suffered from considerable teething troubles, including problems with the tilt mechanism and the hydrokinetic braking system, designed to allow the trains to stop within existing breaking limits. Most of the problems were apparent during press runs, with subsequent complaints about queasiness. There were also gearbox problems. The APT project was finally scrapped in 1986, by which time British Rail was investing heavily in other rolling stock and on a programme of easing, but never eliminating, curves to achieve higher line speeds.

Failure to persist with the APT has cost Britain dearly. It set a British speed record of 163mph, which still holds on 'historic' track. Once other European railway equipment manufacturers mastered the problem, after privatisation Virgin Trains had to buy tilting train technology from Italy. The project had come at a time when Britain was at last putting money into railway research. A similar approach post-nationalisation could have spared the railways, and the taxpayer, much waste and inefficiency from the first generation of diesel locomotives. Research into advanced railway technology had ironically been made easier by the terrible cuts in aircraft programmes during the years of the Wilson Labour government in the 1960s, which had cascaded many talented designers on to other industries.

The substitute for the advanced passenger train was the IC125 or high speed train (HST), a non-tilting diesel electric train, in effect a long single multiple unit with a driving power car and luggage vehicle at each end. In what almost amounted to a re-run of trends in the late 1930s, streamlining was back in fashion on Britain's railways. First entering service in 1974, the HST was streamlined with well-swept and rounded ends, made possible by the use of glass fibre technology to achieve curves that would have been difficult and expensive to produce using steel or aluminium. The carriages were officially termed as Mark III, and followed the later versions of the Mark II in having air conditioning and sealed windows. Unlike the Mark II build, however, the Mark IIIs were a comprehensive spread of carriages, with kitchen and buffet vehicles, whereas passengers had become accustomed to leaving the comfort and smooth riding of the Mark IIs to be served in a noisy and rough riding Mark I buffet, while the dining-car crew attempted to cook meals in similar conditions. Suburban and sleeping-car variations of the Mark III followed.

For the passenger, one big advantage of the HSTs was that it was no longer necessary to avoid using the toilet when the train was standing still. The decision to introduce retention tanks was not out of concern for passenger convenience, nor for the health and hygiene of railway maintenance personnel, whether on the track or under the train at the depot, but for the simple reason that breaking the sealed environment of these trains at high speed would have resulted in the passenger concerned bursting an ear drum.

One missed opportunity of the HST was the decision, on grounds of economy, not to include power-operated doors. This was a major weakness and one that was to have tragic consequences for many passengers. It was wholly unnecessary since trains built for the then CIE, Irish Railways, included power-operated doors, as did the Wessex Expresses built for the final extension of electrification from Bournemouth to Weymouth some years later. The omission of power-operated doors was to have one unforeseen consequence. The Mark III enjoyed integral construction, known as monocoque, with the body providing all of the strength needed and no separate underframe, but with bogies and anything else attached to the body. This method of construction combined lightness with strength, but what had not been foreseen was that such bodies, in order to survive and avoid metal fatigue, had to flex while running at high speed. A long series of mysterious deaths among passengers standing in or passing through the vestibules at the ends of carriages was first attributed to suicide, before finally being traced to doors suddenly flying open at high speed and the draught sucking the hapless passenger out. These problems apart, alighting from the HST entailed passengers opening a door window, and then leaning over a thick and heavy door to operate an external handle – difficult enough for a fit male of around six feet tall, but an obstacle for anyone shorter or perhaps none too steady on their feet. The solution to doors flying open at speed was electric door locking, so that when a train pulled into a station the guard had to press a button to unlock the doors. Power-operated doors would have meant not only not spoiling the ship for a ha'penny worth of tar, but would have saved lives!

The HST brought modular construction to railway carriages for the first time, so that the same construction was used for carriages of either class – fine in first class, with seats matching up with the windows, but not always so good in second class, especially when increased use was made of coach-style seating to increase the number of seats in a carriage. High window sills were another disappointment for young children, and indeed for anyone well below average height.

The HSTs offered acceleration and an official maximum speed of 125mph, when track condition was good enough, although on a test run just over 143mph was achieved, setting a world record for a diesel. The HSTs revolutionised intercity railway travel, but were often not utilised efficiently. On the long run to the south-west of England use of the Berks & Bucks line with its many curves meant that they could not show their true potential, especially before the signalling was revised to account for their higher speeds. Then, on this route after Plymouth, and on services into Wales after Cardiff, the insertion of many stops also made poor use of high-speed stock. The same could be said of services north of Edinburgh in Scotland, and especially on the line to Inverness, where the HST operates even today as a local stopping train.

Nevertheless, the HST was a success. Reliable, long-lasting and comfortable, it bought time for Britain's railways, offering attractive scheduling without the need for special track. Single-handedly it even made railway travel fashionable again, with people actually noticing the trains as they rushed through stations, and even remarking to their acquaintances whenever they had travelled on an HST.

Despite his undoubted political experience and his success with the HST, Marsh was disillusioned by the tight limits on investment in the railways. The Treasury mandarins would look, for example, at a proposal to electrify the west coast route to Scotland, and question why an east coast electrification scheme was also necessary. Electrification in one part of the country, even where there could be no question of competition or duplication of resources, meant nothing elsewhere. At a time in the late 1960s when the Waterloo–Portsmouth service was making an annual profit of around £750,000 and the service to Bournemouth around £500,000, investment in new rolling stock for the thirty-year-old Portsmouth line original electrification stock was denied until it could be shown that a return of 6 per cent could be achieved. Doubtless less strict criteria were applied in the north-west owing to regional development considerations. Nevertheless, before his departure Marsh had achieved several further milestones in the electrification programme with the opening of electrification to Glasgow in 1974 and some additional expansion of the Glasgow suburban network, followed by the King's Cross to Welwyn and Hertford 'Great Northern' scheme in 1976, resurrecting an old pre-grouping title more than half a century after it had disappeared. That same year authority was obtained for electrification between both St Pancras, stuck on the periphery because of Victorian decision-making, and the more convenient new City of London terminus at Moorgate, and Bedford, the so-called 'Bedpan Line'. However, the full introduction of new services on the former was to be delayed until 1983 by an industrial dispute over single manning.

By this time it was Marsh's turn to be shunted out of the way, leaving in September 1976 to give a clear road for his successor, Sir Peter Parker, the man who coined the phrase 'the crumbling edge of quality' to describe British Rail. Parker had extensive business experience, unlike many of his predecessors, but like them he was to be frustrated by the limitations on investment in the railways. His disappointment was all the more acute because he was one of the few to take up his post and find that the situation was actually improving, since the impact of the Public Service Obligation subsidy and the money pumped into regional railway networks by the passenger transport authorities, plus investment funds provided for new projects, meant that the railways were actually making a net surplus on their operating accounts. Undoubtedly one aspect of the improved financial situation was that the responsibility for freight rested with the National Freight Corporation, but almost as part of the death struggles of the Labour administration the Transport Act 1978 transferred control of the NFC back to British Rail. Once back under railway control the old mentality reasserted itself and money was squandered in an attempt to revitalise the wagonload business, despite growing road haulage competition, under the brand of 'Speedlink', with a national network of longer-distance fast goods trains. BR spent the next decade trying to make an impression on the business before finally killing it off in 1991. A brighter spot in the freight business was the market for bulk traffic, including cement, which was expanding steadily with ample investment because of – horror of horrors – the re-emergence of that *bête noire* of railwaymen of old, the private owner's wagon.

The big success in railway and marketing terms over the period following the introduction of the new 'British Rail' corporate identity had been InterCity, advertised under the strapline 'Heart to Heart', to drive home the message that railway stations were closer to the centres of urban areas than airports. The idea of InterCity was a network of express and fast trains usually equipped with catering, for which the brand Travellers' Fare was soon coined, and with seat reservations. Renewed emphasis was also placed on cross-country trains and substantial traffic flows developed on many of what the airline people would describe as 'city pairs', such as York to the West Midlands for example, in addition to some of the longer-standing significant pairs, the most obvious example being Glasgow and Edinburgh. Even so, the ideal also had to face certain practicalities. On the Southern Region, for instance, the often very short turn-around times, especially during the morning and evening peak periods, meant that the promised seat reservations could not always be provided, especially at the busiest periods when this service was most appreciated and sought after by the traveller. Progressively the brand was removed from these services, including even the Waterloo–Southampton–Bournemouth–Weymouth service, which over its entire length was considerably longer than London to Birmingham or Bristol. 'Imitation is the sincerest form of flattery', and the true accolade of InterCity's success was the adoption of this very English title for a revitalised network of express services in what was then West Germany. It has to be said that it wouldn't have happened in France, but then the Germans were increasingly tolerant of the anglicisation of their language, albeit largely owing to American influence.

Even so, while InterCity was supposed to pay its own way there were many voices suggesting that even this prestigious and successful service was not truly capable of doing so.

The period since the end of the Second World War had been marked by what almost amounted to a consensus in British politics. On returning to office in 1951 the Conservative prime minister Sir Winston Churchill decided against denationalisation, even though the Conservatives were to remain in office for twelve years and see private enterprise blossom in road haulage and iron and steel; they allowed a grudging expansion of the role of the private sector in air transport, spurred largely by the unforeseen popularity of the inclusive tour or package holiday that enabled some substantial charter airlines to develop, notably Britannia Airways, at one time the world's largest charter airline. The consensus really amounted to competition between the two main parties in the search for the so-called 'middle ground' of British politics, and was criticised by many on the right of the political spectrum as a form of creeping socialisation, due to a steady leftward drift. This ended at the 1979 general election. Spurred by a 'winter of discontent' that had seen the worst industrial unrest experienced in the UK since the General Strike of 1926, the voters returned a Conservative administration under a new leader, Margaret Thatcher, that was determined to reverse the tide, with lower taxation, deregulation and denationalisation, although this latter policy was to be given the title of 'privatisation', probably justified by the fact that not only was the state to discard its own business interests, but so too were local authorities.

CHAPTER TWELVE

# Privatisation

The Conservative government started privatisation slowly. The policy soon proved popular with an electorate divided between those keen to become members of the share-owning democracy, and those who rapidly realised that in many cases considerable profits could be made by 'stagging' privatisation issues. The way in which the public speculated on shares in privatised industries to gain a quick profit has been criticised, especially by many of those on the left of the political spectrum, often on the grounds that companies were sold off too cheaply. In some cases this was undoubtedly true, but the real issue was that Margaret Thatcher was faced with a difficult political problem. For her the question was not whether to retain nationalised industries or to denationalise, but how to do it. Her every instinct was to give the ordinary people the chance to own these businesses, and so privatisation plans were always laid so that the small shareholder benefited, with special allocations of shares for employees, and with shares in the most popular privatisations rationed. This was popular with the voters, including the employees, but unpopular with the managements and financial advisers of the privatised industries who foresaw the heavy costs of a highly fragmented shareholders' register with many small shareholdings. It was also unpopular with the financial institutions, including the pension funds, who wanted to include such businesses in their portfolios. This meant that there was a ready market among those in the City wanting to acquire substantial blocks of shares, and it was this bait that ensured that the lucky private shareholder could sell the allotment of shares within days, if not hours, of issue at a considerable profit.

Such problems were inevitable, yet unforeseen, as no one had ever privatised on such a scale before. It didn't matter. Privatisation more than doubled the number of individual shareholders in the UK, as well as pointing the way for similar exercises throughout much of Europe, and incidentally providing the City of London with another invisible export in

145

the experience of its privatisation teams. It was very difficult to know just what price a sleeping giant of a nationalised industry could attract, even for those making worthwhile profits. After all, to what extent were these profits made despite poor productivity and feather bedding? Just what potential could the business have in private hands?

## SERPELL AND THE NETWORK

Railway privatisation was not at the top of the list, and in any case the position of the railways became unpredictable when the government started to deregulate road transport. First road haulage and longer-distance express coach services were deregulated, then ordinary bus services. At the same time the nationalised bus companies were privatised, often being sold off to their managements after having been broken down into smaller and more manageable units. Local authorities were also encouraged to sell off their municipal bus companies.

Within the Conservative Party there were many who doubted whether the railways could ever be denationalised. In the United States, the land of free enterprise, passenger railways had effectively been nationalised with the creation of Amtrak. On the other hand it could be argued that the USA was not the UK. Away from the Eastern Seaboard and perhaps southern California and around the Great Lakes, most inter-urban journeys in the USA were over far longer-distances than in the UK and much better suited to air travel than rail which, because of the needs of passengers on such long journeys, was inevitably more expensive. Economy passengers were already catered for by the coach networks, of which the most comprehensive and famous was Greyhound. Even in the USA railways were far from efficient: one reason for the length of many American freight trains headed by three or more locomotives in tandem was the rigid union rules on the number of personnel required for certain distances. It was also the case that in Switzerland and Japan only the main-line trunk railways were in state ownership.

Part of the problem was that even in the Conservative Party there were those, such as the former prime minister and railway director Harold Macmillan, who believed that the country had 'needed the railways', meaning that it needed to own them, although never really explaining why. On the other side of the argument stood those who questioned the cost and efficiency of the railways, and the size of the network, and others who were complete free marketers who would have left the railways to sink or swim. On the fringes stood a small number ready to convert the railways into roads. In the middle there stood a number who believed that the railways could be run more efficiently if returned to private hands, especially if broken down into manageable chunks, and that the taxpayer and traveller could still benefit even if a subsidy continued to be necessary.

It was certainly true that the heavy suburban and commuter loads could only be managed efficiently by railways. It was equally true that a busy main line or suburban line might consist of only two tracks, Up and Down lines, occupying a width, allowing for the body width of the trains and for trackside equipment, of around 24ft, just wide enough for a secondary road, and nowhere near the 90–110ft required for a three-lane motorway. The railway line could carry trains travelling up to 125mph, faster in some circumstances, while in Britain road users were legally limited to just 70mph on motorways and 'unrestricted' dual carriageways – admittedly some way below the usual 85–90mph of the traffic flow in safe conditions. The railway conversion lobby had some successes to point to in support of its arguments, such as the conversion of a main line into Edinburgh, the old Caledonian Railway route, to provide the Western Approach road, a four-lane single-carriageway road.

There was certainly no reason for the railways to hang on to many of their non-core businesses such as hotels and ferries, where there was already private enterprise competition. The ferries had become a sector of their own as Sealink UK, sharing the brand with the ferries operated by French and Belgian railways on the cross-Channel routes. This move recognised that most of their customers were motorists, road hauliers or coach operators, with only a minority using the train. Sealink had a comprehensive ferry network, operating across the Channel and the Irish Sea, to the Channel Islands and the Isle of Wight, and was sold in 1984 to the American-owned but UK-based Sea Containers, which later sold its main services to Stena Line.

British Transport Hotels (BTH) could not be sold as a chain, so were sold off piecemeal. The problem was that while a number enjoyed ideal locations, including some well away from the railway in Scotland, too many had been badly neglected. The hotels were a high-profile reminder that the state had been a poor custodian of the nation's assets.

Meanwhile, the railway workshops had at last been split up between those providing essential maintenance for the operation of trains and those that were involved in production, and who competed with a not insubstantial private sector. This was long overdue, and for years many had questioned whether the railway workshops with their cosy relationship with their main, and usually only, customer (although attempts were made to enter the export market), were truly efficient and provided good value for money. There remained a private sector, whose products had been much favoured not only before the war by the Southern Railway for its main-line electrification schemes, but also by the nationalised London Transport. In many European countries and in North America production and operations had been divided in this way, enabling many rolling-stock manufacturers to maintain a presence in both the railway and tramway markets. The manufacturing interests of British Rail Engineering were sold in 1989.

There were those within the railways themselves who suggested, or perhaps more accurately hoped, that the railways could be seen as being privatised from within through outsourcing of certain services and the growing involvement of the private sector in the provision of goods wagons and terminals. Meanwhile, Parker had in turn been replaced, and his successor was to be a different kettle of fish. Robert Reid, who took over in 1983, was later to become known as 'Bob Reid Mk1' since he was later succeeded by a namesake. He was described by *Modern Railways* as a 'man of iron will, strong political awareness and strong management'. A career railwayman, Reid had been largely instrumental in forcing through sector management in his previous role as chief executive (Railways). Now Reid could claim in the annual report for 1988–9 that the private investment in goods wagons and terminals amounted to £2.7 billion (about £4 billion today). A further development came through the Charterail Consortium when city institutions and GKN joined British Rail in 1990 to provide the railway trunk element of a road–rail service, with BR providing the locomotives to haul rolling stock owned by the consortium. Within two years the consortium fell apart as it ran into financial difficulties amid recriminations over the prices charged by BR and the reliability of the locomotives used.

Meanwhile, the railways had been given yet another thorough review that culminated in the scathing criticism of the Serpell Report, officially the 'Review of Railway Finances', published in January 1983. As usual with such reports it was named after the chairman of the committee, Sir David Serpell, a former permanent secretary at the DoT, and in retirement a part-time member of the British Railways Board. Parker had high hopes of the committee, expecting the basis of a longer-term strategy; certainly the report went far beyond simply looking at finance, and considered relationships between the government and the railways, and such matters as management structures. It also dealt with the relationship between BR and its engineering functions.

Nevertheless, for many Serpell will also be seen as being very nearly a 'Beeching Mk2', for it looked very carefully at the network, and made it clear that the true commercial network was much smaller than anyone had realised. As the maps (shown in the plate section) show, a truly commercial network would have to close the railways north of Edinburgh and Glasgow, and west of Cardiff and Bristol. In the south there would be lines to Dover, Brighton and Eastbourne, as well as to Southampton and Bournemouth, all of which seems very understandable until one looks at Portsmouth, where the line doesn't quite reach the city! In fact, Serpell was a nonsense. The railway line from Havant to Portsmouth Harbour might be loss-making, but without it volumes on Havant to Waterloo would be thin indeed, because travellers from Portsmouth, as with most cities, find the road journey out of the town the most time-consuming part, and so are hardly likely to waste time parking at a station when they can then drive up the clearer stretches of the A3! Indeed, the line to Edinburgh saw trains travelling up the west coast main line (WCML) because the east coast route (ECML) would stop at Newcastle. Again, without traffic from Aberdeen, Dundee and Edinburgh it is doubtful whether the line south of Newcastle really would be profitable.

Compromise seemed to be inevitable so Serpell produced a reduced support network. This was much more realistic, although politically unacceptable as it allowed the lines to Dundee and Aberdeen to survive, but entailed cutting Inverness and Plymouth off the network. Oddly, as we shall see later when looking at the rate of subsidy for the privatised railway, it allowed the line from Ryde to Shanklin on the Isle of Wight to survive.

## TOWARDS PRIVATISATION

Public dissatisfaction with the railways had led to consideration of ways in which they might be privatised. In 1985 the Adam Smith Institute had questioned the prevailing wisdom that public transport should be subject to political control. This was followed by two pamphlets by a former BR management trainee, Kenneth Irvine, with 'The Right Lines' in 1987 and 'Track to the Future' in 1988, proposing separating infrastructure from operating trains and effectively calling for a competitive open access regime. By way of contrast, in the latter year the Centre for Policy Studies produced 'Reviving the Railways: A Victorian Future' by Andrew Gritten, calling for BR to be split into twelve vertically integrated companies and arguing that allowing an infrastructure monopoly would lead to high costs without any incentive for development of the network. Effectively he condemned the legislation of 1921 and 1947, and called for a change in the culture with managements attuned to growth rather than contraction.

In fact, Gritten's proposals were anything but Victorian – simply a freer and less prescriptive variant of the grouping, but in that they could well have offered a practical way forward with none of the unhappy pairings that had led to the creation of the LNER, or the infighting that afflicted the LMS.

Gritten rejected privatising BR as a whole or privatising the sectors, which others had seen as a way forward. 'Sectorisation' had been introduced in 1982, and had been intended to create a more market-orientated railway, with the establishment of InterCity, Freight, London & South-East and Provincial Services sectors. In its implementation, sectorisation was a mixed blessing. Taking a business comparison, the sector directors had to act effectively as marketing or brand management, while the regions, which remained in existence, were in effect product management. They had to produce a service to the specification of the sector management, who would be responsible for selling it. Of course it didn't always work out this way, as the intending passenger could walk into a station booking office and buy a ticket for any two or three out of the passenger sectors, and indeed just one journey could involve three sectors. With the obvious exception of London & South East and, later, Scotland, friction between the sectors and the regions was to become a major stumbling block.

The London & South East sector had one big advantage over all of the other sectors in that it included the whole of the Southern Region; this immediately gave it a framework that was not only integrated but extended to the London ends of the Eastern, Western and London Midland regions. Parts of the Eastern Region, notably the services from Fenchurch Street and from Moorgate, were again entirely L&SE. Under the inspired leadership of Chris Green, who had the vision to see a 'single railway for the South-East', and introduced schemes to encourage greater use of the railway such as the Network Card, offering discounts on rail travel, L&SE, soon to be renamed Network South-East, was an unmitigated success. The Network Card offered holders a third off fares, encouraging greater use of the railways.

Elsewhere, regional management felt that they had ownership of their services and their rolling stock and infrastructure, and that they were being bullied by the sector managers at head office. These feelings were worsened by the growing power of area management. Yet on the roads both National Express and its Scottish counterpart, CityLink, operated as a network with a single distinctive livery, marketing and booking, with the individual local companies retaining ownership and operations.

Provincial services had the leavings from the table, comprising those that were outside the south-east and yet not grand enough for InterCity, including many rural no-hopers. On the other hand this was the sector with access to ambitious and free-spending passenger transport authorities – at least while the going remained good, as Thatcher had local government reform in her sights, abolishing the metropolitan counties that had become massively over-bureaucratic Labour fiefdoms.

Conservative ministers of transport ducked the issue at first, and instead of outright privatisation they proposed private enterprise involvement in railway passenger services. It seems clear that at the time they had in mind similar arrangements to those already in place with the railway freight business. This was not completely impractical. A small number of approaches were made by would-be operators interested in a joint venture with BR, although the latter was concerned that these might dilute its own income. Finally an opportunity arose. Overnight sleeper services had also offered seated accommodation, but this facility was withdrawn in May 1992. The bus and coach operator, Stagecoach, stepped in using six carriages leased from BR but renovated and painted in Stagecoach livery and attached to the sleepers. As with Charterail the charges, which effectively guaranteed BR £860,000 annually for three years, soon proved to be uneconomic, and the operation was withdrawn after just five months. By 1992 privatisation was finally on the political agenda, and mentioned in the Queen's Speech early in May.

When Bob Reid Mk1 had taken over in 1983 he came to his new role at one of the good times for the railways, with buoyant passenger traffic after years of decline, especially in the crucial off-peak business, coinciding with a property boom so that the British Rail Property Board, with all of its prime sites, was able to make a substantial contribution to overall railway revenues, at least for the first five years of Reid's tenure of office.

On the debit side, Reid found that he was now directly responsible to a government that was keen to cut costs and reduce public expenditure. Margaret Thatcher was notorious for having told a conference of railway managers that 'if they were any good, they wouldn't be here'. Her attitude, that the railways were badly run by people who lacked what it took to succeed in the private sector, was undoubtedly harsh and often untrue, but it was also a fair reflection of the attitude of many commuters and many of the people who had returned the Conservatives to power. Sometimes commuter discontent was justified, sometimes it wasn't, and was simply a reflection of even the intelligent person's inability to understand the complexities of railway operation. It was also a reflection of the difficulty of ensuring that every corner of an over-large organisation was managed effectively. Most of those who travelled extensively by train could think of an instance where a train would wait outside a station while a potential connection departed, even though a cross-platform dash was easily achievable. Indeed, when pressed to do this so that passengers on a train from Guildford could connect with one to East Croydon and Victoria at Redhill, the railways eventually gave in and allowed the connection, by bringing the Guildford train in behind the Victoria train!

Reid inherited further electrification projects, with an extension of those from Liverpool Street to Cambridge and Norwich, and a cut-price scheme for Charing Cross and Cannon Street to Hastings. The latter involved stretching the availability of the existing rolling stock pool to the limit and singling the line through Mountfield Tunnel rather than rebuilding this obstacle, but this was better than running down and eventual closure that was seriously considered as an alternative to the politically explosive closure of lines in the far north of Scotland. His great achievement as far as modernisation went was to secure permission to electrify the ECML in 1984, but this was a silver lining in search of a cloud. That same year a lengthy and bitter strike by coal miners forced the railways into a record annual loss of £200 million, which was bad enough in itself, but for the future amounted to a sharp contraction in coal mining and the loss of a staple traffic for the railways; one on which considerable success had been achieved through the merry-go-round system of working, and one of the traffics that had fuelled the railway boom.

Electrification of the ECML included extending the scheme from Edinburgh to Glasgow, but the desire to save money and the number of tunnels on the direct route between the two cities, the line between Edinburgh Waverley and Glasgow Queen Street, as well as the short platform lengths and restricted location of the latter station, meant that the electrified line went into Glasgow Central. Therefore trains effectively ran a dog's leg route down into the borders after leaving Edinburgh, before joining the WCML and running north through Motherwell to Glasgow. A good idea of the time taken comes from the note in the cross-country timetables for trains leaving Edinburgh and travelling south via Glasgow, to the effect that passengers could leave Edinburgh an hour later by catching a following train and changing! Worse than this, cost-cutting beyond the bounds of reason spaced the supports for the overhead wires further apart than was wise, especially on the exposed northern stretches of the line running close to the coast in Northumberland and in Scotland, with the result that high winds – a not unusual occurrence in the east of Scotland – seriously affected operations.

As if these problems weren't enough, there was another problem with this scheme that was to have unforeseen effects for many years following privatisation. A completely new design of rolling stock, sometimes referred to as the Mk4, was introduced, with the sides cambered in towards the roof so that a second build could use tilting technology for an upgrade of the WCML. The Mk4 had at last the power-operated doors denied the Mk3. The second tranche of Mk4s never materialised and production stopped once sufficient trains had been completed, making building additional rolling stock to the same design prohibitively expensive, should either traffic growth or the loss of rolling stock in accidents demand it. This was the penalty of having non-standard rolling stock. An updated version of the Mk3 with power-operated doors, as was built for the Weymouth electrification, would have been more practical and economical when, as it happened, both traffic growth and a series of accidents coincided after privatisation. Initially the Mk4s were plagued by poor reliability with their air conditioning and, even more serious, poor reliability of the Class 91 electric locomotives. An electric version of the successful HST would have been a far safer option.

Electrification more or less coincided with the diversion of the line to avoid the Selby coalfield, funded by the National Coal Board, and which provided the first new stretch of main line in Britain since the extension to Marylebone in 1899.

Cost cutting continued, but as usual the most obvious and biggest cuts come first and the remainder are less obvious and much more difficult. One plan was to close Marylebone station in London and turn it into a coach station, but this was successfully resisted in favour of modernising the remaining lines into this, once the terminus for the Great Central Railway but now bereft of main lines, to serve the affluent commuter areas of Aylesbury, Banbury and High Wycombe; eventually it was to provide a slower but cheaper alternative to Euston for travellers between London and Birmingham. Turning a railway terminus into a coach station recognised that coach commuter traffic had boomed in the wake of deregulation. This was not simply because of cheaper fares, but because many commuters looking for affordable places to live had been forced to find housing well away from good commuter railway stations, and the coaches could serve such areas. Typical of these was Cranleigh, south of Guildford in Surrey, with many new estates but having lost the line from Guildford to Horsham Christ's Hospital in the Beeching cuts. Earlier conversions included the Lord Street railway station in Southport, closed to trains in 1952 and re-opened as a bus station in 1954, or the narrow former terminus of the Jersey Eastern Railway at Snow Hill in St Helier, also converted to become a bus station and, because of its cramped position, retaining the locomotive turntable for buses until it eventually became a car park.

A London terminus was sacrificed that year with the closure of Bishopsgate, next door to Liverpool Street in the City. Unlike Marylebone, always the quietest and even countrified of London termini, Bishopsgate was ready for closure, derelict and for many years without a roof. It was part of the former North London Railway that had seen some of its most promising suburban lines taken over by the expanding tube network between the wars, while the remaining lines that offered great potential for cross-London travel on paper, such as the line from Broad Street to Richmond, in reality meandered and crossed too many junctions to offer slick service and convenient links to attract travellers.

As one would have expected given his earlier experience on the railways, Bob Reid encouraged sector management at the expense of regional management, although one exception to this was further tinkering with the recently enlarged Eastern Region in 1988, when a new Anglia Region was created. It might have been wiser to have stretched the London & South East sector to Norwich, just as trains from Waterloo reached Weymouth, itself not really in the south-east at all and certainly well beyond the limits of the commuter belt on the unhurried southern lines, rather than create a new region with so much of its business already in London & South East sector control. Nevertheless, separation of the services to East Anglia from those of the ECML was logical.

Even for the sectors, stability and continuity proved as elusive as ever. The Freight Sector had started life divided into Railfreight Distribution and Trainload Freight, the latter including the Freightliner services and the merry-go-round operations. These two sub-sectors were for a time merged, although parcels survived briefly as a separate sub-sector. The Other Provincial Services sector was finally transformed by an encouraging name-change to Regional Railways, making it seem less of a repository for the bits that didn't fit elsewhere, while services within Scotland passed to a new sector, ScotRail, only the second example of sector and region being the same and sharing the same manager.

The regions were finally abolished in 1992 by introducing the concept of the 'prime user', so that infrastructure costs could be attributed and the engineering support with them assigned to the managerial control of a sector rather than a region. In theory the concept was sound, but it did lead to some wrangling between sectors, especially as overhead costs were shared out to other sectors by the prime user. The Freight Sector could, for example, make a valid argument that costs on the ECML, for example, were far higher than they needed to be because of the operating standards required for high-speed passenger services. On lines dominated by freight Regional Railways could be hampered by track and signalling better suited to the needs of a goods train than to semi-fast passenger services.

Meanwhile, the imminent approval of the Channel Tunnel by the British and French governments led to plans to resurrect the high-speed link between the coast and London, so that British Rail created a subsidiary, Union Railways, to plan the link, and another subsidiary, European Passenger Services, to plan the future cross-Channel railway services.

The British Rail Property Board (BRPB) was hit by the collapse in property values in 1988. The blow was all the greater because the BRPB had been highly pro-active in property development at many of the London termini, completing major developments at Liverpool Street and Cannon Street in the City of London, and also at Charing Cross in the West End and at Victoria.

## Cost Cutting

Meanwhile, the pressure to cut costs continued and began to intensifybeyond reason. The biggest element by far in non-capital railway costs was labour, and it was here that the pressures to reduce costs were being felt. It was perfectly reasonable to cut costs through having just one man in the cab, but less sensible to have complete single manning of multiple units and the 'open station' concept that did away with barrier checks on tickets. Both policies led to an increase in violence and a rise in fare evasion, despite 'flying squads' of inspection staff. While the unions resisted driver-only operation of multiple units on some lines, especially in the south, all too rarely did the conductor guards leave their compartments to check or issue tickets. To strengthen the hand of the railways, passengers caught travelling without a ticket were subjected to on-the-spot fines, while those travelling in first class with a standard-class ticket already had to pay the complete first-class fare rather than just the difference, as in earlier and more honest times. If ticket offices were closed passengers could avoid the risk of a fine by buying a 'permit to travel' that would indicate at which station their journey had started, leaving them just to pay the difference between the permit price and their fare once approached by a conductor guard on a train. Productivity shot up, and British Rail appeared to have the lowest labour costs and highest productivity of any railway in Europe, but as crimes of violence on stations and on trains increased, off-peak travel, especially in the evenings, fell away even more rapidly. Passengers were robbed on trains, even murdered or raped. In constant terms government funding continued to fall, but no longer could statistics on railway travel be relied upon as so many passengers travelled without tickets.

The Channel Tunnel project was supposed to be an entirely private enterprise project, but even from the outset made heavy demands on the capital investment allowed to British Rail. The dedicated high-speed line to the tunnel was many years away, and it was judged, correctly, that certainly in the early years traffic would not be sufficient to make it necessary anyway. As an interim solution it was decided to run the trains from a new station to be built at the 'Windsor', or northern, end of Waterloo and upgrade the line from there to Ashford and Folkestone. Not only did this require British Rail to rebuild one end of the terminus to create the new Waterloo International station and upgrade the line from London to Folkestone to accommodate the Eurostar trains, including improving power supplies, but a costly connecting link had to be built between the approaches from Clapham Junction to Waterloo to enable the tunnel trains to reach the Folkestone line as, of all the former Southern Railway termini, Waterloo was the only one not to have a line to the Kent coast! The investment came from the dwindling sums available to British Rail, and investment elsewhere suffered. The WCML rolling stock was by now showing its age, while improvements to the track and signalling had been put in abeyance as British Rail pursued its dream of the Advanced Passenger Train that could bring genuine high-speed travel to existing track. This didn't matter to the Treasury, for after all, passengers to Glasgow could now use the ECML, although what those to Birmingham, Manchester and Liverpool were expected to do was another question. Doubtless most galling of all, as passengers struggled into the old Southern termini, investment in new trains for these services was delayed by the demands of the Channel Tunnel. The Southern commuters were still travelling in Mk I rolling stock, designed shortly after nationalisation, with those on the Portsmouth line having received theirs in the late 1960s when the design was already obsolete. Elsewhere the really fortunate had been looking forward to the HST and its Mk III carriages! Even the Waterloo to Exeter line, by now barely even a secondary main line with only a train every two hours west of Salisbury, giving it the highest load factor of any BR service, enjoyed early Mk II rolling stock.

The hopes and aspirations for the Channel Tunnel were beyond all reason and in many ways the death throes of the nationalised railway with its access to taxpayers' money. There were plans for 'Nightstars', overnight sleepers that for the first time on Britain's regular services would provide en-suite cabins (only the touring train, the 'Royal Scotsman', offered this facility), and for Regional Eurostars linking major provincial centres with Paris and Brussels, with the rolling stock for these commissioned and built, but never put to the use for which they were intended. After a period in an army siding the 'Nightstars' were exported, being too heavy to upgrade for the Anglo-Scottish sleeper services, and the Regional Eurostars found other uses, some enhancing GNER's own hard-worked fleet. The problem had been that overnight services were a thing of the past, while these and the Regional Eurostars could not compete on cost and speed with direct-air services, especially once the low-cost airlines appeared on the scene. As an interim measure, services from the regions to Waterloo had been provided by HSTs, a costly exercise that provided some interesting connections to Waterloo from Scotland and South Wales, but the only people allowed to travel on these trains were those who already had a Eurostar booking! This was a ridiculous restriction on trains that were scheduled to run anyway, while the formalities for international travel were not conducted until check-in at the Eurostar terminus at Waterloo International, the result being that these trains often carried just three or four passengers.

Elsewhere, cost-cutting even extended to new work, so that when new signalling was installed on the old London & South Western main line into Waterloo, the work was inadequately supervised and tested, leading to a serious accident just south of Clapham Junction in 1988 in which two trains collided, thirty-five people were killed and almost seventy injured. As in an earlier accident at Harrow & Wealdstone, a train coming in the opposite direction ran into the wreckage, but in this case, fortunately, it was empty. As with most accidents on the railway, a combination of factors came into play, including, as usual with an accident, one train running late – this time as a result of vandalism near Poole the previous evening – but the point was that the signalling system that could have prevented the accident failed to work and protect the first train, which had stopped after the driver saw a red signal light flicker.

It was now the moment for a new chairman to be appointed. This was another Bob Reid, often referred to as 'Bob Reid Mk2' and more formally as Sir Bob Reid to distinguish him from his predecessor. The new chairman took up his post in 1990, by which time privatisation of the railways was moving up the political agenda. Everything that did not relate to the core business had been sold; only the railway itself was left.

## A PRIVATISATION TOO FAR?

The new Bob Reid was not a railwayman at all, but instead had been chairman of Shell (UK), although that company did at least have some transport interests incidental to its business in the energy sector. At the time of his appointment in 1990 British Rail had lost all of its non-core businesses, including the production facilities of British Rail Maintenance, which had been purchased in 1987 by a consortium consisting of the Swedish-Swiss ASEA Brown Boveri and Trafalgar House, plus BREL's management. The question of privatisation of British Rail had not been universally popular within the Conservative Party, which had already had its reputation with the electorate battered by protests over the so-called Poll Tax, the Community Service Charge first introduced in Scotland. One Conservative MP described railway privatisation as 'a poll tax on wheels'.

Different ways of privatising the railways were considered. One was to sell off the entire concern as British Rail plc, while another was to re-create the pre-nationalisation structure to a greater or lesser extent with a number of geographically based companies. Yet another was to establish a separate company for the track and infrastructure with a larger number of companies independent of it operating the trains. The latter had two points in its favour. The first, as always, was the attitude of the Treasury, which saw this as the best means of realising the most money from railway privatisation. The second was that the European Union was by now demanding that there should be 'open access' on railways throughout Europe, and as a step towards this was demanding transparency in charging for the use of track, signals and stations. Until the Channel Tunnel had been built, open access was very much a theory, but now, providing a European operator was prepared to build down to the more restrictive British loading gauge and meet the different power requirements, in theory a European operator could initiate a through service to a UK destination. Eurostar trains could operate on up to three different power systems to accommodate British, French and Belgian requirements. The European ruling was also to enable new operators in the UK itself to emerge over and above the privatised train operating companies.

The formidable Margaret Thatcher was uncharacteristically slow in pressing ahead with railway privatisation, leading many to doubt her commitment; one also ducked by Churchill in the first postwar Conservative administration. Nevertheless, her days in office were limited and, while pre-occupied with European matters, moves to hold a leadership contest were initiated. The outcome was that in late 1990, with the country on the brink of war in the Middle East, Margaret Thatcher was replaced as prime minister by John Major.

Major was a different kind of person from Margaret Thatcher, although he had served in her administration and among other senior positions had been her Chancellor of the Exchequer. He brought some experience of transport, having been at one stage in his life a bus conductor! His big mistake was in looking for a coherent political philosophy of his own, something which falls to no more than one politician in a generation. Realising the importance of consumerism, he introduced a 'Citizen's Charter' and launched a 'Back to Basics Campaign'. He also appealed to the nostalgia for a better age, and part of this was, on one occasion, to remark on just how much he looked forward to a revival of the old Great Western. Despite winning a general election in 1992 and putting his own authority on the government, overall Major was a weak prime minister heading a majority party that included many who resented his putsch against the former leader, while pressures within the party over Europe were even more divisive and, instead of being presented as honest and open debate for the benefit of all, were allowed to fester and create the impression of disunity.

While railway privatisation was Major's 'big idea', he had no understanding of the problems inherent in the detail. Meanwhile, his 'Citizen's Charter' was having an adverse effect on the railways, for which punctuality was the supreme objective. This laudable aim carried to a ridiculous extent on the still-nationalised railway had two unfortunate side effects. Lacking the ability to ensure that operational efficiency alone could ensure punctuality, railway management adopted what might be described as the 'Mussolini' approach to timekeeping: timetables were eased to ensure that late running was minimised, so that many of the best performances disappeared off the timetable and the railways became an even less attractive option for those travellers anxious to make the most of their time. The railway became uncompetitive especially on routes running parallel to a good road, as between Exeter and Plymouth, for example. The other side effect was that railway managers were tempted not to maintain connections. Instead of keeping a connecting service waiting if an arrival was running a little late, the service would have to depart on time to maintain the 'Citizen's Charter' obligation. Punctuality was being measured, missed connections weren't!

Privatisation finally surfaced in a White Paper published in July 1992. The main points were:

1.  Rail freight and parcels should be transferred entirely to the private sector.
2.  Passenger services should be operated as franchises by private companies, who would be subjected to providing a certain pre-determined minimum standard of frequency and service, and would receive grants for uneconomic services, while paying for the right to operate profitable services.
3.  All passenger and freight operators should have the right of access to all parts of the railway network.
4.  The rump of British Rail should survive as the new track and infrastructure authority with a new name, Railtrack, and eventually this too should be privatised.
5.  The railway maintenance and other technical facilities should also be privatised.

Several public appointments were to be essential for the operation of the new railway. Franchising would be overseen by the Director of Franchising. The role of the Office of the Rail Regulator promised open access. The latter would also adjudicate in conflicts over timetabling and paths, which were still as likely to be in short supply as they had ever been at peak periods and at bottlenecks on the network, such as Birmingham New Street, and over junctions and interchange points for most longer-distance cross-country services. There would also be a new quango, the Strategic Rail Authority and, among other things, this would now be the body collecting statistics on railway travel. It also took over control of the British Transport Police.

The privatisation proposals were subjected to considerable public criticism as well as to political opposition, with the Labour Party threatening to reverse the process on being returned to power. Accustomed to intense interest in each successive privatisation, the government was disappointed to find that this was distinctly lacking in the case of the railways. As the legislation was passing through Parliament a number of changes were made, of which the most important was that rolling stock and motive power would be sold to companies set up for this purpose and leased to the franchisees, with the entire British Rail 'fleet' divided among three rolling-stock leasing companies, or ROSCOs. This was just part of the alphabet soup cooked up by privatisation, with other acronyms including TOCs, train operating companies, and TESCOs, technical service companies.

Not all of the criticism was aimed at privatisation as such, but at the fragmentation and division of the railway. The romantics wanted to see the re-creation of the old companies, including some, who would have been too young to remember the 'old' railway, even wanting a return to the pre-grouping days. One prominent journalist yearned for the return of the old London & South Western Railway, and wondered just what colour the carriages would have been. A trip to a decent public library would have answered his question, and he might have discovered that it hadn't been the best of railways! When the American-owned Wisconsin Central showed an interest in acquiring the freight services, one newspaper drew attention to the fact that the company had taken over the railways in New Zealand and re-opened lines and improved services, and suggested that the whole of British Rail be handed over to them.

There were also those, mainly in the transport press, who pointed out that the level of subsidy being offered at the start of the process was far higher than that given to British Rail, and they inevitably questioned the wisdom of this and speculated on just what BR might have achieved with such sums. A glance at some of the decisions taken during the years of the modernisation plan might have provided some clues! Supporters of privatisation pointed out that the level of subsidy would decline over the period of the franchises, with many lines expected to move into profit and then make a contribution to the state. Government ministers talked up the prospects for the future, with one minister talking of 'comfortable services for the businessman and cheap and cheerful services for the secretary'.

As a sop to the travelling public and an incentive to the train-operating companies to keep costs to the minimum, as the first franchises were being let, fares were classified into different categories as 'regulated' and 'unregulated'. On the latter the TOCs could more or less charge what they wanted, but on the former, mainly covering season tickets and off-peak 'saver' tickets, annual fare increases were to be one percentage point below the level of inflation, while a TOC that did not operate satisfactorily could find that certain fares, including season tickets, might even be cut as a form of compensation to the regular customer. The decision to cap season increases in some ways was understandable, as a throwback to the concept of the 'workman's ticket', although it did mean that the discount given to season-ticket holders as a percentage of the standard single or return fare was to grow, even though, by creating hopelessly uneconomic peak periods, commuter traffic created massive problems for the railways. For example, in 2003 the Strategic Rail Authority estimated that it could cost as much as £1,500 per passenger per annum to provide an extra rush-hour train, but that the average season-ticket fare per passenger per annum would be just £560! Far less understandable was the decision to cap 'saver' tickets. This risked not simply continuing but worsening an anomaly on some routes where the off-peak return fare was less than that of the single fare, so that conscientious booking clerks would recommend that the would-be purchaser of a single ticket bought an off-peak return instead. In theory it would be worthwhile for anyone wanting a single ticket to wait at the barrier to see if any passengers would throw away their unwanted returns!

It certainly seemed odd that one company would be allowed to buy the entire network, and others the rolling stock and motive power or the freight services, but that the passenger services, which were the public's point of contact with the railway and which would have the most individual customers, were simply to be franchised off, with the term of seven years being set at the beginning. Seven years was hardly long enough to encourage investment in an industry in which the average life of rolling stock was around four times as long. In theory the rolling-stock leasing companies could always lease the carriages and motive power to the next franchisee, but what if the next one had other ideas? Even on the old nationalised railway cascading rolling stock on to other services was sometimes impractical. There were three traction systems available, diesel, overhead electric and third-rail electric. Even within these divisions there were differences in loading gauge. Traffic patterns also varied. When, for example, it was decided that the first generation of electric multiple units with power-operated doors should be transferred from the Southern Region's Western Division to Merseyside, these four-car units had to be cut down to just three cars: the fourth carriage in each case was retained and inserted into a new-build of EMUs of different design, leaving many of the inner suburban services from Waterloo worked by trains with a distinctly odd and uneven roof line!

The rolling-stock problems were made worse in the run-up to privatisation by an increasingly cautious and bureaucratic acceptance process that meant that new rolling stock could literally take years from production to introduction to service. Problems created by new rolling stock, including interference with signalling systems as well as reliability, were not new, and the trains themselves seldom if ever presented a quantum leap in technology or performance, but there was much time and money spent to see whether anyone had tried to reinvent the wheel.

On 5 November the Railways Act 1993 received the Royal Assent and passed into law. There was a short period of calm before a major restructuring of British Rail occurred the following 1 April, ready for privatisation to start. Although intended to be sold in its entirety, Railtrack was organised into ten regional zones. This was reduced to eight in 1995, few of which related directly to a franchise area, the main exception being Scotland where there was a perfect match. In the Isle of Wight, the franchisee would also be responsible for track maintenance, the only one to have this role. British Rail's passenger services were organised into twenty-five companies ready for the franchising process to start, each with a subsidy profile and some of them having funding from local passenger transport executives as well as from central government.

The franchises were, with those receiving PTE funding marked *:

Anglia Railways
Cardiff Railway
Central Trains*
Chiltern Trains
Gatwick Express
Great Eastern
Great North Eastern Railway
Great Western
InterCity Cross Country
InterCity West Coast
Island Line (Isle of Wight)
LTS Rail (London Tilbury & Southend)
Merseyrail Electrics*

Midland Main Line
North London Railways
North West RR (Regional Railways)*
RR North East (Regional Railways)*
Scotrail*
South Central
South Eastern
South Wales & West
South Western
Thames Trains
Thameslink
West Anglia Great Northern

While the government was still committed to open access for all operators, the initial idea was that the franchisees, or train-operating companies (TOCs), would at first be confined by the terms of their licence to their operating areas. The first franchises were let in time for operations to start early in 1996. Among the first was South West Trains, awarded to the bus operator Stagecoach, which promised to provide two new bus services to link towns off the main-line railway network to their nearest main-line station, with a service from Bordon to Petersfield and from Romsey to Winchester. Yet, when National Express, the long-distance coach operator that had acquired its Scottish counterpart, CityLink, wanted the ScotRail franchise, it was eventually forced to dispose of CityLink. This may have been to protect the Highland lines, where, owing to speed restrictions and a failure to take advantage of the possibility of a road and rail bridge across the Dornoch Firth when a new road-only bridge had been built, it was far quicker to take the coach from Inverness to Wick or Thurso. Coach frequencies in consequence also became greater than those offered on the railway.

Two companies were separate from the TOCs and the franchise process, but were intended to be train operators even so. The first of these was a BR subsidiary known as European Passenger Services, which was intended to operate the Eurostar international trains and also the 'Nightstar' sleepers from provincial centres to Paris and Brussels, although the latter never materialised. The other was a venture by the British Airports Authority, the 'Heathrow Express' service from the airport to Paddington, bringing a small part of the old Great Western route under the wires for the first time.

'Heathrow Express' was undoubtedly an improvement for the airline passenger compared with London's traffic congestion or the cramped and uncomfortable, as well as slow, all-stations service from central London on the Piccadilly Line, although it was unfortunate in having Paddington, one of the least accessible and the most remote of all the London termini, as its 'town-end'. It would have been almost as easy to have run the service to Waterloo, with its direct connection to the City of London via the Waterloo & City Line, by this time transferred at last to London Transport, although this line suffered a serious bottleneck at Richmond and had lost valuable platforms to the Eurostar services. Nevertheless, the 'Heathrow Express' did mark a major shift in railway attitudes for, while the significance of airports as traffic generators had long been recognised, dating back to pre-war days on the Southern Railway, the needs of airline travellers had not previously been fully appreciated. The lesson of the 'Heathrow Express' was that it was not enough to provide a fast non-stop service at a special fare running at frequent intervals over 24 hours; it was important to provide sufficient baggage space. Airport operators were better at designing the interiors of airport trains than railwaymen.

Not only did the passenger franchises begin in 1996, but the rail freight business was finally sold outright to Wisconsin Central that year, with the new owner promptly re-naming its business English, Welsh & Scottish Railway (EWSR), although a number of people suggested that its new name should be British Rail! EWSR got off to an ambitious start with a massive order for new locomotives placed in Canada, but this proved to be over-optimistic despite renewed growth in freight traffic.

New names were also applied by some of the franchisees to their businesses. Some of these were simply minor embellishments, with South Central becoming Network South Central, then Connex South Central and Connex South Eastern, while the West Coast and Cross Country InterCity services, again both acquired by a single franchisee, became first Virgin Cross Country and Virgin West Coast, before finally settling as Virgin Trains. Many companies applied their corporate prefix or, in corporate identity terms, branded identity, to their franchises, not always with the result intended. One passenger remarked when a First Great

Western train passed by suitably marked with the First 'F' logo: 'That train has a lot of first-class accommodation.' Defying all logic was the decision by the operator of LTS Rail, the old London Tilbury & Southend Line, to re-name itself C2C, and North London Railways became Silverlink, adopting a sickening livery of green and purple with yellow doors!

As with the freight services, there was much optimism at first. Indeed there had to be, for many of the TOCs were to face a steeply declining subsidy profile so that by 2002–3 the overall level of subsidy was to be no more than that for British Rail in its final year. In fact, some of their forecasts were hopelessly over-optimistic and were to be thrown out of line by events that were completely unforeseen.

Generating traffic and therefore revenue forecasts was undoubtedly extremely difficult. Most of the TOCs planned to increase business; one created an uproar when it decided that it was not economic to provide extra carriages for its morning peak traffic, and attempted to encourage its customers to take the bus instead. There can be no doubt that the provision of extra carriages, in effect an extra diesel multiple unit, for just one busy journey a day was hopelessly uneconomic when viewed in isolation, but no one seemed to have anticipated this problem when tendering. Far too many franchisees went ahead as if they were blindfolded. Richard Branson, the boss of the Virgin TOCs, complained about having the 'oldest rolling stock on British Rail', but had clearly failed to discover this first, and in any case that doubtful privilege belonged to the three companies that had taken over the old Southern Region. The boss of Sea Containers, awarded the GNER franchise, complained that he had been told that it would have the most modern stock on British Rail, but hadn't realised that there was so little of it. This problem came to light as traffic boomed and the hapless TOC wanted to increase frequencies, but couldn't without a new build of its own special rolling stock, a problem mentioned earlier on page 153. In the end, the problem was resolved in part by hiring the mothballed regional Eurostar trains. This simply highlighted another problem: the bottleneck at the southern end of the ECML at Welwyn, where a tunnel and a viaduct combined to limit the line to just one up and one down line, with the much-desired quadruple tracks available only at an extremely high cost.

The highest level of subsidy per passenger kilometre of any of the TOCs was that of Island Line, operating the 8 miles between Ryde and Shanklin on the Isle of Wight with veteran Northern Line tube trains modified to operate on the third rail and needing 36.9p per passenger kilometre in 2001–2, according to the Strategic Rail Authority. Perhaps Island Line would have done much better if its line had gone all the way to Ventnor. Even ScotRail, with its supposedly uneconomic lines north of Inverness, needed just 8.7p. To be fair, not only was there a chronic imbalance between summer and winter traffic, but in addition to the general decline of the British seaside resorts, the Isle of Wight had lost one of its big markets, South Wales coal miners, following the miners' strike of 1982. Perhaps the solution would have been to have kept the Ventnor and Newport lines and run them as preserved steam railways with enthusiast volunteer labour and seasonal workers for the summer, with a core of full-time employees running a diesel multiple unit service during the winter months.

Not all of the TOCs required subsidies. By 2002 the 'Gatwick Express' was paying 3.5p per kilometre to the SRA, with others in surplus including Anglia at 0.3p, having increased passenger numbers by 60 per cent between 1997 and 2003, Midland Mainline at 0.6p, GNER at 0.8p, First Great Eastern at 1.1p and Thameslink at 2.6p. Thames Trains was unique in neither requiring a subsidy nor paying to the SRA.

At the other end of the spectrum, Cardiff Railway required 23.2p subsidy per passenger kilometre, Arriva Trains Merseyside 21.2p and First North Western 20.5p. Interestingly, despite their high volume of rush-hour commuter traffic, South Central Trains required just 0.7p subsidy, South Western 0.8p, and South Eastern 1.4p, the same as First Great Western, whose revenue-earning power must have been much reduced west of Cardiff and west of Plymouth. Overall, the average subsidy per passenger kilometre was 3.3p.

Many of the TOCs started by ordering new trains. Unfortunately the first orders seemed to be a case of history repeating itself with a re-run of the problems affecting the large-scale diesel orders by British Railways during the 1950s. Both South West Trains and the 'Gatwick Express' received new rolling stock plagued by poor reliability with entry into revenue-earning service much delayed, and the latter TOC even having to keep some of its old and extensively used rolling stock as back-up for when the new trains were not available. South West Trains was at this time under considerable pressure to get rid of its slam-door rolling stock, and the poor availability of the new trains must have cost it dear. Reliability of service was also affected as TOCs 'sweated their assets' in the words of one railway journalist, getting the most out of the equipment and often with insufficient spares ready to take over in the case of a failure. At a conference one railway manager demanded trains that 'worked out of the box'. ScotRail suffered massive delays in introducing new electric trains for its Glasgow suburban network, while new diesel trains for its services between the three main Scottish cities had to be returned to the builders one at a time for further work.

Not all of the problems were with the new rolling stock. The electric IC225s for the ECML had to undergo a major modification programme to enhance the reliability of the Class 91 locomotives, and this was after the carriages had had their air-conditioning problems sorted out.

Even so, many of the new TOCs started to increase frequencies and introduce new routes. Some of these were undoubtedly overdue, such as a service between Bristol and Oxford, until line capacity had to be reviewed to improve the reliability of the existing railway services. An open-access operator, Hull Trains, introduced direct services linking the town with King's Cross, ending a cause for dissatisfaction that had extended back to the days of British Rail. In Scotland the nationalised railway's long-promised doubling of the frequency between Glasgow and Edinburgh to a train every fifteen minutes was only achieved after privatisation.

Privatisation also brought about some curious anomalies. Instead of the Anglo-Scottish sleepers being operated by Virgin or GNER as successors to InterCity, they passed to ScotRail, which concentrated all of these services on Euston. The old Western Region sleeper services found themselves with a new London terminus at Waterloo.

Increasing frequencies, or even maintaining existing frequencies, was not simply a problem of rolling-stock availability or reliability, or even of track and station capacity, although all of these factors undoubtedly were important. Many train operators soon found themselves with shortages of drivers, and this was one of the unforeseen consequences of the excessive fragmentation of the railway. In the old days the same train operator would have been responsible for goods, local and express services, offering drivers, and firemen as well, a natural career progression, with the highest-skilled drivers at a depot, known as the 'top link', receiving the best pay and working the fastest and longest-distance trains. Privatisation destroyed this system, which had worked from the early days of railways, by dividing services into different TOCs for local and long-distance services, with the exception of the three companies responsible for the former Southern Region services. Instead of sitting happily with the same employers and waiting to be promoted, drivers now found that the only way up was to change employers, and as longer-distance travel grew and frequencies increased, naturally enough the main-line operators drew their new drivers from the local TOCs, understandably preferring drivers who had already been trained and were familiar with the railway to raw recruits coming direct from the street to driving a high-speed express!

The victims were the TOCs operating local and regional services, having their drivers poached by the main-line operators able to offer higher pay, reflecting the greater productivity and responsibilities of someone driving a ten-car train non-stop at 100mph or more. Some airlines suffer a similar problem, and resolve it through arrangements with air-taxi operators or regional airlines so that sponsored pilot trainees can work their way up through the system, but even so, putting a graduate from training school direct on to a Boeing 737 or 757, which can happen, is less serious than on the railways since, in addition to conversion training, the new recruit is flying as number two, co-pilot rather than captain. The only way forward for the railways on this would be for the main-line and regional or local companies to come to a similar agreement, but this can hardly be done with any conviction given the short periods of the franchises, and the uncertainty over franchise renewal, even for a successful operator. On the other hand, of course, the solution could lie in fewer but larger franchises, or ending franchising and selling off the railways outright.

It soon transpired that the best way to make money from railway privatisation was to buy a rolling-stock company when one of the ROSCOs changed hands, making its management buy-out team millionaires. The big groups also seemed to be able to acquire a number of first-round franchises, with National Express gaining Central Trains, Gatwick Express, Midland Main Line, North London (or Silverlink) and ScotRail. In addition to its coach operations, National Express was by this time also becoming involved in the ownership and operation of regional airports. Stagecoach acquired not only South West Trains but also Island Line, suitably since most of the railway passengers arriving on the island would have reached Portsmouth by SWT, and Porterbrook, one of the ROSCOs. Later, Stagecoach was to acquire a substantial stake in Virgin Trains. First Bus, later renamed First Group, started with the Great Eastern franchise but later added First Great Western and First North Western. Prism Rail took the franchises for London, Tilbury & Southend, or C2C, as well as Cardiff Railway, South Wales & West and West Anglia Great Northern. In some cases franchises were awarded for more than seven years on condition that the franchisee provided certain agreed improvements, but the longest of these were just for fifteen years, in the case of Connex South Eastern, C2C and Gatwick Express, while Midland Main Line and Great Western Trains were both for ten years.

There were many contradictions in privatisation, which in some ways seems to have been set up to produce exactly the opposite effect from that intended, and despite promises none of these problems were addressed by the Labour administration that took office in 1997.

One good example has been the impact of privatisation on electrification, generally considered to be beneficial, reducing pollution and bringing considerable advances in such matters as reliability and acceleration, as well as reducing dependence upon fossil fuels, especially if nuclear energy can be revived. Yet electrification is no longer as likely or as easily achievable as it once was. This is because the infrastructure provider now has to compensate the train operators whenever work takes place on the line. For example, if the direct line between Edinburgh and Glasgow were to be electrified, ScotRail would have to be compensated for the inevitable delays while work was in progress, and for when trains either had to be diverted, or passengers transferred to buses. Despite the TOC benefiting from electrification, the compensation would increase the cost of the project. Even if the TOC wanted to accept the disruption on the basis of 'present pain for future gain', it would still need compensation as it in turn needed to compensate passengers for the delays, while its ability to increase fares to match rising costs would be placed in jeopardy as the Rail Regulator could ban these or reduce the level of increase until punctuality and reliability improved. Season-ticket holders, and there are many on this line, would be given discounts on renewal.

This is not a hypothetical example, as compensation for disruption has already resulted in mounting costs for the WCML modernisation scheme, and also meant that the 140mph speeds promised once the work is completed have had to be trimmed to 125mph at best, much to the dismay of Virgin Trains with rolling stock capable of attaining the higher speeds. Failure to reach the higher speed not only means that the service becomes less competitive against air and road competition and less attractive to passengers; it also reduces the productivity of the trains, although it also seems that Virgin's original plans for turn-around times were over-optimistic and allowed insufficient leeway to make up for delays to incoming trains. The problem doesn't stop here either, for the entire financial forecasts for the WCML have also been placed in doubt.

# CHAPTER THIRTEEN

# The Railways Today

Opposition to railway privatisation reached a peak when the time came to sell off the infrastructure, grouped together and known as Railtrack, the last major element of the railways to be sold. It included track, signals and major stations. Whether a railway station was operated by a franchisee or by Railtrack depended on how many train-operating companies used it. Sole use meant that it belonged to the TOC with the licence for that area, but if there were several operators, then the station would be operated by Railtrack. Many within the industry objected to these arrangements because of the complex legal agreements required. On a political level, the Labour Party effectively shot itself in the foot by insisting that it would renationalise Railtrack on being returned to power, by this time a very real possibility, and the threat was so successful in diminishing interest in the company that the government was forced to cut the price, and also guarantee the first dividend to those buying shares at the time of flotation. This was almost a return to the days of the railway mania when dividends were often paid out of investments. In short, the most fundamental aspects of any railway operation, track, signals and stations, became a speculative stock in an uncertain political climate.

Separation of the infrastructure from operation of trains had just one advantage in that it did at least guarantee open access and also made adherence to European Union strictures on this and transparency of charging easier. This was not the main reason, however, as the Treasury saw a separate infrastructure company that could be sold off as the means by which the most money could be realised from privatisation. Operational reasons were ignored altogether or overruled completely.

Needless to say, there were those that described privatisation in general as 'selling the family silver', overlooking the fact that much of the silver was not only tarnished but had been, if not exactly stolen, acquired in rather a sharp deal to begin with!

It was to take an unhappy chain of events to bring Railtrack back into state hands. On returning to office in the 1997 general election after eighteen years in the political wilderness, with a massive landslide majority and with the opposition parties emasculated, the new Labour administration stated that they couldn't afford to renationalise Railtrack. This was a marked change in policy. It was not just a volte-face compared with Labour statements when in opposition, but also compared with 1945, when there had been so many more pressing demands on the public purse, and when Parliamentary time and the economy had been in far worse shape than in 1997. The new leader of the Labour Party, Tony Blair, had realised that nationalisation had not been popular with the electorate, while for the most part privatisation had been, as had lower taxes. Railtrack was nevertheless to become the architect of its own misfortunes.

Traditionally, most railways handled all of their own track and signal maintenance, even including extensive renewals, with the chief civil engineer being a senior figure of considerable authority who could even overrule the ambitions of the chief mechanical engineer, responsible for locomotives and rolling stock. While no substantial railway could expect the chief civil engineer to be familiar with every inch of track, area civil engineers could, and were. Before privatisation British Rail had contracted out some work, not always with the desired results. Despite all of this, Railtrack immediately set about disbanding its own maintenance teams, including the workers who monitored track condition as much as every other day on busy stretches of line, and putting the whole business out to tender.

At first, while a few railway journalists complained about the dangers of breaking up teams and of the importance of everyone connected with the railway regarding themselves as part of the railway, there were relatively few murmurs of concern. In one or two cases, when concern did arise, it was prompted by major safety lapses, such as one occasion pre-privatisation when a maintenance worker in a road–rail vehicle drove the wrong way along a railway line seemingly oblivious to the dangers. However, the policy of contracting out has to be viewed in the light of developments elsewhere, with many local authorities doing the same with highway maintenance, or at least setting up a department at arm's length in place of their old direct labour arrangements. To many it seemed to be one way of ensuring transparency of charging and of obtaining lower costs in place of feather-bedded and cosy in-house arrangements.

There was indeed a comparison to be made between using contractors for new highway construction, as in using equipment manufacturers to build new trains, or even new planes, and using one's own personnel for maintenance, whether it be track, signals or vehicles. The big difference between a railway and a highway is the much stronger relationship between operations and infrastructure. On the nationalised railway, burdened by Treasury restrictions on expenditure, British Rail often struggled to achieve 'whole route' modernisation, meaning that trains, track and signals were all upgraded together so that the maximum benefit could be extracted from the investment. There is no point having rolling stock that can run at 125mph if track condition limits the maximum speed to 90mph, and if signals cannot cope with the extra stopping distances. Indeed, on the East Coast Main Line, GNER has trains, at one time known as IC225s for their maximum speed in kilometres, capable of 140mph, but nowhere is the line capable of supporting this, with 125mph the best that can be achieved. Even the lower speed is possible only on certain stretches.

Even so, the cost of upgrading lines started to rise under Railtrack. Improving the loading gauge on the route between the container port at Southampton and the Midlands to take higher containers was estimated at £3 million per mile, putting the viability of the operation in doubt.

Even Railtrack's custodianship of the existing railway infrastructure was soon called into question by a series of accidents. Two of these involved collisions: at Southall and outside Paddington. Then there were two accidents caused by track defects: first at Hatfield involving a northbound GNER express running over track that had been noticeably deteriorating for some time, and then a WAGN train running from King's Cross to Cambridge found defective points at Potters Bar.

Such was the media interest in these accidents that even before the Potters Bar accident, when a Land Rover Defender towing a trailer came off a motorway and plunged down an embankment, derailing another GNER express that then struck a freight train head on, railway journalists called for radio interviews had their work cut out emphasising that the accident was not the fault either of Railtrack or of GNER! Strange that in a country festooned by an over-abundance of traffic speed cameras, no one thought at first of blaming the motorist! The trouble with the railways by this time was that the growing unpopularity of privatisation had seeped through to the media which, smelling weakness, went in for the kill.

Of all of these the Hatfield disaster was the one that did most to damage the reputation and eventually the finances of Railtrack. The state of the track revealed by the accident and the poor standard of inspection and programming of maintenance, as well as glaring deficiencies in the reporting mechanism, resulted in an emergency programme of track inspection, temporary speed limits and repairs, including the closure of almost the entire network for a weekend. Typical of the chaos, overnight sleepers between Scotland and London were withdrawn at short notice, leaving passengers stranded, so that large sections of the WCML could be inspected – no one seems to have considered the possibility of sending the trains down the ECML, from which they could still have reached Euston. Railway schedules fell apart under the pressures imposed by the speed limits and diversions or closures for repairs. The quantity of materials required for track replacement meant that track was even imported, and on one occasion had to be taken up again after being laid as it was not of the required quality. These emergency, even panic-stricken, measures were costly both to Railtrack and to the TOCs. Indeed, Railtrack was hit twice over with the cost of the work and the need to compensate the train operators. Commentators began describing the crisis in terms such as 'meltdown'.

What happened next saw political opportunism and cowardice at its worst. Railtrack sought additional funding from the government, seeking an advance on money due for modernisation, but the Minister of Transport, Stephen Byers, stalled, and on a Sunday in October 2001 sought to put the company into administration. The shareholders, many of whom were or had been employees, were offered a minimal value for their shares later, and although this was raised after the threat of court action, most of them still lost money. This was due in no small part to many of the institutional fund managers accepting the revised offer – after all, it was not their money – even though it was less than the individual investors would have wanted; but the former held the majority of the shares and the latter lacked organisational strength or the funding for a court case that still might not have improved their compensation.

Byers had the idea of a 'not for profit company' that would raise funds on the market. This was a case of legerdemain as the concept was created so that any borrowing by the new Railtrack, or Network Rail as it was re-named, would not be counted as public borrowing by the government. But given the company's record, the only way in which it could raise money would be if the financial institutions understood that all of its borrowing would be underwritten by the government! Eventually the entire affair and the controversy it aroused led to Byers's resignation. On its own, the act of creating Network Rail out of Railtrack cost the taxpayer £70 million in fees for accountants, bankers and lawyers. Put another way, this kind of money would have paid for a single substantial infrastructure improvement, such as 7 miles of TGV-standard track, or 70 good- quality railway carriages!

## FRANCHISE RENEWAL

Byers had already shown a complete lack of understanding of the realities of railway management, putting off the politically sensitive issue of renewing franchises by extending most of the existing franchise terms by two years, officially to encourage investment in new rolling stock. As one railway manager put it, it would be 'hard to select and order new rolling stock within that period, let alone get it built, delivered, approved for operation and into service'. Part of the problem with franchise renewal was the intention of Virgin Trains to tender for the ECML franchise as well as for renewal of the WCML and cross-country franchises it already held, offering the prospect of a monopoly on the Anglo-Scottish routes. Virgin plans for the east coast route included a substantial section of new high-speed railway, but by this time it was already clear that Virgin's plans for the west coast were running into difficulty, and had been over-ambitious.

The much-delayed renewal of the first generation of franchises finally started in 2003. It had been delayed by Byers and then by his departure, and by a new regulatory system. Meanwhile, there had been some extensions conditional on investment criteria being met, with Chiltern Trains, one of the success stories, having its franchise changed, with a new twenty-year extension being introduced before its original franchise expired.

Also in 2003 South West Trains was awarded a three-year extension of its franchise, with a subsidy of £170 million annually, with £6 million to fund improvements but, needless to say, a whole raft of improvements, including additional carriages to strengthen existing sets, proposed in return for a twenty-year franchise renewal, were not included!

Earlier it had come as no surprise that Connex Central lost its franchise for the old Central Division of what had been the Southern Region of British Railways. Nor did it come as a great surprise in 2003 when the Strategic Rail Authority took away the Connex South Eastern franchise, on the grounds of financial management issues and Connex's failure to implement a detailed programme of improvements. After the termination of the franchise the services were effectively renationalised and operated by a SRA subsidiary known as South Eastern Trains, while a new franchise holder was sought and the franchise itself changed to include not only the old SECR services, but also high-speed domestic services using the Channel Tunnel Rail Link. On the other hand, when it was decided to merge the Anglia and Great Eastern franchise to create a new Greater Anglia franchise, it was a surprise that the incumbent at Great Eastern, First Group, was not short-listed, since the franchise had been seen as one of the more successful.

The one improvement of the second-generation franchises has been longer franchise periods. Merseyrail received a 25-year franchise on renewal. It is open to question whether changes to franchise boundaries in themselves would be a benefit or drawback, although plans to reduce the number of them, despite such additions as Wessex Trains, seem to contradict plans for reductions. It is also open to question whether it was wise to propose a new franchise for Wales, with a substantial track mileage outside the principality, while the Welsh Assembly, unlike the Scottish Parliament, has no powers over transport. Creating a Welsh version of ScotRail nevertheless was typical of an administration that placed too much emphasis on show and spin, and too little on substance. The Welsh Assembly members started to press for transport powers, which in many ways might appear logical, but Wales is not Scotland. The traffic flow in Scotland passes through or is concentrated on the Central Belt, Edinburgh and Glasgow, while that in Wales is far more closely tied into that of England, regardless of cultural and other differences. This is not because of the longer union between the principality and England, but because of topography and industrial development. Traffic flows in Wales are predominantly east–west, to Merseyside and Manchester in North Wales, to Birmingham and the Midlands in mid-Wales, and towards Bristol in South Wales. Only in the south, with the lines in the valleys and the Swansea–Cardiff–Newport corridor, does one find anything to compare with the situation in Scotland.

## NETWORK RAIL AND PUNCTUALITY

Meanwhile, the new Network Rail had profligate spending habits and mounting debts, worrying the Rail Regulator. In the year to the end of March 2003 Network Rail lost £290 million, and many financial commentators feel that the true figure could have been worse. The government was effectively underwriting £21 billion of debts, not far short of one year's defence budget and equivalent to more than half the money paid annually in taxes of all kinds by road users. All this was despite the fact that Network Rail was due to receive £12 billion of taxpayers' money in subsidy for the three years to 2006!

A good idea of just how far costs have been escalating out of control can be judged from the fact that Network Rail originally planned to spend £15.8 billion by April 2006, but by June 2003 this figure had risen to £27.8 billion. This has meant that many desirable 'in-filling' electrification schemes that would allow rationalisation of rolling stock and motive power, such as Ashford–Hastings, have been shelved because the costs are now so high. The Rail Regulator complained that it was far harder to control Network Rail than Railtrack as any fines or penalties came not from the pockets of shareholders but from either the state or Network Rail's customers, the train operating companies. Indeed, instead of shareholders, Network Rail is run by a management team answerable to a membership of 116 people drawn from a wide variety of organisations, with only a minority having anything to do with railways. Out of the total just 31 come from the industry, including the TOCs, with another 34 from public bodies, such as the Cyclists' Touring Club, trade unions, the Crime Concern Trust and the Royal Association for Disability and Rehabilitation, while the remainder, 51 people, are there as individuals.

The impact of the problems of reliability that followed from the Hatfield accident was that between 1997 and 2003, on the former InterCity routes the number of train kilometres rose by 44 per cent, but the number of passenger kilometres rose by just 5 per cent. The extra trains plus the inadequacies of much of the network, even before temporary speed limits and the crash programme of track renewal put further pressure on timekeeping, were such that by 2003, only 80 per cent of trains were reaching their destinations on time, by now interpreted as being within five minutes of the right time compared to the actual on-time performance figures of the old companies! On the longer-distance former InterCity routes, timekeeping in the first quarter of 2002 was 75.9 per cent of trains on time, but this fell to 73 per cent for the corresponding quarter of 2003. The new Head of the Strategic Rail Authority, Richard Bowker, responded by calling for cuts in the number of trains so that those that did run had a better chance of being punctual, in effect cutting capacity so that it reflected demand for longer-distance travel. A number of commentators also proposed longer trains to avoid over-crowding on the busier routes, although lengthening trains can be more difficult than it seems as many stations are limited in the length of train that they can handle safely and efficiently not just by platform length – which certainly can be a problem – but also by the position of signals, points, bridges and other line-side structures at the ends of platforms. In short, lengthening trains brings heavy costs well in excess of the cost of additional rolling stock. It is also a problem that a long train will often not be evenly loaded, especially on commuter services. In vain did the management of British Railways Southern Region point out in the late 1960s and 1970s that trains with passengers standing at the front, so that they would be close to the barrier when the train reached its London terminus, often had empty seats at the back, but a quick spot survey on many routes proved the SR to be right more often than not.

In contrast to most countries where the slick punctual trains tended to be the great expresses, in Britain during 2003 the best timekeeping of all was the 8-mile stretch of the isolated Island Line between Ryde and Shanklin on the Isle of Wight, with 98 per cent of trains on time! Worst was Virgin Cross Country, with the distinction between the two parts of Virgin Trains still maintained in official figures, at just 67.8 per cent of trains on time compared to 72.4 per cent a year earlier. Midland Mainline also only managed 69.1 per cent on time compared to 77.6 per cent a year earlier.

Cross-country trains have always been the most difficult to run on time, running across many boundaries; at one time it was a question of company boundaries, then it was regional boundaries, but now it isddifferent Network Rail zones and TOC territories. Most of the cross-country services also ran through that bottleneck of bottlenecks, Birmingham New Street. Contended with this congested scene, what did Virgin Cross Country do? It replaced its eight carriage HST fleet with four-car Voyagers and five-car Super Voyagers, doubling many frequencies in a complete shake-up of the cross-country timetable known as 'Operation Princess', which obviously added to the capacity problem. Unfortunately the new trains had far less seating capacity, despite being very cramped, than the trains they replaced, so at peak periods the trains were crowded, and station dwell times were extended while passengers struggled to collect their luggage and get off, and then others struggled to find a place on the train. 'Operation Princess' was to be the shortest duration railway timetable since the emergency timetable introduced shortly after the outbreak of the Second World War. The idea of running a more frequent service but with shorter trains, or in the case of other modes of transport, smaller buses or aircraft, has much to commend it, often increasing traffic, but everything depends on the situation. Too many flights can lead to congestion at airports, and too many trains can cause congestion at pinch points on the railway network. Costs rise, as each train needs a driver, while a longer train can provide a full refreshment service more efficiently and economically. There are certain peak periods, such as the rush hours, when large numbers need to travel at the same time, and to provide enough seats is a necessity.

The growth in services and in passenger numbers has not been uniform across the system – it never could be. In many conurbations frequencies had increased along with passenger numbers but, inevitably, there were those areas where passenger numbers had grown, especially at peak periods, but frequencies hadn't and nor had the lengths of trains!

The Strategic Rail Authority simply promised to prepare 'route strategies' over the three years 2003–6, and stuck to its plans for 25 per cent passenger growth by 2010. One strong disincentive for passenger growth of the order predicted came in June 2003, when the secretary of state for transport, Alistair Darling, decided to remove the cap on fare increases for regulated fares, and instead of restricting the TOCs to increases of a percentage point below inflation, allowed them to raise fares at a percentage point above inflation for three years. This was at a time when the economy was suffering some of the effects of deflation, so one might be excused for asking why annual fare increases needed to be considered at all. Passenger groups pointed out that the net effect of the permitted increase would be to give the train-operating companies an extra £15 million per annum, *less* than Network Rail's daily operational and maintenance expenditure of £16 million!

Meanwhile, as if proof was needed that railway finances were indeed a moving target, in mid-2003 a further blow was the announcement by the Post Office that the railways would no longer be used for the carriage of mail. This bombshell seems to have been entirely unexpected, despite the fact that the Post Office itself was struggling with a massive deficit and had been making greater use of road and air transport over the years. It had also had to make some considerable adjustments to maintain services in the post-Hatfield chaos and, like other customers, could not accept lengthy closures of lines following accidents. The fact that the railways had carried mail since 1830 did not mean that they could carry it for all time – although this fact of life seemed to pass unnoticed by many.

CHAPTER FOURTEEN

# A Future for the Railways?

Today Britain's railways remain fragmented with a complete lack of vertical integration, and with insufficient tenure for the train-operating companies, although this benefit has been accorded everyone else. Regardless of what the government might claim, the infrastructure has been re-nationalised, and given the alarming rate at which public expenditure increased at the start of the new century, there can be few who believe that Network Rail will be allowed to spend its way out of the current problems afflicting the railways. Indeed, the rate at which money is being spent is alarming the regulator and the government, while the soaring costs of infrastructure projects has alarmed the railway press, and no doubt depressed the managements of those TOCs with long-term plans.

The way in which train services have been cut to match the infrastructure resources available is a pointer to the future. This is rationing in one form, albeit a hidden and dishonest one that leaves the TOCs to face public dissatisfaction with the railways. The way in which the state looked after the railways when it previously owned them suggests strongly that too much hope cannot be placed in it now. The one constant in British political life is the Treasury, whose mandarins earlier saw that only one route to Scotland needed to be modern, forgetting those places along the way, or indeed just off it, which fed into the east and west coast main lines.

At the same time the modernisation plan saw a colossal sum of money pumped into the railways, but much of it was wasted. The nationalised railway, still busy building and rebuilding steam locomotives, which might have been acceptable for a couple of years as wartime losses were replaced, also neglected many routes, especially those that had benefited from the pre-war electrification work of the Southern Railway. Viewed in this light, the Treasury attitude becomes a little more understandable, as it is clear that whatever sum of money offered to the railways will be spent, not always wisely. No one in British Railways, or British Rail, or Railtrack, or Network Rail, could match that inspired and inspiring figure, Sir Herbert Walker, last general manager of the London & South Western Railway and first general manager of the Southern Railway, who really knew how to modernise without wasting money.*

Regardless of the dissatisfaction felt with the railways today, the truth is that the state is not, and never has been, a good custodian of the nation's assets, in transport as elsewhere. If anyone doubts this, forget the other pressing priorities such as hospitals and schools and instead just look at the road network, inadequate for a modern industrialised society and with tremendous arrears of maintenance. This is the other clue to the inability of the state to provide. Road users are taxed to provide a sum equivalent each year to a tenth of government expenditure, but they are rationed by shortages, one of the methods used by the postwar Labour administrations to augment the official rationing scheme, especially as regarded allocations of material to industry. The argument that providing more roads will only mean more traffic is never used for hospitals or schools. It also ignores the situation in London and the south-east, where there is a single road around the capital, the M25 motorway, often known as the London Orbital Car Park, and closer to the centre the less satisfactory North Circular and its other half, the South Circular, not a through road like the North Circular but a series of local roads with a through route that exists only in the imagination of the planners. At one stage, postwar, it was reckoned that as many as five roads around London would be needed. After all, within the M25 lives a population greater than that of Greece, Sweden or Portugal, and greater than that of Norway

---

* When he took up the post of general manager of the London & South Western Railway in 1912, Walker found the rebuilding of Waterloo in full progress. This was an ambitious plan to create a single grand station out of four that had been built at intervals as the LSWR had expanded. The newest part of the station served the Windsor platforms and Walker famously decided that this should not be rebuilt as it was so recent. This not only saved money, but the economy affected not at all the grand sweep of the new station. At the Southern Railway, rather than spend considerable sums of money on corporate identity consultants, Walker bought a length of green cord from an optician, cut off a length for each of his four subordinates, declared the colour to be the new official livery for the company, and told them that the remainder of the cord would be held in his office as the standard to which they should refer!

and Denmark combined. There are many who would argue that current demographic trends will mean that traffic growth, on the roads as elsewhere, will eventually level off. The official mindset is incapable of envisaging an investment plan for the railways without balancing one route off against another, or even one region against another, or a road improvement versus an upgraded railway.

It is also true that trying to upgrade the west coast main line (WCML), at a total cost of £9.8 billion, is now more costly than building a completely new line in the first place. Those who advocate a new main line are themselves often unrealistic. A new railway line causes as much commotion and disturbance as a new motorway. A high-speed line such as those in France means that either trains have to leave it and rejoin the historic route to reach existing stations, or the line avoids the town centres and passengers have to travel to and from new stations, with the journey time for this eating into the time savings offered by the high-speed route. This is only part of it. Even HSTs are the Concordes of the railway network, and are only viable when there are substantial distances that can be run non-stop between stations. If using the HSTs on services with many stops west of Cardiff and Plymouth, and north of Edinburgh, has been a nonsense, just how much more so would it be to do the same with a British *Train Grande Vitesse* (TGV)? Concorde was never designed for short hops!

Building new railways is an option, but not a course to be taken lightly. When the London & South Western Railway decided to move its London terminus from Nine Elms to the more convenient Waterloo, 700 homes had to be destroyed for a much smaller railway than we see over the same route today. Many more homes were destroyed in the building and extension of Waterloo.

On the other hand, there are a number of schemes that will need to be tackled, such as a Crossrail for London, linking east and west, and then later enhancing the capacity of north–south movements. The cost of these will be such that Parliament will not only be involved in the legislative process, but will have to consider using taxpayers' money. It is not simply a question of whether or not private funding can afford it, as faced by the Victorians – the cost of building a new railway line through congested London has risen out of all proportion. In the nineteenth century putting the railways underground was practical and affordable. Today, with the mass of utilities lying deep in the ground and the deep foundations of skyscraper office blocks, driving a route below the surface is costlier than ever and the construction of stations a daunting task, as indeed is the question of where to put them in the first place. Suggestions that the bed of the River Thames provides an unused route overlook the fact that this is crossed not just by bridges but by four tube lines, and indeed the fact that the river is far from straight for any distance.

While new lines should never be ruled out, one has to question the huge cost and effort of building the Channel Tunnel Rail Link (CTRL) to St Pancras, which will be used by a relatively limited market, when the available funding could have produced a far greater improvement for many more travellers every day had it been used to fund the Crossrail link in London. Even without the CTRL, certain Eurostar trains from Waterloo International provide the fastest intercity departures from London with end-to-end speeds of 106mph (170.5kph), while inbound trains are faster, at up to 108mph (174.5kph). The CTRL will cut the London–Paris schedule from 2hr 50min to 2hr 35min.

One prominent railway journalist, Roger Ford of *Modern Railways*, has coined the phrase 'boiling frogs syndrome' for the way in which current railway modernisation projects are handled. The rationale is that if you drop a frog into hot water it immediately jumps out. On the other hand, if you put the frog into cold water and gradually turn up the heat it doesn't notice and gets boiled. In financial terms this means that if you tell the customer just how much a project will cost, the answer is 'no', but if you submit a lower figure you get the contract and the cost can be steadily increased over a number of years.

The big difference in practice is that either the costs are too high so a project gets shelved, or the gradual cost increases either bankrupt the organisation or force it to reduce the specification. The latter is what has happened to the WCML upgrade, so that Virgin Trains' new 140mph 'Pendolino' tilting trains will not be able to run at anything like the projected speed. This means that the passenger appeal will be much less, reducing revenue, while trains will not be able to provide the productivity gains expected, thus raising costs.

Having stood by its plans to spend £10.4 billion more over the next ten years than permitted by the regulator, Network Rail has been attacked by the rail regulator, Tom Winsor, who demanded that it cut £2 billion a year from its spending, by cutting out waste and further delaying improvements to the WCML. Winsor claimed that maintenance contracts were being mismanaged and that the amount spent on maintenance had doubled over three years to £6 billion. The delays to the WCML work north of Crewe would provide a saving in 2003–4 of £1 billion but mean that plans to cut London–Glasgow journey times by a fifth would be delayed by a year, and also affect services to Carlisle and Preston, Liverpool and Blackpool. Improvements to services to Birmingham and Manchester were already running late, delayed until September 2004, and the call for further delays produced an angry response from Virgin's MD Chris Green, who stated that 'applying stop-go tactics at the 11th hour can only damage the rail industry. . . . We have invested £1 billion in new trains and would be deeply concerned over yet another delay to the West Coast upgrade and its benefits to passengers.'

The £9.8 billion cost of the WCML upgrade had been criticised by many, both for the cost increases over the life of the programme and for the delays to it. Worse, the rail regulator had found that signalling was costing twice as much on the WCML as elsewhere, while new track was costing 43 per cent more. It was also the case that the section north of Crewe was less heavily used, and that there were more urgent priorities elsewhere on the network. Winsor maintained that if Network Rail was inefficient or overspent, he would not allow the company to pass this on to its customers, the TOCs, in the form of higher charges.

Costs have been running out of control elsewhere, *Modern Railways* reported. A plan to extend the Chiltern Railways network to Kidderminster using the preserved Severn Valley Railway had gone ahead, but only four trains a day could be provided while Chiltern wanted to operate an hourly service. This required new points, for which Network Rail demanded £500,000, rejected as too costly by Chiltern. They then offered a simpler job incorporating a disused siding at £250,000, although this meant that instead of having trains stabled at Kidderminster, the ideal location, they would have to be left at Stourbridge. The job completed, Network Rail demanded £750,000, three times the original estimate!

Far worse was a plan to upgrade the line between Blaenau and Llandudno, 28 miles of single track used by single railcars, but which had been built and maintained to a far higher specification to transport heavy nuclear flasks for a power station. Plans to recycle slate waste offered the prospect of the line carrying heavy trains on a trial basis, which if successful could lead to a 5-mile conveyor belt being built to connect the waste tips to a new purpose-built terminal on the main line near Bangor. Upgrading was necessary to carry the waste trains, weighing 800 tonnes and with axle loadings of 25.4 tonnes, to prevent the track being damaged. An initial survey found that the cost should be £2 million, or £4 million if passing loops were installed to allow line capacity to rise to five slate trains a day. Network Rail then decided that the entire line needed relaying, ideally with a complete blockade that would mean the existing passenger service being replaced by a bus, and costing up to £20 million. The cost of £740,000 per mile seemed steep, but when challenged by members and officials of the Welsh Assembly, a revised estimate was produced of between £15 million and £230 million. In itself, the wide difference in costs is almost unbelievable, but the higher figure is £8.2 million a mile, against £10 million per mile for the Leuven–Liege line for the French TGV Est! The frustrated slate industry even considered using the narrow-gauge Festiniog Railway, which had after all been built for just this purpose, and the railway found that it could cope, but this fall-back scheme failed because the port facilities at Portmadoc could not cope with large modern bulk carriers without extensive and costly work.

## LOOKING TO THE FUTURE

There can be no doubt whatsoever that Britain's railways have lost their way after more than a hundred years that have seen them fragmented and owned by more than a hundred companies, taken temporarily into state hands twice, merged and then nationalised 'for good', privatised, and then the infrastructure re-nationalised again. Added to this there have been two periods of war, a prolonged period of economic recession and deflation between the wars, then strong competition from road transport and the private car. Along the way many commentators on the industry feel that much has been lost in the form of experienced and dedicated railwaymen. On the other hand, those running the railways between the wars and their shareholders were such people, but where did it get them? As we saw earlier, Hugh Dalton added insult to the injury of nationalisation with mean compensation by describing the railways as 'a poor bag of assets'.

Now the boot is on the other foot, with many refuting the claims made by Network Rail and the Strategic Rail Authority that the railways had been run down over several decades and that British Rail had done nothing to modernise the system. These claims are in turn also nonsense, since BR did electrify the two longest trunk routes, plus several suburban systems, plus the main lines from London into East Anglia, as well as completing Southern main-line electrification. It also produced an outstanding success in the HST, putting strong passenger appeal back into rail travel. During its lifetime the nationalised railway ensured that all main lines, and many branches, received continuous welded track and saw widespread introduction of automatic warning system (AWS), which with all of its shortcomings compared with what can now be achieved, nevertheless was a marked step forward in safety and operational efficiency. Did it do enough? No. Why not? It wasn't allowed to do so.

Similarly, the Big Four grouped companies did not do enough, not because they weren't allowed to, for there were incentives, but because most of them couldn't afford to. Part of this was owing to the state of the British economy, part of it was owing to the lack of forward thinking on behalf of those who imposed the grouping on the companies, and partly it was down to both the legislative framework that prevented the grouped companies from rationalising the traffic handled and their network properly. It also has to be said that for every hard-headed improvement that paid its way, such as the main-line electrification schemes in the south, there was another that lost money. Scarce financial resources were squandered on prestige trains whose earning potential was limited.

Taken at face value, the implication is that nothing has worked as well as it ought to since 1922, but that, of course, is nonsense. The pre-grouping companies were a mixed bag. Only the naïve believe that private enterprise is always excellent and the same can be said about those who believe that state control is the answer. British Rail was not all bad, the old companies were not all good, and even the performances of the grouped companies varied.

It is time to consider what should be done for the future. In the second generation franchising, Merseyrail has a 25-year franchise, an improvement on seven years, but this begs the question of what does a franchisee do as time runs out? In any case, how do franchisees who are transient creatures establish customer and staff loyalty? How does a franchisee that has lost its franchise, especially after having worked hard to develop it, handle the remaining months after the franchise has been handed to someone else?

Network Rail is running out of control and, as the Rail Regulator has remarked, it is harder to control than a private enterprise company, since any penalties do not come from the shareholders' pockets but from those of either the customer, meaning the train operators, or the taxpayer.

While Network Rail has been described as a 'not for profit' company and lacks shareholders, it has certainly not been a 'not for bonuses' company, since the directors, unable to be 'incentivised' by share options, have provided adequate incentives for themselves by awarding substantial bonuses. This news originally surfaced at a time when only 79 per cent of trains were arriving 'on time' – within five minutes of the scheduled time! The best that Railtrack had achieved had been 90 per cent.

Sooner or later the government of the day will have to return to the fray and examine what can be done about the railways. It will have to consider whether or not the industry is too fragmented, with too many train operators, but maintain a balance between establishing operators big enough to provide a sensible route structure and also capable of dealing with surplus rolling stock, and not providing over-large and over-centralised complacent railway operators. It certainly must not repeat the waste of good-quality middle-aged rolling stock that has followed the introduction of the Pendolino to the WCML.

The most obvious change has to be that rolling stock and infrastructure should once again be owned by and at the service of train operators. It should also go one step further, for there is no reason why a passenger-train operator should not also handle freight. This will take political courage, as it also implies that some operators might not invest heavily enough, but on those routes where subsidies are still needed the government will have a substantial amount of leverage. It must be recognised that the railways are not the answer to every transport question. Air transport can provide more direct routes from a wider variety of originating points to a wider variety of destinations and often at a lower price, as well as being able to follow the changing market better than the railways ever could. In Scotland journalists and politicians look to France and the TGV lines for inspiration, but should they not instead look to Norway, a country whose best railway is that to Stockholm in neighbouring Sweden? The Norwegians instead rely heavily on ferries and air travel.

Finally, now that rolling stock manufacture and maintenance have been separated, isn't it time for the manufacturers to offer standard trains, for suburban, rural and intercity use – basically requiring three different types of rolling stock, which could be sold on to other train operators if no longer needed? After all, no airline today expects airliners to be designed and built entirely to its specification, but instead buys standard models, often available with different fuselage lengths, off the shelf. Today many people, told that aircraft should be designed to suit one airline's needs, would laugh, but that is to forget history and the way that airlines once did things. Imperial Airways specified the Empire flying-boat, British European Airways specified the Vanguard and Trident airliners, British Overseas Airways Corporation specified the VC10, and most of these aircraft were commercial failures. Imperial's rival, the original British Airways, and operators such as Railway Air Services, bought aircraft in the de Havilland Dragon series off the shelf; BEA's rivals bought One-Elevens off the shelf.

The government itself shouldn't become too involved with the question of the 'standard' train, since the history of government involvement with and interference in manufacturing industry has not been good. What it can do is take a strategic and long-term view of the franchising arrangements.

Privatisation and franchising are not compatible. If the former is to work, the latter has to be abolished. There has to be a return to the vertically integrated railway with infrastructure and rolling stock owned and controlled by the operator of the trains, and instead of franchising, ownership should be on offer, giving a degree of involvement and permanence that is today sadly lacking. This is no longer the railway age, but the state was happy to privatise British Airways once and for all, and to do the same with the British Airports Authority.

We also need to look at the structure of the railways and accept that not only was nationalisation a bad move, but also that the grouping was a move too far. The priority is to ensure self-sufficient and logical operational units, big enough to provide networks of their own and yet small enough to be manageable, with some opportunities for an entrepreneurial approach. Given the current shape of the network, the new railways with some provisional titles, should be:

1.  Southern Railway – covering the area of the old 1923 company as far as Exeter, but with opportunities to operate further westwards, and including Island Line, which is already in the hands of the same franchisee as South West Trains.
2.  Great Western Railway – also covering the area of the 1923 company and including operations in South and Mid-Wales, with opportunities to return to Birmingham.

3. Great Eastern Railway – covering the area of the pre-1922 company, with the addition of the London Tilbury & Southend Railway since current practice involves a number of trains on this route being diverted into Liverpool Street in the evenings.
4. North Eastern Railway – operations from King's Cross including suburban and main-line services as far as Edinburgh and Glasgow, but with the opportunity to operate through to Aberdeen.
5. Midland Railway – operations from St Pancras.
6. North Western Railway – operations from Euston including suburban and main-line services as far as Edinburgh and Glasgow, but with the opportunity to operate through to Aberdeen.
7. Lancashire & Yorkshire – operations across the Pennines.
8. Merseyside – the existing Merseyrail franchise, which is largely self-contained and has few other operations through it.
9. Scottish Railway – ScotRail as it is, but with services and the routes from Carlisle to Glasgow and Berwick-on-Tweed to Edinburgh in the hands of the North Western and North Eastern as already mentioned.
10. North London Railway – essentially the Silverlink network as at present.
11. Chiltern Trains – services from Marylebone.
12. Clydeside – the Glasgow suburban network, although this could remain part of the Scottish Railway.

This makes eleven or twelve companies, depending on the treatment of the Glasgow suburban network, many of them operating a mixture of services, and which should also be allowed to operate goods as well as passenger services to make the maximum use of their assets. While the operations of EWS, for example, should be left alone, it could be that this would become a largely franchise-based operation, with the railway companies providing traction and rolling stock. The 'InterCity' brand could also be revived and marketed as a network, but once again based on the rolling stock of the railway companies, as with National Express and Scottish CityLink.

The appeal of these companies to investors clearly varies. In some cases denationalisation should be simple and complete, while in others, a state–private enterprise partnership, or even a local authority–private enterprise partnership, could be the solution, through a jointly owned operation. Using private-sector management companies is not really a solution, since this implies a continuation of franchising.

This leaves the question of getting there. At the time of writing only the South Central franchise is a problem, since this has recently been re-let, while Merseyrail has been let for a lengthy period, but this is a largely self-contained network and can be treated as such. In any event, franchises should be written to allow further adjustment to operating areas within the franchise period.

The advantage of this system is that it creates a series of managerially viable operations with vertical integration, allowing no dodging of responsibility. It is not a question of 'back to the future', since the operation is stronger than the pre-grouping structure and the privatisation structure, but less centralised than the grouping.

Does this mean a better railway? In one sense it does, in that it would achieve the balance between a railway network in units of manageable size but without excessive fragmentation. On the other hand, as we have seen, no one structure and no one type of ownership guarantees consistent quality. The old railway companies were a mixed bag, with the Midland Railway being far and away the best from the point of view of the passenger, although in terms of operations and finance its lack of powerful locomotives was a failing. The grouped companies also varied, with the Great Western and the Southern doing their best for everyone, while the LMS and LNER concentrated on the prestigious expresses, but the big failing was state interference, attempting to regulate too far and basing everything on the 1913 revenues at a time of unprecedented competition on the roads, the start of competition from the air and economic recession. In fact, the period between the two wars should have acted as a warning that the railways were no longer suitable for almost every type of traffic and every journey.

The nationalised railway had its high spots, its achievements, but once again was the sum of its component parts, and for every success there was a failure. Faced with rising costs and competition from road and air, and from the private car, it made two big mistakes. The first was that it often wasted large sums of taxpayers' money; the second was that it increasingly came to see itself as providing a service for those who had no choice but to travel by train, either because they couldn't drive or couldn't afford a car, or because the train was the only practical way to commute to work.

The privatised railway was also good in parts and bad in others. The concept was flawed by excessive fragmentation and by an absence of vertical integration, setting different parts of the industry against one another. Only a madman could have conceived a system that works against electrification, for example, by requiring the owner of the infrastructure to compensate the train operators for delays incurred during the installation of overhead wires or a third rail. Even so, companies such as ScotRail, with doubled frequencies between Edinburgh and Glasgow, Chiltern, with improvements and a new route between London and Birmingham offering a slower service at a much cheaper price, and Anglia have all shown just what can be done.

In no area of business life does one find that every company provides the same high standard of service. The railways are no different. If you look at the supermarket chains each has its strengths and weaknesses. One can say the same about airlines and airports. London's Heathrow Airport may seem over-large and a nightmare for those passing through for the first time, but it offers unrivalled international and domestic connections, something that cannot be said for smaller, and more pleasant, airports such as Edinburgh or Glasgow.

There is no guarantee that the structure proposed will give everyone an improved service, but it does have a better chance than the existing structure, the overblown nationalised railway, or the grouped companies struggling with poverty and internal politics. Only the naïve believe that any one structure will provide an answer. The mature will also realise that success and failure are also part of life.

Have a good journey!

# Appendix

## The Grouping of 1923

Companies were defined as constituent companies if they were major elements in the grouping, being merged or amalgamated with one another, or subsidiary companies if they were minor companies that could be acquired rather than given the status of being 'merged'. In anticipation of the grouping, there were a number of acquisitions of smaller railways in the year or so before the grouping took effect on 1 January 1923.

The Railways Act 1921 defined the new shape of the railways as consisting of a 'Southern Group', a 'Western Group', a 'North Western, Midland, and West Scottish Group', and a 'North Eastern, Eastern, and East Scottish Group', which, of course, became the Southern, Great Western, London Midland & Scottish and London & North Eastern respectively.

This meant that the **Great Western Railway** had as its constituent companies the original GWR itself, plus the Barry Railway; Cambrian Railway; the Rhymney Railway; the Taff Vale Railway and the Alexandra (Newport and South Wales) Docks & Railway; with, as subsidiary companies, the Brecon & Merthyr Tydfil Junction Railway; Burry Port & Gwendraeth Valley Railway; Cleobury Mortimer & Ditton Priors Light Railway; Didcot Newbury & Southampton Railway; Exeter Railway; Forest of Dean Central Railway; Gwendraeth Valleys Railway; Lampeter Aberayron & New Quay Light Railway; Liskeard & Looe Railway; Llanelly & Mynydd Mawr Railway; Mawddwy Railway; Midland & South Western Junction Railway; Neath & Brecon Railway; Penarth Extension Railway; Penarth Harbour Dock & Railway; Port Talbot Railway & Docks; Princetown Railway; Rhondda & Swansea Bay Railway; Ross & Monmouth Railway; South Wales Mineral Railway; Teign Valley; Van Railway; Welshpool & Llanfair Light Railway; West Somerset Railway; and the Wrexham & Ellesmere Railway.

The **London & North Eastern Railway**'s constituent companies were the Great Central Railway; Great Eastern Railway; Great North of

192

Scotland Railway; Great Northern Railway; Hull & Barnsley Railway; North Eastern Railway and the North British Railway; while as subsidiaries there were the Brackenhill Light Railway; Colne Valley & Halstead Railway; East & West Yorkshire Union Railway; East Lincolnshire Railway; Edinburgh & Bathgate Railway; Forcett Railway; Forth & Clyde Junction Railway; Gifford & Garvald Railway; Great North of England Railway; Clarence & Hartlepool Junction Railway; Horncastle Railway; Humber Commercial Railway & Dock; Kilsyth & Bonnybridge Railway; Lauder Light Railway; London & Blackwall Railway; Mansfield Railway; Mid-Suffolk Light Railway; Newburgh & North Fife Railway; North Lindsey Light Railway; Nottingham & Grantham Railway; Nottingham Joint Station Committee; Nottingham Suburban Railway; Seaforth & Sefton Junction Railway; Stamford & Essendine Railway; and the West Riding Railway Committee.

The **London Midland & Scottish** had as its constituent companies the Caledonian Railway; Lancashire & Yorkshire Railway, which had already reached an agreement to be purchased by the London & North Western Railway; Glasgow & South Western Railway; Highland Railway; Midland Railway; North Staffordshire Railway and the Furness Railway; with subsidiaries including the Arbroath & Forfar Railway; Brechin & Edzell District Railway; Callander & Oban Railway; Cathcart District Railway; Charnwood Forest Railway; Cleator & Workington Junction Railway; Cockermouth Keswick & Penrith Railway; Dearne Valley Railway; Dornoch Light Railway; Dundee & Newtyle Railway; Harborne Railway; Leek & Manifold Valley Light Railway; Maryport & Carlisle Railway; Mold & Denbigh Junction Railway; North & South Western Junction Railway; North London Railway; Portpatrick & Wigtownshire Joint Committee; Shropshire Union Railways & Canal; Solway Junction Railway; Stratford-upon-Avon & Midland Junction Railway; Tottenham & Forest Gate Railway; Wick & Lynster Light Railway; Wirral Railway; and the Yorkshire Dales Railway.

As the smallest of the 'Big Four' grouped companies, the **Southern Railway** consisted of three constituent companies, the London Brighton & South Coast Railway; the London & South Western Railway; and the South Eastern & Chatham Railway Companies Managing Committee, itself representing two companies, the South Eastern Railway and the London Chatham & Dover Railway, retained their own assets and shareholders. The subsidiaries were the Bridgwater Railway; Brighton & Dyke Railway; Freshwater Yarmouth & Newport (Isle of Wight) Railway;

Hayling Railway; Isle of Wight Central Railway; Isle of Wight Railway; Lee-on-Solent Railway; London & Greenwich Railway; Mid Kent Railway; North Cornwall Railway; Plymouth & Dartmoor Railway; Plymouth Devonport & South Western Junction Railway; Sidmouth Railway; and the Victoria Station & Pimlico Railway.

Within each of the Big Four many of the minor companies were already operated or managed by the constituent companies.

# Bibliography

In dealing with a subject as vast as the railways, a bibliography could fill a volume on its own, but instead here is a selection of books that cover the subject in some breadth and depth. Those who want further reading will find that every railway company has at least one, and usually many more, books covering their history, and often this is covered from many different angles, with separate books on passenger and freight rolling stock, and another on locomotives, with yet others on stations or signalling. Old copies of *Bradshaw's Railway Guide*, published monthly when they can be found, are illuminating, and the reprints by David & Charles are better value than the originals, now collectors' items.

Bailey, B., *George Hudson: The Rise and Fall of the Railway King* (Stroud, Alan Sutton Publishing, 1995)

Beaumont, R., *The Railway King: A Biography of George Hudson, Railway Pioneer and Fraudster* (London, Review, 2002)

Gourvish, T., *British Railways 1948–73* (Cambridge University Press, 1987)

——, *British Rail 1974–1997* (Oxford University Press, 2002)

Gritten, A., *Reviving the Railways: A Victorian Future?* (London, Centre for Policy Studies, 1998)

Jackson, A.A., *London's Termini* (Newton Abbot, David & Charles, 1969)

Nock, O.S., *Britain's Railways At War 1939–1945* (Shepperton, Ian Allan, 1971)

St John Thomas, David, *A Regional History to the Railways of Great Britain* (Newton Abbot, David & Charles, several volumes, 1960 onwards with reprints, 1960)

Simons, J. and Biddle, G., *The Oxford Companion to Railway History from 1603 to the 1990s* (Oxford University Press, 2000)

Smullen, I., *Taken for a Ride* (London, Herbert Jenkins, 1968)

# Index